Fact File

A Sea Bird

Horned Puffin
(Fratercula corniculata)

habitat range

Horned puffins grow to be ten inches tall and they weigh about a pound. These birds spend most of their lives on the open ocean. Horned puffins are sometimes found along the California coast.

Puffins keep the same mate for life, and both mother and father help hatch the egg and take care of the baby.

HOUGHTON MIFFLIN

California Science

HOUGHTON MIFFLIN   BOSTON

Program Authors

William Badders
Director of the Cleveland Mathematics and
Science Partnership
Cleveland Municipal School District, Cleveland, Ohio

Douglas Carnine, Ph.D.
Professor of Education
University of Oregon, Eugene, Oregon

James Feliciani
Supervisor of Instructional Media and Technology
Land O' Lakes, Florida

Bobby Jeanpierre, Ph.D.
Assistant Professor, Science Education
University of Central Florida, Orlando, Florida

Carolyn Sumners, Ph.D.
Director of Astronomy and Physical Sciences
Houston Museum of Natural Science, Houston, Texas

Catherine Valentino
Author-in-Residence
Houghton Mifflin, West Kingston, Rhode Island

Primary Grade Consultant

Kathleen B. Horstmeyer
Past President SEPA
Carefree, Arizona

Content Consultants

See Teacher's Edition for a complete list.

California Teacher Reviewers

Robert Aikman
Cunningham Elementary
Turlock, California

Christine Anderson
Rock Creek Elementary
Rocklin, California

Dan M. Anthony
Berry Elementary
San Diego, California

Patricia Babb
Cypress Elementary
Tulare, California

Ann Balfour
Lang Ranch Elementary
Thousand Oaks, California

Colleen Briner-Schmidt
Conejo Elementary
Thousand Oaks, California

Mary Brouse
Panama Buena Vista Union
School District
Bakersfield, California

Monica Carabay
Four Creeks Elementary
Visalia, California

Printed in the U.S.A.

ISBN-13: 978-0-618-68617-9
ISBN-10: 0-618-68617-7

Science Content Standards for California Public Schools reproduced by permission, California Department of Education, CDE Press, 1430 N Street, Suite 3207, Sacramento, CA 95814.

3 4 5 6 7 8 9-CRK-15 14 13 12 11 10 09 08 07

California Teacher Reviewers (cont'd.)

Sheri Chu
Vineyard Elementary
Ontario, California

Teena Collins
Frank D. Parent Elementary
Inglewood, California

Gary Comstock
Cole Elementary
Clovis, California

Jenny Dickinson
Bijou Community School
South Lake Tahoe, California

Cheryl Dultz
Kingswood Elementary
Citrus Heights, California

Tom East
Mountain View Elementary
Fresno, California

Sharon Ferguson
Fort Washington Elementary
Fresno, California

Robbin Ferrell
Hawthorne Elementary
Ontario, California

Mike Freedman
Alta-Dutch Flat Elementary
Alta, California

Linda Gadis-Honaker
Banyan Elementary
Alta Loma, California

Lisa Gomez
Marshall James Elementary
Modesto, California

Lisa Green
Jordan Elementary
Orange, California

Carey Iannuzzo
Fitzgerald Elementary
Rialto, California

Teresa Lorentz
Banta Elementary
Tracy, California

Christine Luellig
Henderson Elementary
Barstow, California

Peggy MacArthur
Montevideo Elementary
San Ramon, California

Jeffrey McPherson
Parkview Elementary
Garden Grove, California

Susan Moore
Lang Ranch Elementary
Thousand Oaks, California

William Neddersen
Tustin Unified School District
Tustin, California

Josette Perrie
Plaza Vista School
Irvine, California

Lisa Pulliam
Alcott Elementary
Pomona, California

Jennifer Ramirez
Skyline North Elementary
Barstow, California

Nancy Scali
Arroyo Elementary
Ontario, California

Janet Sugimoto
Sunset Lane School
Fullerton, California

Laura Valencia
Kingsley Elementary
Montclair, California

Sally Van Wagner
Antelope Creek Elementary
Rocklin, California

Jenny Wade
Stockton Unified School District
Stockton, California

Judy Williams
Price Elementary
Anaheim, California

Karen Yamamoto
Westmore Oaks Elementary
West Sacramento, California

Contents

Activities

Mount Shasta

Contents

UNIT B
Patterns in the Sky

Big Idea Objects in the sky move in regular and predictable patterns.

**Joshua Tree National
Monument**

Contents

UNIT C
Matter

Big Idea Energy and matter have multiple forms and can be changed from one form to another.

California gold nugget

Activities

Yosemite National Park

Contents

UNIT D
Energy

Big Ideas Energy and matter have multiple forms and can be changed from one form to another. Light has a source and travels in a direction.

Roaring Camp Railroad
Felton, California

Activities

California

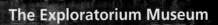

The Exploratorium Museum

Using Your Textbook

Science is an adventure. People all over the world do science. You can do science, too. You probably already do.

The Nature of Science

In the front of your book, you will be introduced to scientists and to ways of investigating science.

Every unit in your book has two or more chapters.

LIFE SCIENCE

UNIT A

Survival of Living Things

Chapter 1
Adaptations to Land and Water...................2

Independent Books
• Adaptations to Land and Water
• Amazing Adaptations
• Life on the Serengeti

Chapter 2
When Environments Change......................38

Independent Books
• When Environments Change
• Wild Adaptations
• Forced Out

Chapter 3
Organisms of Long Ago 66

Independent Books
• Organisms of Long Ago
• Amber
• Mary Anning, Fossil Hunter

Big Idea!

Standard Set 3.
Life Sciences

Adaptations in physical structure or behavior may improve an organism's chance for survival.

Polar bears in the frozen Arctic

1

Independent Books are books you can read on your own.

Big Idea! tells you the part of your **California Science Standards** that connects the Main Ideas of each lesson.

Lesson Preview gives information and asks questions about each lesson.

Writing Journal tells you to write or draw answers to the questions.

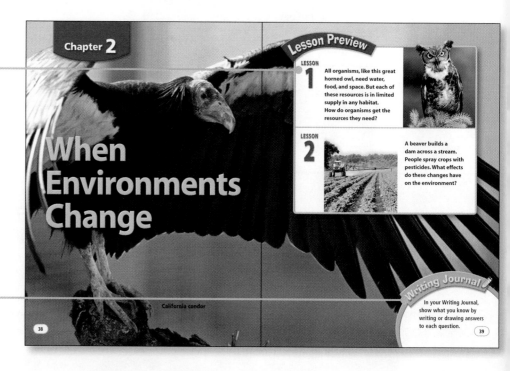

Chapter 2

When Environments Change

California condor

38

Lesson Preview

LESSON 1
All organisms, like this great horned owl, need water, food, and space. But each of these resources is in limited supply in any habitat. How do organisms get the resources they need?

LESSON 2
A beaver builds a dam across a stream. People spray crops with pesticides. What effects do these changes have on the environment?

Writing Journal!

In your Writing Journal, show what you know by writing or drawing answers to each question.

39

Vocabulary Preview

introduces important science terms, with pictures, and vocabulary skills.

California Science Standards are identified for each chapter.

Every lesson in your book has two parts.
Lesson Part 1: Directed Inquiry

Building Background gives you science facts and information.

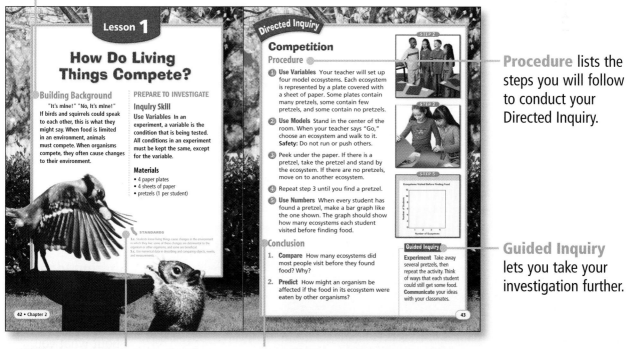

Procedure lists the steps you will follow to conduct your Directed Inquiry.

Guided Inquiry lets you take your investigation further.

California Science Standards appear in blue throughout each lesson.

Conclusion guides you in thinking about your investigation.

Lesson Part 2: Learn by Reading

Vocabulary lists the new science words that you will learn.

Main Idea tells you what is important.

Reading Skill helps you understand and organize information as you read.

Lesson Wrap-Up

Visual Summary shows you different ways to summarize what you've read.

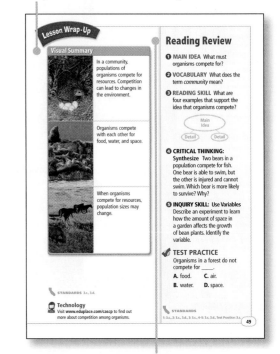

Reading Review lets you check your understanding after you read.

Focus On

Focus On lets you learn more about a key concept in a chapter.

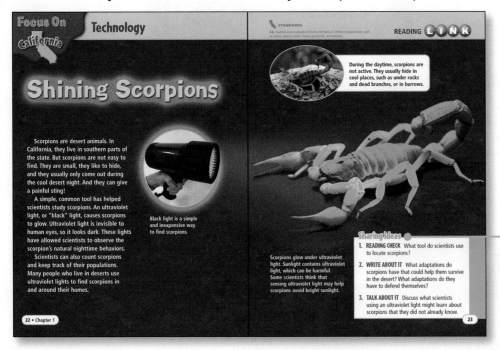

Focus On types include: History of Science, Technology, Primary Source, Literature, and Readers' Theater.

Sharing Ideas has you check your understanding and write and talk about what you have learned.

Extreme Science

Compares and contrasts interesting science information.

Writing Journal provides writing guidance for the Extreme Science lesson.

Links and Careers/People in Science

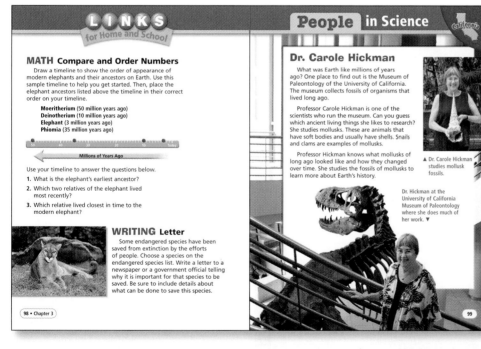

Links connects science to other subject areas.

Careers/People in Science tells you about the work of real scientists.

Chapter and Unit Review and Test Practice

Helps you to know you are on track with learning California science standards.

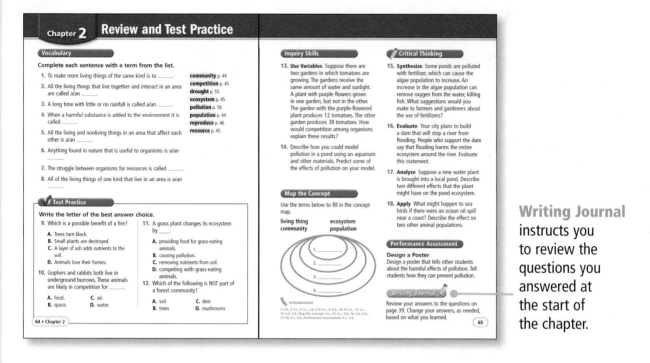

Chapter 2 — Review and Test Practice

Vocabulary

Complete each sentence with a term from the list.

1. To make more living things of the same kind is to _____.
2. All the living things that live together and interact in an area are called a/an _____.
3. A long time with little or no rainfall is called a/an _____.
4. When a harmful substance is added to the environment it is called _____.
5. All the living and nonliving things in an area that affect each other is a/an _____.
6. Anything found in nature that is useful to organisms is a/an _____.
7. The struggle between organisms for resources is called _____.
8. All of the living things of one kind that live in an area is a/an _____.

community p. 44
competition p. 45
drought p. 55
ecosystem p. 45
pollution p. 58
population p. 44
reproduce p. 46
resource p. 45

Test Practice

Write the letter of the best answer choice.

9. Which is a possible benefit of a fire?
   A. Trees turn black.
   B. Small plants are destroyed.
   C. A layer of ash adds nutrients to the soil.
   D. Animals lose their homes.

10. Gophers and rabbits both live in underground burrows. These animals are likely in competition for _____.
   A. food.   C. air.
   B. space.   D. water.

11. A grass plant changes its ecosystem by _____.
   A. providing food for grass-eating animals.
   B. causing pollution.
   C. removing nutrients from soil.
   D. competing with grass-eating animals.

12. Which of the following is NOT part of a forest community?
   A. soil   C. deer
   B. trees   D. mushrooms

64 • Chapter 2

Inquiry Skills

13. Use Variables Suppose there are two gardens in which tomatoes are growing. The gardens receive the same amount of water and sunlight. A plant with purple flowers grows in one garden, but not in the other. The garden with the purple-flowered plant produces 12 tomatoes. The other garden produces 38 tomatoes. How would competition among organisms explain these results?

14. Describe how you could model pollution in a pond using an aquarium and other materials. Predict some of the effects of pollution on your model.

Map the Concept

Use the terms below to fill in the concept map.

living thing   ecosystem
community   population

1. _____
2. _____
3. _____
4. _____

Critical Thinking

15. Synthesize Some ponds are polluted with fertilizer, which can cause the algae population to increase. An increase in the algae population can remove oxygen from the water, killing fish. What suggestions would you make to farmers and gardeners about the use of fertilizers?

16. Evaluate Your city plans to build a dam that will stop a river from flooding. People who support the dam say that flooding harms the entire ecosystem around the river. Evaluate this statement.

17. Analyze Suppose a new water plant is brought into a local pond. Describe two different effects that the plant might have on the pond ecosystem.

18. Apply What might happen to sea birds if there were an ocean oil spill near a coast? Describe the effect on two other animal populations.

Performance Assessment

Design a Poster
Design a poster that tells other students about the harmful effects of pollution. Tell students how they can prevent pollution.

Writing Journal

Review your answers to the questions on page 39. Change your answers, as needed, based on what you learned.

65

STANDARDS
1: 3.d., 2: 3.c., 3: 3.c., 4-8: 3.c., 9: 3.d., 10-12: 3.c., 13: 3.c., 14: 3.d., 5.d., Map the Concept: 3.c., 15: 3.c., 3.d., 16: 3.d., 5.d., 17-18: 3.c., 3.d., Performance Assessment: 3.c., 3.d.

Writing Journal instructs you to review the questions you answered at the start of the chapter.

Unit Wrap-Up

Learn more about science using the **Discover More** question. Also find a link to a simulation on the EduPlace web site.

Unit A — Wrap-Up

You Can... Discover More

Polar bears are adapted to the cold, icy environment of the Arctic. Thick fur and a layer of fat keep them warm in freezing temperatures. Even their paws are adapted for their environment. These adaptations make it easy for polar bears to walk on ice without slipping.

Polar bears have four paws that can be over 25 cm (about 10 in.) wide. Each paw has five toes, and each toe has a long sharp claw. These claws help polar bears grip the ice.

Each polar bear paw has seven footpads. The footpads are made of a thick, black layer of skin and are covered with small bumps. The bumps on the bear's footpads are like the treads on a sport shoe. They grip the ice and keep the bear from slipping when it runs.

Long fur between the footpads and toes keeps polar bears from slipping, too. Webbing that is under the fur between the toes helps polar bears swim.

Simulations Go to www.eduplace.com/cascp to see how polar bears and other animals adapt to their environments.

104 • Unit A

References

The back of your book includes sections you will refer to again and again.

Index

A
atom (AT uhm) The smallest particle of some kinds of matter that has the properties of

Glossary

Health and Fitness Handbook

Science and Math Toolbox

Science and Math Toolbox

Using a Hand Lens H2
Making a Bar Graph H3
Using a Calculator H4
Making a Tally Chart H5
Using a Tape Measure or Ruler H6
Measuring Volume H7
Using a Thermometer H8
Using a Balance H9
Making a Chart to Organize Data H10
Reading a Circle Graph H11
Measuring Elapsed Time H12
Measurements H14

Start with Your Standards

Your California Science Standards

Your California Science Standards

Welcome to the adventure of science!

Many famous scientists and inventors have lived and worked in California. Someday, you could be one, too!

Your science standards tell you what you should know by the end of Grade 3. They also tell what you should be able to do when you investigate and experiment. When you use your science book, you will find the standards printed next to each section of the lesson and chapter.

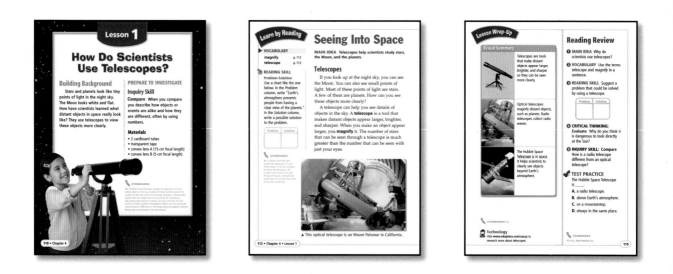

Houghton Mifflin Science will lead you to mastering your standards. Along the way, you will ask questions, do hands-on investigations, think critically, and read what scientists have discovered about how the world works. You will also get to know real people who do science every day.

How Families Can Help

- Get to know the California Science Content Standards on the pages that follow. If you want to learn more about science education, you can find the Science Framework for California Public Schools online at **www.cde.ca.gov/ci/**

- Relate the science of the standards to activities at home such as cooking, gardening, and playing sports.

- Get to know your child's science textbook, encouraging him or her to use the table of contents, index, and glossary. Point out the importance of titles and headings as a means to finding the information needed.

- Help your child choose library books to read about science, nature, inventors, and scientists. You can use the Recommended Literature for Math & Science online database at **www.cde.ca.gov/ci/sc/ll/**

- Find opportunities for your child to use numbers and mathematics skills and to measure and to estimate measurements, such as when planning a trip.

- Encourage your child to do experiments and enter science fairs.

Vasquez Rocks, California

Science Content Standards

These Science Content Standards are learning goals that you will achieve by the end of third grade. Below each standard is the unit or chapter in this book where that standard is taught. In that unit and chapter, there are many opportunities to master the standard—by doing investigations, reading, writing, speaking, and drawing concept maps.

Set 1

Physical Sciences (Energy and Matter)

Energy and matter have multiple forms and can be changed from one form to another. As a basis for understanding this concept:
Unit C: Matter; Unit D: Energy

1.a. *Students know* energy comes from the Sun to Earth in the form of light.
Chapter 8: Forms of Energy; Chapter 9: Light

1.b. *Students know* sources of stored energy take many forms, such as food, fuel, and batteries.
Chapter 8: Forms of Energy

1.c. *Students know* machines and living things convert stored energy to motion and heat.
Chapter 8: Forms of Energy

1.d. *Students know* energy can be carried from one place to another by waves, such as water waves and sound waves, by electric current, and by moving objects.
Chapter 8: Forms of Energy

1.e. *Students know* matter has three forms: solid, liquid, and gas.
Chapter 6: Properties of Matter

1.f. *Students know* evaporation and melting are changes that occur when the objects are heated.
Chapter 6: Properties of Matter

1.g. *Students know* that when two or more substances are combined, a new substance may be formed with properties that are different from those of the original materials.
Chapter 7: Chemical Changes

1.h. *Students know* all matter is made of small particles called atoms, too small to see with the naked eye.
Chapter 6: Properties of Matter

1.i. *Students know* people once thought that earth, wind, fire, and water were the basic elements that made up all matter. Science experiments show that there are more than 100 different types of atoms, which are presented on the periodic table of the elements.
Chapter 7: Chemical Changes

Set 2

Physical Sciences (Light)

Light has a source and travels in a direction. As a basis for understanding this concept:
Unit D: Energy

2.a. *Students know* sunlight can be blocked to create shadows.
Chapter 9: Light

2.b. *Students know* light is reflected from mirrors and other surfaces.
Chapter 8: Forms of Energy

2.c. *Students know* the color of light striking an object affects the way the object is seen.
Chapter 8: Forms of Energy

Coit Tower, San Francisco

2.d. *Students know* an object is seen when light traveling from the object enters the eye.
Chapter 8: Forms of Energy

Set 3 Life Sciences

Adaptations in physical structure or behavior may improve an organism's chance for survival. As a basis for understanding this concept:

Unit A: Survival of Living Things

3.a. *Students know* plants and animals have structures that serve different functions in growth, survival, and reproduction.
Chapter 1: Adaptations to Land and Water

3.b. *Students know* examples of diverse life forms in different environments, such as oceans, deserts, tundra, forests, grasslands, and wetlands.
Chapter 1: Adaptations to Land and Water

3.c. *Students know* living things cause changes in the environment in which they live: some of these changes are detrimental to the organism or other organisms, and some are beneficial.
Chapter 2: When Environments Change

3.d. *Students know* when the environment changes, some plants and animals survive and reproduce; others die or move to new locations.
Chapter 2: When Environments Change
Chapter 3: Organisms of Long Ago

3.e. *Students know* that some kinds of organisms that once lived on Earth have completely disappeared and that some of those resembled others that are alive today.
Chapter 3: Organisms of Long Ago

Beavertail cactus flowers

Set 4

Earth Sciences

Objects in the sky move in regular and predictable patterns. As a basis for understanding this concept:

Unit B: Patterns in the Sky

4.a. *Students know* the patterns of stars stay the same, although they appear to move across the sky nightly, and different stars can be seen in different seasons.
Chapter 5: Cycles and Patterns in Space

4.b. *Students know* the way in which the Moon's appearance changes during the four-week lunar cycle.
Chapter 5: Cycles and Patterns in Space

4.c. *Students know* telescopes magnify the appearance of some distant objects in the sky, including the Moon and the planets. The number of stars that can be seen through telescopes is dramatically greater than the number that can be seen by the unaided eye.
Chapter 4: Our Solar System
Chapter 5: Cycles and Patterns in Space

4.d. *Students know* that Earth is one of several planets that orbit the Sun and that the Moon orbits Earth.
Chapter 4: Our Solar System
Chapter 5: Cycles and Patterns in Space

4.e. *Students know* the position of the Sun in the sky changes during the course of the day and from season to season.
Chapter 5: Cycles and Patterns in Space

Radio telescope in Goldstone, California

Investigation and Experimentation

Scientific progress is made by asking meaningful questions and conducting careful investigations. As a basis for understanding this concept and addressing the content in the other three strands, students should develop their own questions and perform investigations. Students will:

Directed Inquiry and Guided Inquiry investigations in every lesson.

5.a. Repeat observations to improve accuracy and know that the results of similar scientific investigations seldom turn out exactly the same because of differences in the things being investigated, methods being used, or uncertainty in the observation.
Directed Inquiry and Guided Inquiry investigations

5.b. Differentiate evidence from opinion and know that scientists do not rely on claims or conclusions unless they are backed by observations that can be confirmed.
Directed Inquiry and Guided Inquiry investigations

5.c. Use numerical data in describing and comparing objects, events, and measurements.
Directed Inquiry and Guided Inquiry investigations

5.d. Predict the outcome of a simple investigation and compare the result with the prediction.
Directed Inquiry and Guided Inquiry investigations

5.e. Collect data in an investigation and analyze those data to develop a logical conclusion.
Directed Inquiry and Guided Inquiry investigations

The Nature of Science

Science is an adventure. People all over the world do science. You can do science, too. You probably already do.

Big Idea

Scientific progress is made by asking meaningful questions and conducting careful investigations.

Start With Your Standards

STANDARD SET 5. Investigation and Experimentation

5. Scientific progress is made by asking meaningful questions and conducting careful investigations. As a basis for understanding this concept and addressing the content in the other three strands, students should develop their own questions and perform investigations. Students will:

5.a. Repeat observations to improve accuracy and know that the results of similar scientific investigations seldom turn out exactly the same because of differences in the things being investigated, methods being used, or uncertainty in the observation.

5.b. Differentiate evidence from opinion and know that scientists do not rely on claims or conclusions unless they are backed by observations that can be confirmed.

5.c. Use numerical data in describing and comparing objects, events, and measurements.

5.d. Predict the outcome of a simple investigation and compare the result with the prediction.

5.e. Collect data in an investigation and analyze those data to develop a logical conclusion.

The Nature of Science

You Can...

Do What Scientists Do

Meet Dr. Caitlin O'Connell. She is a scientist at Stanford University in Palo Alto, California. But her work takes her far away, often to Africa and Asia. She studies elephants.

As Dr. O'Connell could tell you, elephants make very loud calls. One call is a greeting. Another call warns of danger. The third call means, "Let's go!"

When elephants are near each other, they can easily hear one another's calls. Yet Dr. O'Connell had an idea that elephants could sense calls from far away, too. Her idea was that certain calls make the ground shake a little, almost like a tiny earthquake. Elephants feel the shaking ground with their feet.

STANDARDS

5.a. Repeat observations to improve accuracy and know that the results of similar scientific investigations seldom turn out exactly the same because of differences in the things being investigated, methods being used, or uncertainty in the observation.

Dr. O'Connell worked with a team of scientists to test her ideas. With experiments, they showed that the shaking from elephant calls travels as far as 2 kilometers (1.2 miles) or even farther.

In one experiment, a group of elephants bunched closely together when the "danger" call was played through the ground. This observation supported Dr. O'Connell's ideas.

Scientists interpret their observations.

All elephants are different, and no two may behave exactly the same way. However, if other scientists ran Dr. O'Connell's experiments, their observations should be similar to hers. Such results would further support her ideas.

Conclusions in science are drawn from data, which are facts that have been observed or measured. Scientists do not accept a conclusion that is an opinion or a made-up story.

Dr. O'Connell spent many hours observing elephants and testing her ideas with experiments. She shares details of her work with other scientists. They will judge her claims and conclusions based on her data and methods.

You Can...

Think Like a Scientist

The ways scientists ask and answer questions about the world around them is called **scientific inquiry.** Scientific inquiry requires certain attitudes, or ways of thinking. To think like a scientist you have to be:

- curious and ask a lot of questions.

- a careful investigator.

- willing to listen to the ideas of others but reach your own conclusions.

- open to change what you think when your investigation results surprise you.

- willing to question what other people tell you.

What attracts the bee to the flower? Is it color, odor, or something else?

Use Critical Thinking

When you think critically you make decisions about what others tell you or what you read. Is what you heard or read fact or opinion? A *fact* can be checked to make sure it is true. An *opinion* is what you think about the facts.

Did anyone ever tell you a story that was hard to believe? When you think, "That just can't be true," you are thinking critically. Critical thinkers question what they hear or read in a book.

It looks like bees are attracted to certain flowers. I wonder if they use color, smell, or something else, to tell one flower from another?

I read that bees are attracted to flowers by their smell, but they identify different flowers by their color and shape.

Bees

Science Inquiry

Applying scientific inquiry helps you understand the world around you. Say you have decided to keep Triops, or tadpole shrimp.

Observe You watch the baby Triops swim around in their tank. You notice how they swim.

Ask a Question When you think about what you saw, heard, or read you may have questions.

Hypothesis Think about facts you already know. Do you have an idea about the answer? Write it down. That is your *hypothesis.*

Experiment Plan a test that will tell if the hypothesis is true or not. List the materials you will need. Write the steps you will follow. Make sure that you keep all conditions the same except the one you are testing. That condition is called the *variable.*

Conclusion Think about your results. What do they tell you? Did your results support your hypothesis or show it to be false?

Describe your experiment to others. Communicate your results and conclusion. You can use words, numbers, charts, or graphs.

STANDARDS

5.a. Repeat observations to improve accuracy and know that the results of similar scientific investigations seldom turn out exactly the same because of differences in the things being investigated, methods being used, or uncertainty in the observation.

My Triops Experiment

Observe Light appears to cause Triops to change how they move.

Ask a Question I wonder, do Triops like to swim more in the daytime or the nighttime?

Hypothesis If I watch the Triops in dim light and then in bright light they will move differently.

Experiment I'm going to observe how the Triops move in dim light. Then I'm going to turn on a light and observe any changes. I will repeat my observations a few times and compare them.

Conclusion When I turn on a bright light, the Triops speed up in the water. The results support my hypothesis. Triops are more active in bright light than in dim light.

Inquiry Process

Here is a process that some scientists follow to answer questions and make new discoveries.

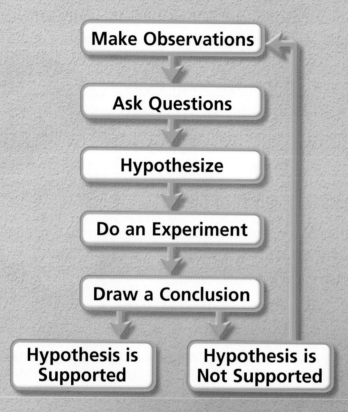

Make Observations

Ask Questions

Hypothesize

Do an Experiment

Draw a Conclusion

Hypothesis is Supported

Hypothesis is Not Supported

Science Inquiry Skills

You'll use many of these inquiry skills when you investigate and experiment.

- Ask Questions
- Observe
- Compare
- Classify
- Predict
- Measure

- Hypothesize
- Use Variables
- Experiment
- Use Models
- Communicate
- Use Numbers

- Record Data
- Analyze Data
- Infer
- Collaborate
- Research

Try It Yourself!

Experiment With a Matter Masher

To use the Matter Masher, put foam cubes or mini marshmallows in the bottle and screw on the cap. Then, push the top part of the cap up and down to pump air into the bottle.

1 Make a list of questions you have about the Matter Masher.

2 Think about how you could find out the answers.

3 Describe your experiment. Predict what the results would be if you did your experiment.

You Can...

Be an Inventor

Jonathan Santos

Jonathan Santos has been an inventor all his life. His first invention was a system of strings he used to switch off the lights without getting out of bed.

As a teenager, Jonathan invented a throwing toy called the J-Boom. He read about boomerangs. Then he planned his own toy with four arms instead of two. He built a sample, tried it out, and made improvements. Then he sold it in science museum gift shops.

Today, Jonathan works as a computer software engineer. He invents new ways to use computers. Jonathan is still inventing toys. His latest idea is a new kind of roller coaster!

His invention earned him his own trading card!

J-Boom

"As a kid I quickly discovered that by using inventiveness you can design things and build things by using almost anything."

What Is Technology?

The tools people make and use and the things they build with tools are all technology. A wooden flying toy is technology. So is a space shuttle.

Scientists use technology, too. For example, a microscope makes it possible for them to see things that cannot be seen with just the eyes. Scientists also use measurement tools to make their observations more exact.

Many technologies make the world a better place to live. But sometimes a technology that solves one problem can cause other problems. For example, riding in cars or buses makes it easier for people to travel long distances. But the fuel that powers cars and buses pollutes the air. Air pollution causes health problems for people and other living things.

USA

VASA
scovery

A Better Idea

"I wish I had a better way to _____". How would you fill in the blank? Everyone wishes they could find a way to do their jobs more easily or have more fun. Inventors try to make those wishes come true. Inventing or improving an invention requires time and patience.

Many inventors have improved video game controllers. Maybe, someday, you will invent a new way to play video games.

Video Game Controller

joystick

buttons to choose actions

direction button

How to Be a Good Inventor

1. **Identify a problem.** It may be a problem at school, at home, or in your community.

2. **List ways to solve the problem.** Sometimes the solution is a new tool. Other times it may be a new way of doing an old job or activity.

3. **Choose the best solution.** Decide which idea will work best. Think about which one you can carry out.

4. **Make a sample.** A sample, called a *prototype,* is the first try. Your idea may need many materials or none at all. Choose measuring tools that will help your design work better.

5. **Try out your invention.** Use your prototype or ask some else to try it. Keep a record of how it works and what problems you find.

6. **Improve your invention.** Use what you learned to make your design work better. Draw or write about the changes you made and why you made them.

7. **Share your invention.** Show your invention to others. Explain how it works. Tell how it makes an activity easier or more fun. If it did not work as well as you wanted, tell why.

Make Decisions

Troubles for Baby Turtles

Each spring adult female sea turtles come out of the ocean in the dark of night. They crawl onto sandy beaches and dig nest holes. They lay their eggs, cover them with sand, and slip back into the ocean.

A few weeks later, and all at once, the babies hatch and climb out of the nest. Attracted to nature's bright lights, the turtles should crawl toward the lights of the night sky shining on the ocean. But on many beaches, the lights from streetlights or houses are much brighter. The baby turtles crawl away from the ocean and toward the electric lights. Instead of finding their home in the sea, many of them die.

Deciding What to Do

How could you help save the most baby turtles?

Here's how to make your decision about the baby turtles. You can use the same steps to help solve problems in your home, in your school, and in your community.

Learn → Learn about the problem. Take the time needed to get the facts. You could talk to an expert, read a science book, or explore a web site.

List → Make a list of actions you could take. Add actions other people could take.

Decide → Think about each action on your list. Decide which choice is the best one for you or your community.

Share → Communicate your decision to others.

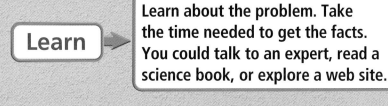

Sea Turtles

Science Safety

☑ Know the safety rules of your school and classroom and follow them.

☑ Read and follow the safety tips in each Investigation activity.

☑ When you plan your own investigations, write down how to keep safe.

☑ Know how to clean up and put away science materials. Keep your work area clean and tell your teacher about spills right away.

☑ Know how to safely plug in electrical devices.

☑ Wear safety goggles when your teacher tells you.

☑ Unless your teacher tells you to, never put any science materials in or near your ears, eyes, or mouth.

☑ Wear gloves when handling live animals.

☑ Wash your hands when your investigation is done.

Caring for Living Things

☑ Learn how to care for the plants and animals in your classroom so that they stay healthy and safe. Learn how to hold animals carefully.

Survival of Living Things

California Connection

Visit www.eduplace.com/cascp to find out how California zoos and wildlife refuges help living things survive.

Let's Go!

California Field Trip

La Brea Tar Pits

This model shows how mastodons probably became trapped in the tar pit at the end of the Ice Age.

More than one million fossils, including this mammoth skeleton, have been found at La Brea.

Fossils of giant sloths, shown in these models, have been found at La Brea.

Survival of Living Things

Adaptations in physical structure or behavior may improve an organism's chance for survival.

Polar bears in the frozen Arctic

Chapter 1

Adaptations to Land and Water

California sea otter eating a sea star

LESSON 1

Some living things live in wooded forests. Others live in dry grasslands. What helps these organisms survive in these environments?

LESSON 2

The tundra is frozen for much of the year. The desert is hot and dry. What body structures and behaviors help plants and animals survive in such harsh surroundings?

LESSON 3

Many types of living things make their homes in and around water. How do these living things survive?

Writing Journal

In your Writing Journal, show what you know by writing or drawing answers to each question.

Vocabulary Preview

Vocabulary

Glossary

Vocabulary Skill

Homographs

desert

Homographs are words that are spelled the same way but have different meanings. They may also be pronounced differently.

Look at the definition of the word *desert* (DEHZ urt) shown at the right. The homograph *desert* (dih ZURT) means "to leave empty or alone."

tundra

A cold, treeless area that has short, cool summers and long, cold winters.

behavior

The way an organism usually acts in a certain situation.

desert

An area that receives less than about 25 cm (10 in.) of rain in a year.

Start with Your Standards

Standard Set 3. Life Sciences

3.a. *Students know* plants and animals have structures that serve different functions in growth, survival, and reproduction.

3.b. *Students know* examples of diverse life forms in different environments, such as oceans, deserts, tundra, forests, grasslands, and wetlands.

Standard Set 5. Investigation and Experimentation covered in this chapter: 5.a., 5.b., 5.d.

adaptation

A behavior or body part that helps a living thing survive in its environment.

What Organisms Live in Forests and Grasslands?

Building Background

The forest is home to birds and other animals that eat katydids. Green katydids look just like the leaves they live on. This helps them survive in their forest home. All living things have body structures or behaviors that help them survive.

STANDARDS

3.a. *Students know* plants and animals have structures that serve different functions in growth, survival, and reproduction.
5.a. Repeat observations to improve accuracy and know that the results of similar scientific investigation seldom turn out exactly the same because of differences in the things being investigated, methods being used, or uncertainty in the observation.

PREPARE TO INVESTIGATE

Inquiry Skill

Experiment When you experiment, you collect data that either supports a hypothesis or shows that it is false.

Materials

- foods: wheat nugget cereal, shredded wheat cereal softened in water, sunflower seeds, grapes
- plastic bottle with water
- tools: tweezers, chopsticks, dropper, salad tongs, pliers, hand-held strainer or slotted spoon
- goggles

Science and Math Toolbox

For step 1, review **Making a Chart to Organize Data** on page H10.

Best Bird Beak

Procedure

1. **Record Data** In your *Science Notebook*, make a chart like the one shown. **Safety:** Wear goggles during this activity. Do not eat any of the foods.

Material	Best Tool
softened shredded wheat	
wheat nuggets	
sunflower seeds	
grapes	
water	

2. **Experiment** Use each tool several times to pick up softened shredded wheat. Each tool represents a type of bird beak. Decide which tool works best. Write the name of that tool next to "softened shredded wheat" on your chart.

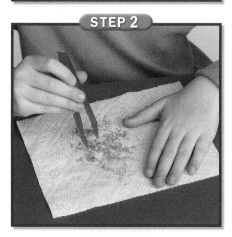

3. Repeat step 2 for each of the other materials. Record results in your chart.

4. The bottle of water represents a flower containing a liquid called nectar. Repeat step 2 to remove water from the bottle.

5. **Communicate** Share your results with your classmates. Then decide which tool is best for handling each material.

Conclusion

1. **Analyze Data** For each tool that you used, were the results the same each time you tried it?

2. **Use Models** Which tool would be best for getting nectar from a flower?

3. **Infer** From your results, make an inference about how the shape of a bird's beak is related to what it eats.

Guided Inquiry

Experiment Use a book about birds to observe the shapes of bird beaks. Think of another tool you could use to represent a bird beak. **Use models** to see if the tool works to pick up different foods.

7

VOCABULARY

adaptation	p. 8
behavior	p. 12
biome	p. 8
forest	p. 8
grassland	p. 10
habitat	p. 12

READING SKILL

Classify

As you read, classify different organisms as living in a forest or a grassland.

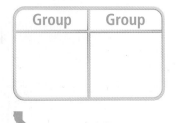

Group	Group

STANDARDS

3.a. *Students know* plants and animals have structures that serve different functions in growth, survival, and reproduction.
3.b. *Students know* examples of diverse life forms in different environments, such as oceans, deserts, tundra, forests, grasslands, and wetlands.

Forest and Grassland Biomes

MAIN IDEA Forests and grasslands have different characteristics, such as amount of water, temperature, and organisms. Different organisms have adapted to survive in each of these environments.

Living in the Forest

A **forest** (FAWR ihst) is a large area in which there are many trees growing close together. Besides trees, many other kinds of plants as well as animals live in the forest biome (BY ohm). A **biome** is a large area that has similar living things and about the same temperature and rainfall throughout.

The living things, or organisms, that live in a forest have adaptations (ad dap TAY shuhnz) that help them survive there. An **adaptation** is a way of acting or a body part that helps a living thing survive.

Growing taller than other forest plants is an adaptation of trees that allows leaves to reach sunlight. Low-growing ferns are adapted to surviving in shade.

An adaptation of some forest animals, such as squirrels, is the ability to live in trees. Sharp claws help these animals climb tree trunks. Long tails allow them to balance on high branches.

CLASSIFY Name two plants and two animals that live in a forest.

Forest Life

Hawks have excellent eyesight, which helps them hunt for food.

Living in trees helps keep squirrels safe from animals that live on the ground and might hunt them.

When threatened, a skunk can release a bad-smelling spray from its body.

When a deer senses danger, its strong legs allow it to run away quickly.

Grassland Survival

A grassland is another biome. A **grassland** is an area made up of large, flat land that is covered with grasses. The grassland is dry at some times of the year. When there is rainfall, the grasses that live there grow quickly.

Many animals of the grassland, such as zebras, eat grasses. Some animals, such as lions, eat other animals. The sharp teeth and claws of a lion are adaptations that help it catch and eat other animals.

CLASSIFY Name two plants and two animals that live in a grassland.

A zebra's stomach can break down tough grasses.

Lions have good eyesight, sharp claws, and coloring that blends with the grass. They also hunt in teams.

Hippopotamuses live in shallow water. Their eyes and nostrils are at the tops of their heads. This helps them see when they are underwater.

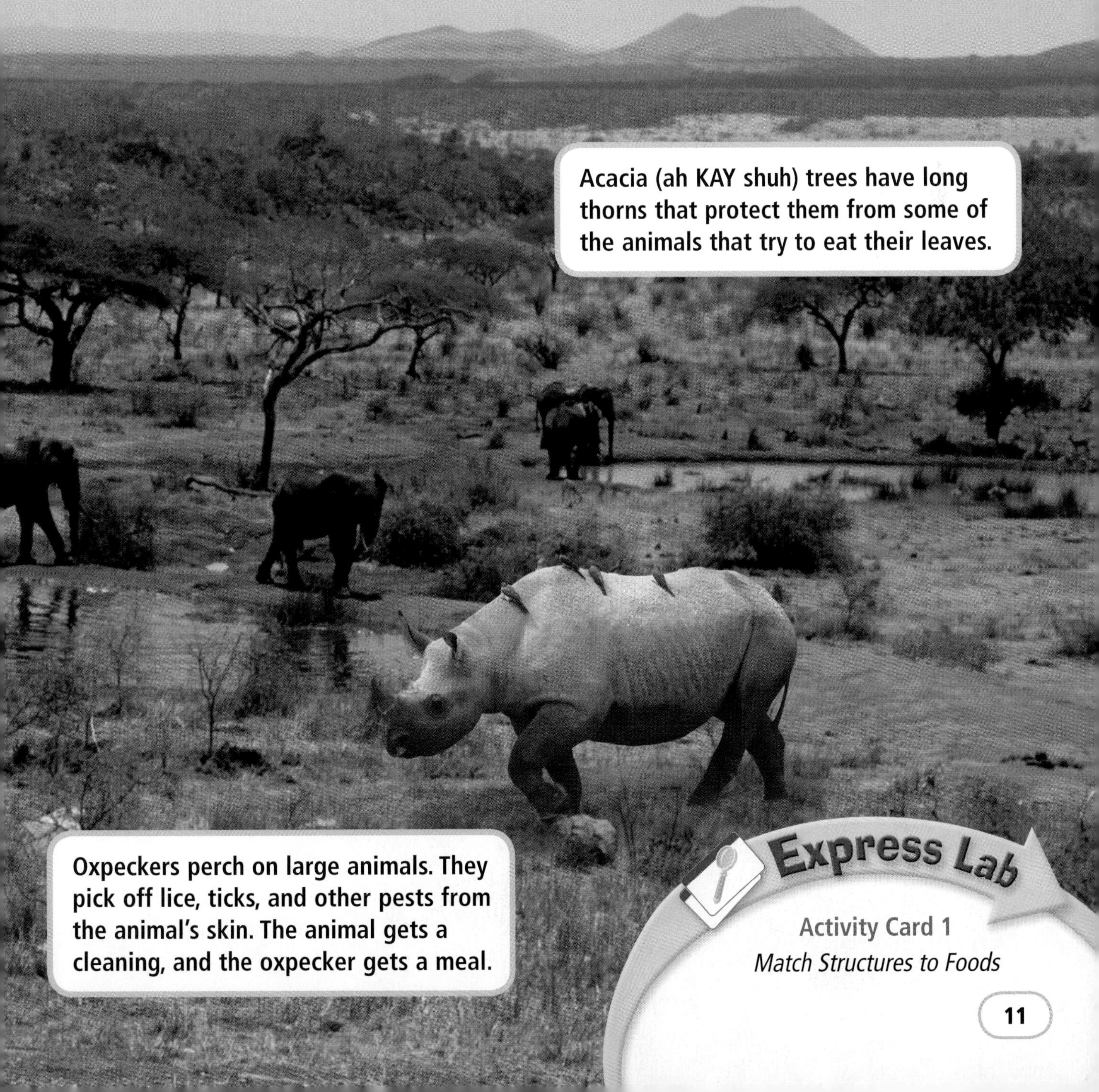

Acacia (ah KAY shuh) trees have long thorns that protect them from some of the animals that try to eat their leaves.

Oxpeckers perch on large animals. They pick off lice, ticks, and other pests from the animal's skin. The animal gets a cleaning, and the oxpecker gets a meal.

Express Lab

Activity Card 1
Match Structures to Foods

11

▲ Spiders are born knowing how to spin webs.

Types of Adaptations

All organisms have adaptations that help them survive in their habitat (HAB ih tat). A **habitat** is the place where a plant or animal lives. In a grassland habitat, a giraffe's long neck helps it reach the leaves of high trees. A giraffe's neck is a structural adaptation.

Spiders use silk to build webs that trap insects for food. Body parts that make silk are structural adaptations. Web-building is an adaptation that is a behavior. A **behavior** is the way an organism typically acts in a certain situation. Both adaptations help a spider survive.

To hunt mice, a cat must sneak up slowly and pounce quickly. Hunting in this way is a behavioral adaptation that helps a cat survive.

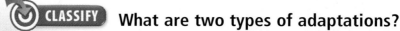 **CLASSIFY** What are two types of adaptations?

A cat's strong hind legs help it pounce on its meal. ▼

◀ Giraffes are adapted to eat leaves in high trees.

Lesson Wrap-Up

Visual Summary

A forest is an area in which most of the plants are trees. Many organisms are adapted to forest life.

A grassland is a large area of flat land that is covered with grasses. Many organisms are adapted to grasslands.

Adaptations can be body parts or behaviors. An organism's adaptations help it survive in its habitat.

STANDARDS 3.a., 3.b.

Technology
Visit **www.eduplace.com/cascp** to find out more about adaptations.

Reading Review

1 MAIN IDEA What helps an organism survive in its habitat?

2 VOCABULARY Describe a forest.

3 READING SKILL Would an animal that needs large amounts of water more likely live in a forest, or in a grassland?

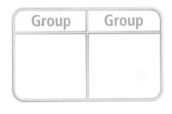

Group	Group

4 CRITICAL THINKING: Synthesize Would a plant that has adaptations to survive in a shady forest be able to survive in a grassland? Explain.

5 INQUIRY SKILL: Experiment Design an experiment to test this hypothesis: A green frog is better adapted to hiding in leaves than is a yellow frog.

✔ TEST PRACTICE

A spider uses _____ to help it survive.

A. only body parts

B. body parts and behaviors

C. only behaviors

D. habitats

STANDARDS
1: 3.a., 2–3: 3.b., 4: 3.a, 3.b., 5: 3.a, Test Practice: 3.a.

13

What Organisms Live in Tundra and Deserts?

Building Background

In the desert, it may not rain for months. Rivers are dry for most of the year. The Sun beats down on the organisms that live here. But plants such as cactuses and animals such as burros are able to survive there.

PREPARE TO INVESTIGATE

Inquiry Skill

Infer When you infer, you use facts you know and observations you have made to draw a conclusion.

Materials

- cactus
- hand lens
- tweezers
- plastic spoon
- sheet of paper

Science and Math Toolbox

For steps 3 and 4, review **Using a Hand Lens** on page H2.

STANDARDS

3.a. *Students know* plants and animals have structures that serve different functions in growth, survival, and reproduction.
5.b. Differentiate evidence from opinion and know that scientists do not rely on claims or conclusions unless they are backed by observations that can be confirmed.

Desert Plant

Procedure

1. **Record Data** Work with a partner. Observe a cactus. In your *Science Notebook*, make a sketch of the cactus.

2. Use tweezers to pull a spine off the cactus. **Safety:** Never touch a cactus. Cactus spines can be sharp.

3. **Observe** Look at the spine with a hand lens. Record your observations.

4. **Observe** Use a plastic spoon to gently move some of the soil around the base of the cactus. Use the spoon to remove a small amount of soil. Put the soil on a sheet of paper. Observe the soil with a hand lens. Record your observations.

5. Continue to move soil around the base of the cactus until you can see some roots. Sketch them in your *Science Notebook*. Note whether the roots grew deeply or were close to the surface of the soil.

6. **Infer** Under your sketch of the cactus, describe the habitat in which you think it might be found.

Conclusion

1. **Infer** Based on your observations, where do you think a cactus lives?

2. **Infer** How do the parts of a cactus help it survive where it lives?

STEP 2

STEP 3

STEP 4

Guided Inquiry

Ask Questions Ask other students their opinion about whether a cactus would likely live in a wet habitat. **Research** whether cactus live in rainforests. Present the evidence that you find.

Tundra and Desert Biomes

MAIN IDEA The tundra and the desert are two extreme environments. One is very cold, and the other is very dry. Organisms in these biomes have adaptations that help them survive.

Surviving on the Tundra

The **tundra** (TUHN drah) is a cold, treeless area that has short, cool summers and long, cold winters. Snow covers the ground in the tundra for most of the year. It can be difficult to survive in this harsh environment (ehn VY-ruhn muhnt). An **environment** is all the living and nonliving things that surround and affect an organism. Organisms in a tundra biome have adaptations that help them survive.

Tundra in Spring

The arctic fox has small ears, short legs, and a thick coat. These adaptations help it keep heat close to its body.

Tundra plants are short, which helps protect against wind.

During the short summer, the ground of the tundra is covered with mosses, grasses, and wildflowers. These plants tend to grow close to the ground, which helps them withstand strong winds. Small tundra plants lose little water when it's windy. The fact that plants grow quickly during the short growing season is also an adaptation of tundra plants.

The coats of some tundra animals change color from brown to white in winter. This makes it easier to hide from other animals in the snow. Most of the animals that live on the tundra, such as caribou, have thick fur and layers of fat, which keep them warm. Some animals survive the cold by spending the winter resting in a shelter.

▲ The ptarmigan changes color with the seasons.

PROBLEM AND SOLUTION What adaptation helps tundra plants stay out of the wind?

Tundra in Winter

Mosses are plants that can survive under the snow. Caribou dig through the snow to find and eat mosses.

During the winter, the entire tundra is covered with snow and ice.

Surviving in the Desert

A **desert** is an area that receives less than about 25 cm (10 in.) of rain in a year. Deserts are also often very hot. Many organisms that live in the desert have adaptations that help them find and keep water.

Some desert organisms have tough skin or scales that hold in water and protect them from the Sun. Animals such as lizards and rattlesnakes have hard scales. Jackrabbits have large ears that release extra heat into the air.

Organisms also use behavioral adaptations to survive in the desert. Ground squirrels and other animals live underground, where it is cooler. Other animals come out only in the cool of night.

prickly pear cactus

black-collared lizard

roadrunner

The white-tailed antelope squirrel lives in a burrow underground. The burrow keeps the squirrel cool.

Express Lab

Activity Card 2
Choose a Habitat

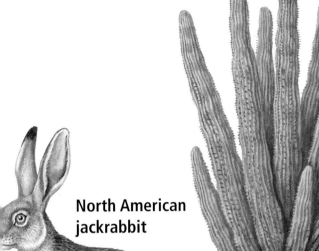

organ pipe cactus

turkey vulture

North American jackrabbit

coyote

The tough scales of a rattlesnake help save water. Also, rattlesnakes hunt in the morning and evening, when it is cooler.

The evening primrose opens its flowers only in the cool evening.

Plants in the desert have many adaptations to help them save water. Most have shallow roots that can quickly absorb rainwater before it runs off. Cactuses have thick, waxy stems that can hold water for the dry months. Some small plants grow quickly after a rain. Their seeds lie in the sandy soil until the next rain, when they will sprout.

PROBLEM AND SOLUTION How do desert plants get and store water?

▲ The barrel cactus is covered with long, sharp spines that help keep animals away.

Self-Defense

No matter in which habitat they live, most organisms have adaptations for self-defense. These are behaviors or body parts that help keep an organism from being eaten by enemies. For example, when an enemy approaches, some animals run away or hide. Other animals group together to overpower an enemy. Many large animals will fight an animal that threatens them. Tough skin and sharp horns help them fight.

Desert plants are in danger from animals that want to get water from their leaves or stems. Cactuses have spines that prevent animals from getting at their water-rich stems. Some plants and insects contain bad-tasting chemicals. The bad taste makes them a poor choice for a meal.

PROBLEM AND SOLUTION **What are two ways that animals defend themselves?**

To protect their young, musk oxen stand in a circle with their sharp horns facing out. The young oxen stay in the middle. ▼

Visual Summary

Plants and animals in the tundra are adapted to long, cold, snowy winters.

Organisms in a desert must adapt to a dry environment and extreme temperatures.

Most organisms have structures or behaviors that help protect them from enemies.

STANDARDS 3.a., 3.b.

Technology
Visit **www.eduplace.com/cascp** to learn more about tundra and desert biomes.

Reading Review

1 MAIN IDEA What is a desert?

2 VOCABULARY Write a sentence using the word *tundra*.

3 READING SKILL What is one way that the arctic fox is adapted to the tundra?

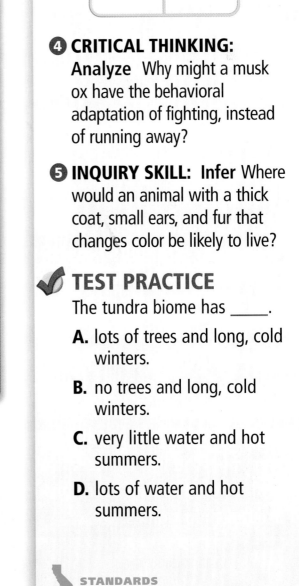

Problem	Solution

4 CRITICAL THINKING: Analyze Why might a musk ox have the behavioral adaptation of fighting, instead of running away?

5 INQUIRY SKILL: Infer Where would an animal with a thick coat, small ears, and fur that changes color be likely to live?

✓ TEST PRACTICE

The tundra biome has _____.

A. lots of trees and long, cold winters.

B. no trees and long, cold winters.

C. very little water and hot summers.

D. lots of water and hot summers.

STANDARDS
1–2: 3.b., 3–4: 3.a., 5: 3.a., 3.b., Test Practice: 3.b.

Shining Scorpions

Scorpions are desert animals. In California, they live in southern parts of the state. But scorpions are not easy to find. They are small, they like to hide, and they usually only come out during the cool desert night. And they can give a painful sting!

A simple, common tool has helped scientists study scorpions. An ultraviolet light, or "black" light, causes scorpions to glow. Ultraviolet light is invisible to human eyes, so it looks dark. These lights have allowed scientists to observe the scorpion's natural nighttime behaviors.

Scientists can also count scorpions and keep track of their populations. Many people who live in deserts use ultraviolet lights to find scorpions in and around their homes.

Black light is a simple and inexpensive way to find scorpions.

3.b. *Students know* examples of diverse life forms in different environments, such as oceans, deserts, tundra, forests, grasslands, and wetlands.

During the daytime, scorpions are not active. They usually hide in cool places, such as under rocks and dead branches, or in burrows.

Scorpions glow under ultraviolet light. Sunlight contains ultraviolet light, which can be harmful. Some scientists think that sensing ultraviolet light may help scorpions avoid bright sunlight.

Sharing Ideas

1. **READING CHECK** What tool do scientists use to locate scorpions?

2. **WRITE ABOUT IT** What adaptations do scorpions have that could help them survive in the desert? What adaptations do they have to defend themselves?

3. **TALK ABOUT IT** Discuss what scientists using an ultraviolet light might learn about scorpions that they did not already know.

What Organisms Live in Water Habitats?

Building Background

Sharks are well adapted to living in water. Their body shape and fins help them swim. By using their strong sense of smell, they can find food that is many kilometers away. Their gills allow them to breathe underwater.

STANDARDS

3.a. *Students know* plants and animals have structures that serve different functions in growth, survival, and reproduction.
5.d. Predict the outcome of a simple investigation and compare the result with the prediction.

PREPARE TO INVESTIGATE

Inquiry Skill

Predict When you predict, you state what you think will happen based on observations and experiences.

Materials

- spoon
- tub
- clock
- disposable gloves
- solid vegetable shortening
- 2 plastic bags
- masking tape
- cold water

Science and Math Toolbox

For step 4, review **Measuring Elapsed Time** on page H13.

Cold-Water Adaptation

Procedure

1 Work with a partner. Wear disposable gloves. Have your partner hold open a plastic bag and use a spoon to half-fill it with solid vegetable shortening. **Safety:** Do not eat the shortening.

STEP 1

2 **Experiment** Place one gloved hand in the bag with the shortening. Have your partner press on the outside of the bag until the shortening covers the glove. Place your other gloved hand in an empty plastic bag. Have your partner use masking tape to seal both bags around your wrists.

STEP 2

3 **Predict** Record how long you think you will be able to hold each hand in cold water before feeling the cold.

4 **Measure** Place both covered hands in a tub of cold water. Keep the tops of the bags above the water level. Remove each hand from the water when it feels cold. Have your partner time and record how long you kept each hand in the water.

STEP 4

Conclusion

1. **Analyze Data** Which hand did you remove from the water first? Compare your results with your prediction.

2. **Infer** Shortening is a kind of fat. How might a layer of fat help an ocean animal survive in cold water?

Guided Inquiry

Experiment Choose another material to cover your gloved hand. Repeat the experiment with the new material. **Hypothesize** about whether or not this material would keep an animal warm in cold water.

Aquatic Habitats

VOCABULARY

aquatic habitat   p. 26

READING SKILL

Compare and Contrast
Use the diagram to compare and contrast different aquatic habitats.

Compare	Contrast

STANDARDS

3.a. *Students know* plants and animals have structures that serve different functions in growth, survival, and reproduction.
3.b. *Students know* examples of diverse life forms in different environments, such as oceans, deserts, tundra, forests, grasslands, and wetlands.

MAIN IDEA Many habitats are partly or completely underwater. The organisms in these habitats must adapt to living in water to survive.

Life in a Tide Pool

If you have been to the ocean shore, you have probably seen a tide pool. Tide pools are pools of seawater left behind when the ocean tide goes out. A tide pool is an example of an aquatic (uh KWAT ihk) habitat. An **aquatic habitat** is a place where organisms live in or around water.

Plants and animals in and around a tide pool have adaptations that help them live in this saltwater habitat. To survive, organisms in a tide pool must eat, grow, and stay safe.

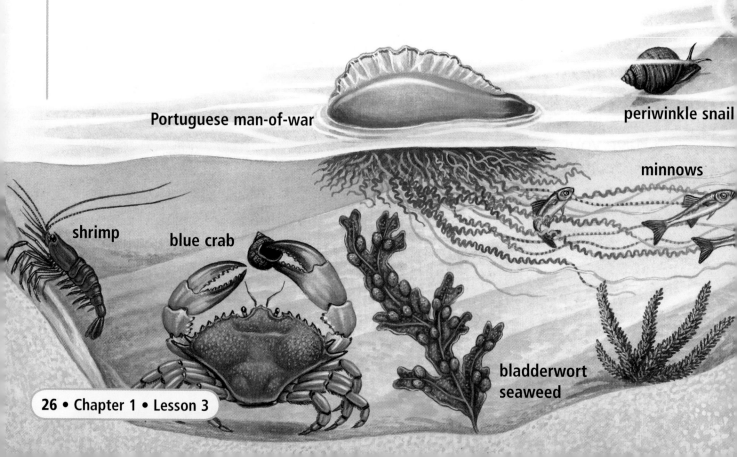

Portuguese man-of-war

periwinkle snail

minnows

shrimp

blue crab

bladderwort
seaweed

Some animals, such as an oyster, have a shell that can close tightly. This keeps the animal moist when the tide pool dries up. Sea birds have long legs that help them wade through the water.

COMPARE AND CONTRAST Compare an adaptation of an animal that lives in an aquatic habitat to one that lives on land.

oystercatcher bird

cordgrass

oyster

sea star

Adaptations to Tide Pools

Cordgrass
This grass survives in salt water by releasing extra salt from its leaves.

Periwinkle snail
This snail goes inside its shell to hide from enemies.

Blue crab
This crab uses its strong claws to capture and eat snails.

Drift kelp is a plantlike organism that lives in the ocean. It floats near the surface, where it uses sunlight to make food.

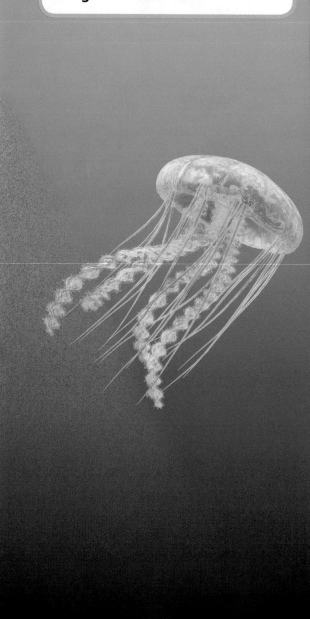

Life in the Ocean

From the surface, the ocean may look lifeless. But the ocean contains some of the most unusual organisms on Earth.

Water temperature is warm at the surface and there is a lot of sunlight. Plantlike organisms such as seaweed live here. Shellfish, mammals, and fish also live near the surface of the ocean.

As the ocean gets deeper, there is less and less sunlight. The water gets colder. There are no plantlike organisms here. But there are squid, octopus, jellies, and other animals.

At the deepest levels, the ocean is totally black. Some animals in the deep ocean have lighted body parts that help them catch food.

COMPARE AND CONTRAST In what ways is living near the surface of the ocean different from living close to the ocean floor?

These dolphins, like humans, are mammals. They breathe air. Dolphins, whales, and porpoises have an opening on the tops of their heads. This blowhole allows them to breathe air without leaving the water.

The giant Pacific octopus can live in very deep water. It can change the color of its skin instantly to blend in with its surroundings.

The lanternfish has tiny lights all along its body. The lights may attract small animals that the lanternfish eats. It has gills that allow it to breathe under water.

Express Lab

Activity Card 3
Model an Adaptation

Wetlands

A wetland is an aquatic habitat that is partly covered with shallow water. The organisms that live there have adaptations that help them survive.

Wetland birds, such as herons and pelicans, have long legs that allow them to wade in water. They also have long, sharp bills that help them catch the fish they eat.

The plants in a wetland have adaptations that help them live partly or fully in water. For example, water lilies have long stems that keep their leaves on top of the water, where sunlight can reach them.

COMPARE AND CONTRAST How are herons and pelicans similar?

Herons use their long legs and bills to help them fish in shallow water.

Pelicans have a large pouch under their bills. They use this pouch to hold fish.

Mangrove roots hold the tree up. These roots do not rot in salt water.

Fish have gills that allow them to breathe in water.

Visual Summary

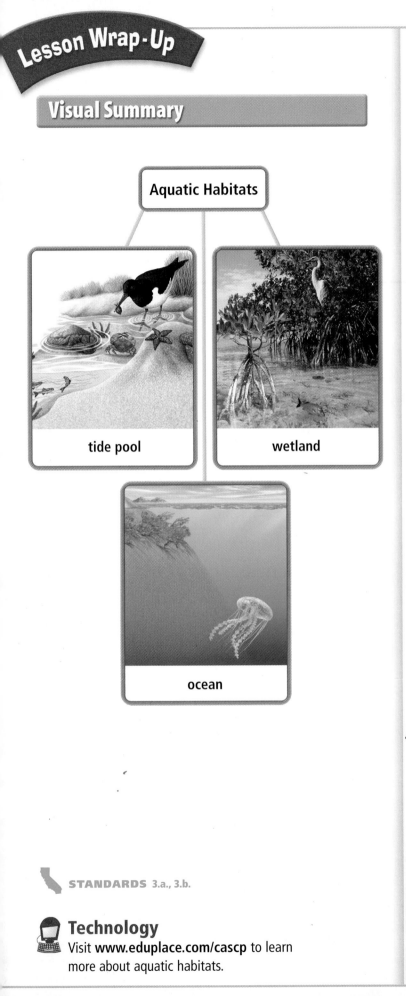

Aquatic Habitats

tide pool

wetland

ocean

STANDARDS 3.a., 3.b.

Technology
Visit **www.eduplace.com/cascp** to learn more about aquatic habitats.

Reading Review

1 **MAIN IDEA** What are three aquatic habitats?

2 **VOCABULARY** Use the term *aquatic habitat* in a sentence.

3 **READING SKILL** How are a tide pool and deep ocean alike and different?

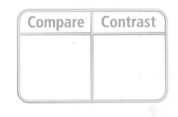

Compare	Contrast

4 **CRITICAL THINKING: Compare and Contrast** What adaptations do organisms in aquatic habitats have that organisms on land do not?

5 **INQUIRY SKILL: Predict** Some wetlands are freshwater habitats. Predict what would happen to a freshwater plant if it were placed in an ocean tide pool. Describe an experiment to test your prediction.

✓ TEST PRACTICE

A lantern fish's lights are most likely an adaptation to _____ at the bottom of the ocean.

A. the cold water

B. the complete darkness

C. the lack of food

D. many enemies

STANDARDS

1–3: 3.b., 4: 3.a., 5: 5.d., Test Practice: 3.a.

STANDARDS **3.a.** *Students know* plants and animals have structures that serve different functions in growth, survival, and reproduction.

Big Mouth!

Its jaws are as long as a rowboat. The underside of its throat can expand like an accordion. Its nostrils are at the top of its head. Everything about the humpback whale is adapted to gulping gallons of seawater.

Why would a whale take in so much water? Huge humpback whales eat tiny animals called krill. But they don't eat them one at a time—they eat them by the ton! The whale takes in a huge amount of water and krill in one gulp. Then, it pushes the water out between comb-like plates in its jaw called baleen. The krill are left behind for the whale's meal.

Krill are tiny animals similar to shrimp. One of their adaptations is to produce so many young that at least some survive.

No teeth, no problem! Instead of teeth, the humpback has baleen. These comb-like plates hang from the whale's upper jaw. They trap krill and let seawater flow out.

Writing Journal

In your writing journal, tell why you think that living in water could be considered an adaptation of whales—the largest creatures on Earth.

33

MATH Compare Fractions

This map shows the location of five biomes of the world. The circle graph shows the fraction of Earth's surface that is covered by each biome. Use the circle graph to answer the following questions.

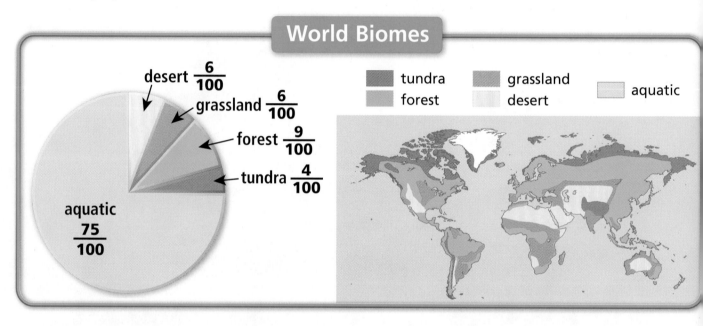

World Biomes

desert $\frac{6}{100}$
grassland $\frac{6}{100}$
forest $\frac{9}{100}$
tundra $\frac{4}{100}$
aquatic $\frac{75}{100}$

tundra   grassland
forest   desert   aquatic

1. Which two biomes cover an equal amount of Earth's surface?

2. Which biome covers the largest surface area?

WRITING Descriptive

You are a nature guide leading a tour group through a habitat. Choose a land or aquatic habitat. Write a description of it for your group. Describe three organisms that live there and adaptations that help them survive.

Dr. Jane Goodall

What can you learn about animals by observing them? Just ask Jane Goodall, the world's leading expert on chimpanzees.

Over the past 40 years, Dr. Goodall has been observing chimps in the African rainforest. As a young woman, she was able to observe chimp behaviors that no one had seen before. She was the first to record the chimps' ability to use tools—an important adaptation in these animals. She also learned that chimps communicate with each other and form family relationships.

Today, Jane Goodall travels the world teaching people about chimpanzees and the importance of protecting their tropical forest habitat.

In 1977, Jane Goodall founded the Jane Goodall Institute, which works to protect wildlife.

Vocabulary

Complete each sentence with a term from the list.

1. The way an organism acts in a situation is a/an _____.

2. A place where organisms live in or on water is a/an _____.

3. There are many trees growing close together in a/an _____.

4. A behavior or body part that helps a living thing survive in its environment is a/an _____.

5. Everything that surrounds and affects an organism is a/an _____.

6. A flat land area covered with grasses is a/an _____.

7. The place where an organism lives is that organism's _____.

8. A cold, treeless area is a/an _____.

9. A large area that has similar living things and about the same temperature and rainfall throughout the year is a/an _____.

10. An area that receives less than about 25 cm (10 in.) of rain in a year is a/an _____.

adaptation p. 8
aquatic habitat p. 26
behavior p. 12
biome p. 8
desert p. 18
environment p. 16
forest p. 8
grassland p. 10
habitat p. 12
tundra p. 16

Test Practice

Write the letter of the best answer choice.

11. A desert animal would most likely have which adaptation?

   A. ability to breathe underwater
   B. a warm coat
   C. ability to dig an underground burrow
   D. ability to live in salt water

12. A wetland is _____.

   A. a habitat formed by pools of seawater.
   B. a habitat partially covered by water.
   C. an ocean biome.
   D. a type of forest.

13. Which of the following is a behavioral adaptation?

   A. hunting at night
   B. sharp teeth and claws
   C. long thorns on trees
   D. eyes near the top of the head

14. Which of the following would the organisms on the tundra most likely need to adapt to?

   A. salt water   **C.** heat
   B. total darkness   **D.** cold

Inquiry Skills

15. **Infer** You purchase a potted plant with a tag that tells you that the plant needs a lot of water. But you suspect that the tag is incorrect. You think that the plant is a desert plant that does not need to be watered often. What adaptations would you look for to support your opinion?

16. Suppose you are investigating how many kinds of living things are found in a tide pool near your home. Why would it be important to visit the tide pool more than one time?

Map the Concept

Use the terms below to fill in the concept map.

desert
aquatic habitat
grassland
forest

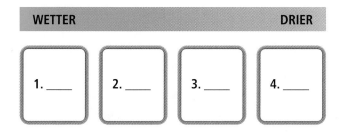

WETTER   DRIER

1. ____   2. ____   3. ____   4. ____

Critical Thinking

17. **Analyze** Use what you know about the adaptations of tundra plants to explain why there are no trees in the tundra.

18. **Evaluate** You observe the skeleton of an animal in a museum. The animal has sharp teeth and long claws. Your friend says the skeleton probably came from a plant-eating animal. Do you agree with your friend? Explain.

19. **Synthesize** Suppose that over the next several hundred years, less and less rain falls on a grassland. What type of biome will it most likely become? Explain.

20. **Apply** List some of the adaptations a seal needs to live in an aquatic habitat.

Performance Assessment

Design an Organism
Choose a biome. Design an organism that could survive in that biome. Be sure to list the adaptations that the organism uses to survive.

Writing Journal

Review your answers to the Lesson Preview questions on page 3. Change your answers, as needed, based on what you learned.

STANDARDS

1: 3.a., 2–3: 3.b., 4: 3.a., 5–10: 3.b., 11: 3.a., 3.b., 12: 3.b., 13: 3.a., 14: 3.a., 3.b., 15: 3.a., 16: 3.b., 5.a., Map the Concept: 3.b., 17: 3.a., 3.b., 18: 3.a., 19: 3.b., 20: 3.a., 3.b., Performance Assessment: 3.a., 3.b.

Chapter **2**

When Environments Change

California condor

LESSON

1

All organisms, like this great horned owl, need water, food, and space. But each of these resources is in limited supply in any habitat. How do organisms get the resources they need?

LESSON

2

A beaver builds a dam across a stream. People spray crops with pesticides. What effects do these changes have on the environment?

Writing Journal

In your Writing Journal, show what you know by writing or drawing answers to each question.

39

Vocabulary Preview

Vocabulary

Glossary

Vocabulary Skill

Prefix/Suffix

competition

Word endings can help you figure out the meaning of a word. The word ending *-tion* can turn a verb into a noun. The verb *compete* means to work or fight against another for a goal. The word *competition* is the noun form of *compete*. It means the act of working or fighting another for a goal.

drought
A long time with little or no rain.

pollution
The addition of any harmful material to the environment.

ecosystem
All of the living and nonliving things that exist and interact in one place.

population

All the organisms of the same kind that live in one place.

Start with Your Standards

Standard Set 3. Life Sciences

3.c. *Students know* living things cause changes in the environment in which they live: some of these changes are detrimental to the organism or other organisms, and some are beneficial.

3.d. *Students know* when the environment changes, some plants and animals survive and reproduce; others die or move to new locations.

Standard Set 5. Investigation and Experimentation covered in this chapter: 5.c., 5.e.

How Do Living Things Compete?

Building Background

"It's mine!" "No, it's mine!" If birds and squirrels could speak to each other, this is what they might say. When food is limited in an environment, animals must compete. When organisms compete, they often cause changes to their environment.

PREPARE TO INVESTIGATE

Inquiry Skill

Use Variables In an experiment, a variable is the condition that is being tested. All conditions in an experiment must be kept the same, except for the variable.

Materials

- 4 paper plates
- 4 sheets of paper
- pretzels (1 per student)

STANDARDS

3.c. *Students know* living things cause changes in the environment in which they live: some of these changes are detrimental to the organism or other organisms, and some are beneficial.
5.c. Use numerical data in describing and comparing objects, events, and measurements.

Competition

Procedure

① **Use Variables** Your teacher will set up four model ecosystems. Each ecosystem is represented by a plate covered with a sheet of paper. Some plates contain many pretzels, some contain few pretzels, and some contain no pretzels.

② **Use Models** Stand in the center of the room. When your teacher says "Go," choose an ecosystem and walk to it. **Safety:** Do not run or push others.

③ Peek under the paper. If there is a pretzel, take the pretzel and stand by the ecosystem. If there are no pretzels, move on to another ecosystem.

④ Repeat step 3 until you find a pretzel.

⑤ **Use Numbers** When every student has found a pretzel, make a bar graph like the one shown. The graph should show how many ecosystems each student visited before finding food.

STEP 2

STEP 3

STEP 5

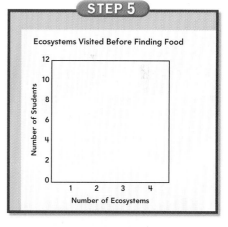

Ecosystems Visited Before Finding Food

Number of Students

Number of Ecosystems

Conclusion

1. **Compare** How many ecosystems did most people visit before they found food? Why?

2. **Predict** How might an organism be affected if the food in its ecosystem were eaten by other organisms?

Guided Inquiry

Experiment Take away several pretzels, then repeat the activity. Think of ways that each student could still get some food. **Communicate** your ideas with your classmates.

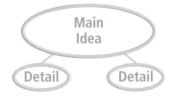
Organisms Compete

MAIN IDEA In all environments, there is a limited amount of food, water, and shelter. Organisms must compete for these and other resources. Competition causes changes in the environment.

Competing for Food and Water

All the mice that live in a field make up a population (pahp yuh LAY shuhn). A **population** is all the organisms of the same kind that live in an area.

All the populations in an area make up a community (kuh MYOO nih tee). A **community** is a group of organisms that live in the same area and interact with each other. For example, populations of grass, coyotes, snakes, skunks, and prairie chickens are all part of a grassland community.

snake

In a grassland community, coyotes, snakes, and skunks compete with each other for prairie chicken eggs.

coyote

skunk

prairie chicken eggs

An **ecosystem** (EE koh SIHS tuhm) is all the living and nonliving things that exist and interact in one place. A pond ecosystem is home to animal and plant populations. These living things must be able to get enough resources (REE sawrs-ehz) to survive. A **resource** is a thing found in nature that is useful to organisms.

Food, water, shelter, and air are resources. Often there is not enough of a resource for all the organisms that need it. Then, organisms in the ecosystem are involved in competition (kom PIH tish-uhn) for that resource. **Competition** is the struggle of one organism against another to gain resources.

Competition among organisms can lead to changes in the environment. If there are not enough resources to meet the needs of all the organisms, some will die. If there are too many frogs, some will not catch enough insects to survive.

Organisms from different populations compete as well. As you can see on page 44, several populations compete for prairie chicken eggs.

above surface

below surface

▲ **Pond Community**
Water lilies need sunlight to make food. They compete for space and for nutrients in the water.

MAIN IDEA What are two resources for which living things compete?

Express Lab

Activity Card 4
Compete for Resources

Competing for Space

In addition to food and water, organisms need living space. Many birds need tree branches or holes in tree trunks to build nests. Trees and other plants need space for their leaves to capture energy from sunlight. They also need space for their roots to spread as they grow toward sources of water.

▲ Wolf packs may move to new areas to find more space.

Wolves live in family groups called packs. Sometimes there isn't enough space for all the wolf packs in an area to live, reproduce (ree proh DOOS), and raise young. To **reproduce** is to make new living things of the same kind. Sometimes, when there are too many wolves in one area, one pack may leave to find more space.

Sea lions live on rocks at the edge of the ocean. If a sea lion population in a rocky area becomes too crowded, the animals will compete for space.

Sea lions compete with one another for space. ▼

Moose are big animals. They need large areas where they can roam in search of food, water, and shelter. Sometimes humans build houses in areas where moose live. The moose no longer have enough space to meet their needs. As moose populations become crowded, moose wander into areas where humans live. This can be dangerous for both the moose and the humans.

People need space, too. When people are crowded together, as in some large cities, they may compete for space. Competition for space might take place on a busy street or on a crowded bus.

▲ In a crowded city, people compete for space.

MAIN IDEA **What can happen if a population becomes too crowded?**

▼ Moose often roam into areas where humans live.

Resources and Population Size

The resources in an area affect the size of the populations that depend on those resources. One hundred years ago, wild horses roamed the desert in Nevada. The horses ate grasses and small shrubs that grew there. Some horses were killed by animals such as mountain lions. This kept the horse population from becoming too large, even as the horses reproduced.

As humans moved into the area, they hunted and killed many of the mountain lions. With fewer enemies, the wild horse population grew. The horses continued to reproduce until they consumed almost all of the food resources in the area. As more horses competed for fewer resources, many began to starve and die.

Today, when the number of horses becomes too great for the food resources, the United States government captures some horses. The government finds new homes for them. This allows the plant population to grow again.

MAIN IDEA What caused the wild horse population to decrease?

The size of a population of wild horses is limited by the amount of food resources that are available. ▼

Visual Summary

In a community, populations of organisms compete for resources. Competition can lead to changes in the environment.

Organisms compete with each other for food, water, and space.

When organisms compete for resources, population sizes may change.

STANDARDS 3.c., 3.d.

Technology
Visit **www.eduplace.com/cascp** to find out more about competition among organisms.

Reading Review

❶ MAIN IDEA What must organisms compete for?

❷ VOCABULARY What does the term *community* mean?

❸ READING SKILL What are four examples that support the idea that organisms compete?

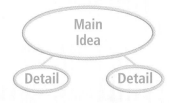

❹ CRITICAL THINKING: Synthesize Two bears in a population compete for fish. One bear is able to swim, but the other is injured and cannot swim. Which bear is more likely to survive? Why?

❺ INQUIRY SKILL: Use Variables Describe an experiment to learn how the amount of space in a garden affects the growth of bean plants. Identify the variable.

✔ **TEST PRACTICE**
Organisms in a forest do not compete for _____.

A. food.   **C.** air.

B. water.   **D.** space.

STANDARDS

1: 3.c., 2: 3.c., 3: 3.d., 3: 3.c., 4–5: 3.c, 3.d., Test Practice: 3.c.

49

STANDARDS 3.c. *Students know* living things cause changes in the environment in which they live: some of these changes are detrimental to the organism or other organisms, and some are beneficial.

Termite Skyscrapers

Who builds the tallest structures on Earth? Not humans! If you compare the size of the builder to the structure it builds, termites make the tallest dwellings anywhere.

How do such small creatures build such giant structures? By itself, each termite cannot change its surroundings much. But by working together, the millions of termites in a colony can greatly change their environment. Alone, a single termite may not be able to compete well with other kinds of organisms for resources. But as part of a colony, it can better compete for resources.

Defenders Soldiers with powerful jaws protect the colony from animals that might want to eat the termites—or compete with them for food or space.

This tower is about 4 m (13 ft) tall. This would be like a human skyscraper thousands of meters high!

These long ventilation shafts provide fresh air for the nest and help keep the tower from overheating.

The fungi garden is the main source of food for the termites.

Writing Journal

In your writing journal, tell how you think termite towers affect other organisms in the termites' community. Then tell if you think this effect is positive or negative.

51

How Do Living Things Change Environments?

Building Background

You may have seen headlines about an oil tanker accidentally spilling oil into ocean water. The oil coats the fur and feathers of water animals. Oil-coated sea birds cannot float or fly, and may drown. The actions of living things often change environments. Organisms are affected in different ways when their environments change.

PREPARE TO INVESTIGATE

Inquiry Skill

Use Models You can use a model of an object, process, or idea to better understand or describe how it works.

Materials

- water
- dropper
- baby oil
- balance
- disposable gloves
- aluminum pan
- large feather

Science and Math Toolbox

For step 3, review **Using a Balance** on page H9.

STANDARDS

3.c. *Students know* living things cause changes in the environment in which they live: some of these changes are detrimental to the organism or other organisms, and some are beneficial.
3.d. *Students know* when the environment changes, some plants and animals survive and reproduce; others die or move to new locations.
5.e. Collect data in an investigation and analyze those data to develop a logical conclusion.

Feather Failure

Procedure

① **Communicate** Work with a partner. In your *Science Notebook*, make a two-column chart with the headings *Dry* and *Oily*.

② **Observe** Examine a feather. Smooth it with your fingers. Wave it in the air. Record your observations.

③ **Measure** Use a balance to find the mass of the feather. Record the mass.

④ **Experiment** Smooth the feather. With a dropper, sprinkle several drops of water on the feather. Record your observations.

⑤ **Use Models** Put on disposable gloves. Model what can happen to a sea bird when there is an ocean oil spill. Pour baby oil into an aluminum pan. Dip the feather into the oil. Spread the oil over the entire feather.

⑥ Using the oily feather, repeat steps 2, 3, and 4.

STEP 4

STEP 5

STEP 6

Conclusion

1. **Infer** What features of the dry feather might help a bird survive?

2. **Hypothesize** How did the oil affect the feather? How might an oil spill affect the sea bird population in the area of the spill?

Guided Inquiry

Experiment Design an experiment to find out how to remove the oil from the feather. Get permission from your teacher to carry out your experiment. **Compare** your results with classmates.

Habitats Change

MAIN IDEA Changes to the environment are caused by living and nonliving factors. Changes can be both harmful and helpful.

Fire

After a forest fire, small plants that are the food source of some animals are destroyed. Thick bushes that provide shelter may vanish. Trees are scorched and ash covers the soil. The habitats of most of the organisms in that part of the forest are changed.

But a change that is harmful to some organisms can be good for others. A fire can create new habitats by clearing out underbrush. Wood ash contains nutrients that help new plants sprout. These new plants can provide food for animals. The organisms that can take advantage of the changed ecosystem will survive.

Lodgepole pine trees are adapted to fire. They will only release their seeds after the high temperatures of a forest fire. After a fire in Yellowstone Park, new lodgepole pines have sprouted. ▶

▲ In some areas yearly floods leave behind nutrient-rich soil, which helps plants grow.

▲ Droughts can kill plants and animals, and drive animals into other areas.

Flood and Drought

After a flood, people and wildlife may lose their homes. Plants die as muddy water covers them and blocks sunlight. But when the water dries up, nutrient-rich soil is left behind. New plants can grow where they might not have grown before there was a flood.

A **drought** is a long period of time with little or no rainfall. During a drought, many plants can die from lack of water. The animals that eat these plants must move to a new area, or they may starve. Organisms that eat dead plant and animal material may thrive under these conditions.

CAUSE AND EFFECT What effects can a forest fire have on an ecosystem?

Express Lab

Activity Card 5
Experience Feather Failure

55

▲ Eurasian water milfoil can quickly take over a pond. It uses up resources such as gases and nutrients in the water.

▲ Kudzu is from Japan. It grows so fast that it can cover signs, cars, and even houses.

Plants Cause Change

Plants can change the environment around them. When a tree grows in an open area, it produces shade. It takes nutrients from the soil around it. Grasses and bushes that may have grown in that area before can no longer survive. But the shade and shelter provided by the tree can also mean that other plants and animals can now live in the area.

Some plants have been brought from one ecosystem to another. The populations of these plants can grow very quickly. They can cause great changes to the new ecosystem.

Kudzu is a vine that was brought to the southern United States. It grows so quickly that it can cover trees, blocking sunlight from reaching the trees.

Animals Cause Change

Animals also change the environment. Herds of grass-eating animals can trim the tops of grass plants across an entire grassland ecosystem. Elephants push down trees and dig watering holes in the soil. As animals travel from place to place, seeds caught in their fur are spread to new areas. This can result in new kinds of plants growing where they have never grown before.

Beavers build dams across streams, causing water to build up behind the dam. A pond may form, overflowing onto nearby land. Plants or animals that lived in the once dry area may die or have to find new homes. However, new plants and animals may make the pond their habitat.

CAUSE AND EFFECT **What are some ways plants affect their environment?**

Beavers cut down trees to build dams. The areas where the trees once grew now get more sunlight. ▼

▲ Pollution can destroy
wildlife habitats.

Pollution

Some human activities harm the environment, and some help it. People are always building. They build houses, roads, farms, and cities. In the process, they may destroy the habitats of plants and animals.

Human activities can produce pollution (puh LOO shuhn). **Pollution** is the addition of any harmful materials to the environment. For example, chemicals that are dumped into rivers can cause fish to die. An ocean oil spill can kill large numbers of sea plants and animals.

Smoke can pollute air, harming the organisms that breathe it. Garbage dumps pollute the land when harmful materials buried in them leak into water or soil.

Not all human activities are harmful. People can also help protect the environment. One way is by passing laws that protect natural resources. Laws that limit hunting and fishing help protect wildlife populations. Wildlife habitats are also protected by laws. In some places, land has been set aside for parks and wildlife preserves. Farmers can help keep soil free of pollution by avoiding the use of poisons to kill insect pests.

CAUSE AND EFFECT **In what ways do people protect the environment?**

Visual Summary

Natural events change the environment. The effects may harm some organisms and benefit others.

Plants and animals can affect the organisms around them in good or bad ways.

Pollution is the addition of harmful materials to the environment. Pollution can result in harm to living things.

STANDARDS 3.c., 3.d.

Technology
Visit **www.eduplace.com/cascp** to learn more about changes to environments.

Reading Review

① MAIN IDEA What can cause changes to an environment?

② VOCABULARY What is pollution?

③ READING SKILL How can a beaver dam form a pond?

④ CRITICAL THINKING: Evaluate You see a news report that claims that a forest fire has no benefits for any organism in the forest. Is this statement accurate? Explain.

⑤ INQUIRY SKILL: Use Models A lot of water is added to a terrarium with several kinds of plants in it. Some of the plants die. Others grow taller. What event has been modeled?

✓ TEST PRACTICE

Which of the following is a change to the environment caused by people?

A. Rainfall floods a town.

B. Lightning burns a forest.

C. There is a drought.

D. A highway is built.

STANDARDS
1: 3.c., 2–5: 3.c., 3.d., Test Practice: 3.c.

59

The *Wump World* and *Deer, Moose, Elk & Caribou* are books about how animals adapt to changing environments. Wumps are fictional creatures. They are forced to live underground when their planet becomes polluted. In the book *Deer, Moose, Elk & Caribou*, real-life deer survive by adapting to changes in their habitat.

THE WUMP WORLD
written and illustrated by BILL PEET

The Wump World
by Bill Peet

. . . the poor Wumps remained underground wandering aimlessly through the caverns feeding on the fuzzy green moss growing on the ledges and the mushrooms clustered in the crannies, and sipping the sweet water from pools fed by underground springs. But they were very unhappy. For all they knew, they might have had to spend the rest of their days down there.

STANDARDS

3.d. *Students know* when the environment changes, some plants and animals survive and reproduce; others die or move to new locations.

READING LINK

Deer, Moose, Elk & Caribou

by Deborah Hodge

To survive, the deer family needs wild, wooded areas. When people clear land for houses and roads, wild areas get smaller. The number of cougars and wolves also shrinks. With fewer enemies, too many deer end up in one area. Food becomes scarce, and some deer die. Others eat farmers' crops to stay alive.

Sharing Ideas

1. **READING CHECK** How did the Wumps adapt when their environment became polluted?

2. **WRITE ABOUT IT** Write a story about a group of fictional characters that must adapt to a changing environment.

3. **TALK ABOUT IT** Discuss with classmates why you do or do not think that deer can adapt to changes. Give reasons for your answer.

LINKS

for Home and School

MATH Bar Graph

The peppered moth is a common insect in England. It has two forms, one with light-colored wings and the other with dark-colored wings. Moths that can blend with their environment are less likely to be eaten by birds.

Light-colored moths were most common before air pollution darkened the tree bark on which they lived. Then the dark-colored moths became more plentiful. As air pollution was cleaned up, light-colored moths returned. Use the graph to answer these questions.

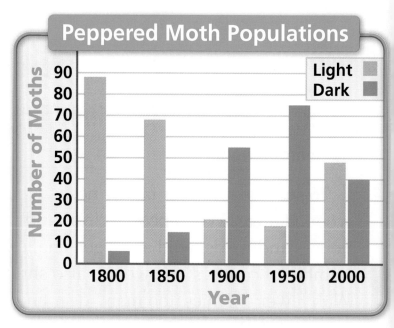

Peppered Moth Populations

1. In which year was the population of light moths the greatest and dark moths the least?

2. In which year was the population of dark and light moths almost the same?

WRITING Letter

Think of a place that you have seen in which you noticed there was some form of pollution. Pollution can be litter, dirty water, dirty air, or even excessive light or noise. Write a letter to a person in your local government. Describe the pollution problem. Ask for help correcting the situation. Describe how the pollution may affect both local wildlife and people.

Farmer

Farming is one of the most important jobs. Farmers must know about competition among plants in order to control weeds in their fields. They must also know how plants change their environment. Today's farmers must make sure that their crops and livestock do not pollute the land.

What It Takes!

- Courses in agriculture and business
- Energy for hard outdoor work

Marine Biologist

Much of the work of a marine biologist is done in a laboratory on land. These biologists use computers to track the movements of sea creatures such as whales, dolphins, and manatees. Understanding the habits of these creatures can help scientists protect them.

What It Takes!

- A degree in biology, oceanography, or zoology
- The ability to work with computers

Vocabulary

Complete each sentence with a term from the list.

1. To make more living things of the same kind is to _____.

2. All the living things that live together and interact in an area are called a/an _____.

3. A long time with little or no rainfall is called a/an _____.

4. Adding a harmful substance to the environment results in _____.

5. All the living and nonliving things in an area that affect each other is a/an _____.

6. Anything found in nature that is useful to organisms is a/an _____.

7. The struggle between organisms for resources is called _____.

8. All of the living things of one kind that live in an area is a/an _____.

community p. 44
competition p. 45
drought p. 55
ecosystem p. 45
pollution p. 58
population p. 44
reproduce p. 46
resource p. 45

Test Practice

Write the letter of the best answer choice.

9. Which is a possible benefit of a fire?

    A. Trees turn black.
    B. Small plants are destroyed.
    C. A layer of ash adds nutrients to the soil.
    D. Animals lose their homes.

10. Gophers and rabbits both live in underground burrows. These animals are likely in competition for _____.

    A. food.   C. air.
    B. space.   D. water.

11. A grass plant changes its ecosystem by _____.

    A. providing food for grass-eating animals.
    B. causing pollution.
    C. removing nutrients from soil.
    D. competing with grass-eating animals.

12. Which of the following is NOT part of a forest community?

    A. soil   C. deer
    B. trees   D. mushrooms

Inquiry Skills

13. Use Variables Suppose there are two gardens in which tomatoes are growing. The gardens receive the same amount of water and sunlight. A plant with purple flowers grows in one garden, but not in the other. The garden with the purple-flowered plant produces 12 tomatoes. The other garden produces 38 tomatoes. How would competition among organisms explain these results?

14. Describe how you could model pollution in a pond using an aquarium and other materials. Predict some of the effects of pollution on your model.

Map the Concept

Use the terms below to fill in the concept map.

living thing   ecosystem
community   population

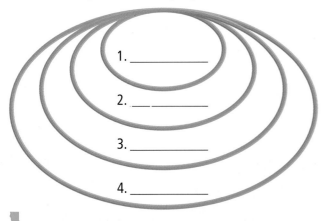

1. _____
2. _____
3. _____
4. _____

STANDARDS

1: 3.d., 2: 3.c., 3: 3.c., 3.d., 4–8: 3.c., 9: 3.d., 10–12: 3.c., 13: 5.c., 14: 3.d., 5.d., Map the Concept: 3.c., 15: 3.c., 3.d., 16: 3.d., 5.d., 17–18: 3.c., 3.d., Performance Assessment: 3.c., 3.d.

Critical Thinking

15. Synthesize Some ponds are polluted with fertilizer, which can cause the algae population to increase. An increase in the algae population can remove oxygen from the water, killing fish. What suggestions would you make to farmers and gardeners about the use of fertilizers?

16. Evaluate Your city plans to build a dam that will stop a river from flooding. People who support the dam say that flooding harms the entire ecosystem around the river. Evaluate this statement.

17. Analyze Suppose a new water plant is brought into a local pond. Describe two different effects that the plant might have on the pond ecosystem.

18. Apply What might happen to sea birds if there were an ocean oil spill near a coast? Describe the effect on two other animal populations.

Performance Assessment

Design a Poster
Design a poster that tells other students about the harmful effects of pollution. Tell students how they can prevent pollution.

Writing Journal

Review your answers to the questions on page 39. Change your answers, as needed, based on what you learned.

Chapter 3

Organisms of Long Ago

Model of *Parasaurolophus* at the
University of California, Berkeley

Lesson Preview

LESSON
1

Populations of some living things, such as this California riparian brush rabbit, may be in danger of dying out. What causes a population of living things to decrease in size?

LESSON
2

Pieces of bone, feathers, and leaves become trapped inside rocks. What can these fossils tell scientists about life in the past?

LESSON
3

Scientists find a fossil and compare it to a living thing that appears similar. What are some organisms from the past that resemble living things of today?

Writing Journal

In your Writing Journal, show what you know by writing or drawing answers to each question.

Vocabulary Preview

Vocabulary

Glossary

Vocabulary Skill

Sentence Context

fossil

Sometimes you can learn the meaning of a word by reading the sentence in which it appears. For example, read this sentence: *The scientists use fossil bones to construct skeletons of dinosaurs.* You can use what you know about dinosaur bones and skeletons to help you figure out the meaning of the word *fossil*.

fossil

The preserved remains of an organism that lived long ago.

extinct species

A species that has died off.

paleontologist

A scientist who studies fossils and forms of life that no longer exist.

endangered species

A species that has so few members that the entire species is at risk of dying out.

Start with Your Standards

Standard Set 3. Life Sciences

3.d. *Students know* when the environment changes, some plants and animals survive and reproduce; others die or move to new locations.

3.e. *Students know* that some kinds of organisms that once lived on Earth have completely disappeared and that some of those resembled others that are alive today.

Standard Set 5. Investigation and Experimentation covered in this chapter: 5.b., 5.c.

What Threatens the Survival of Species?

Building Background

The giant panda eats only bamboo. To survive, it needs to eat large amounts of this plant. People have cut down bamboo plants to use the land it grows on for other purposes. Because there is less bamboo for pandas to eat, their survival is in danger.

PREPARE TO INVESTIGATE

Inquiry Skill

Use Numbers You use numbers to describe and compare objects, events, and measurements.

Materials

- number cube
- Mammoth Key A Support Master
- Mammoth Key B Support Master

STANDARDS

3.d. *Students know* when the environment changes, some plants and animals survive and reproduce; others die or move to new locations.
5.c. Use numerical data in describing and comparing objects, events, and measurements.

Causes of Extinction

Procedure

1. **Record Data** Use a chart like the one shown. You will model what can happen to a herd of 10 woolly mammoths over 40 years. Each roll of a number cube represents what happens to one mammoth in a 20-year period.

2. **Use Models** You and a partner will use different Mammoth Keys. Roll the cube once. Follow the directions on your Mammoth Key for that number. Record what happens to the first mammoth.

3. **Use Numbers** Roll the cube once for each remaining mammoth. Record on the chart what happens to each animal. Record the total mammoths left in the herd at the end of 20 years (Trial 1).

4. **Use Numbers** For Trial 2, draw circles to represent the number of remaining mammoths in the herd. Repeat step 3 for the remaining mammoths. Record the total mammoths left in the herd at the end of 40 years (Trial 2).

Conclusion

1. **Use Numbers** Share your results with your partner. How does the number of mammoths left in each herd compare?

2. **Hypothesize** What do the results suggest about how a type of living thing can become extinct, or die off?

STEP 1

Trial	Mammoths at Start of Trial	Mammoths at End of Trial
1	00000 00000	
2		

STEP 2

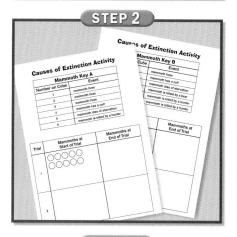

STEP 3

Guided Inquiry

Ask Questions Ask a question about what happened to real woolly mammoths. Based on the activity, **infer** what happened to them. Then, do research to check your inference.

Species in Danger

MAIN IDEA A kind of organism that once lived on Earth but no longer exists is extinct. A kind of organism that is almost extinct is called endangered.

VOCABULARY

endangered
   species   p. 76
extinct species   p. 72
species   p. 72

READING SKILL

Cause and Effect
As you read, use the chart to record causes of organisms becoming endangered or extinct.

| Cause | → | Effect |

STANDARDS

3.d. *Students know* when the environment changes, some plants and animals survive and reproduce; others die or move to new locations.
3.e. *Students know* that some kinds of organisms that once lived on Earth have completely disappeared and that some of those resembled others that are alive today.

Natural Threats

You probably know that dinosaurs were animals that lived millions of years ago. There were many species (SPEE sheez) of dinosaur. A **species** is a group of the same type of living thing that can mate and produce other living things of the same kind.

All of the different species of dinosaur became extinct (ihk STIHNGKT) long ago. An **extinct species** is a species that has died off. Dinosaurs became extinct because they were unable to survive changes in their environment.

Many different species of dinosaurs existed during the millions of years that these animals lived on Earth. During this long time period, some species became extinct due to natural causes. But new species of dinosaurs developed.

Most scientists think that a large rock from space, called a meteorite, struck Earth about 65 million years ago. This collision produced a long period of darkness as well as cold temperatures. It is thought that these conditions caused the extinction of all species of dinosaurs then alive.

CAUSE AND EFFECT What do most scientists believe caused the extinction of dinosaurs?

▲ The diplodocus (dih PLAHD uh kuhs) may have become extinct because the plants it ate died out.

Modern organisms also face natural threats that could lead to their becoming extinct. Events such as volcanic eruptions, earthquakes, and fires can threaten the survival of a species. For example, the olive ridley sea turtle is nearly extinct. In 2004 an earthquake caused a tsunami, or giant wave. The tsunami struck the coast of India and other countries. It killed many olive ridley sea turtles. It also damaged the beaches where they lay their eggs.

CAUSE AND EFFECT **What natural events can cause a species to become extinct?**

The olive ridley sea turtle may soon be an extinct species. ▶

Human Threats

Many species have become extinct in the last few hundred years. Most did not die out from natural causes. They disappeared because of human activities.

Some species have become extinct because people hunted them. As many as 30 million American bison (BY suhn) once lived in North America. Huge herds of American bison once roamed the plains.

During the 1800s, settlers moved westward across America. These settlers hunted bison both for their meat and for sport. As a result, so many bison were killed that the species was close to becoming extinct.

In 1890 there were only 750 bison left. In recent years, humans have helped the bison population grow again. The remaining animals were moved to protected parks and wildlife reserves.

The bison population has increased to about 80,000 today. ▼

▲ The Pyrenean ibex became
extinct when hunters killed
the last of these animals.

▲ The dodo had a very
large body with short
wings. It could not fly.

Other organisms have become extinct when
humans brought new species into an area. Dodos
were flightless birds that lived on an island. When
human ships arrived on the island, pigs, rats, and
dogs came with them. These animals ate the dodos
and their eggs. People also hunted dodos.

Many species become extinct because humans
change or destroy their habitat. People construct
buildings and roads. They cut down forests to
grow crops. These changes reduce the amount of
food, water, and shelter available to other species.
Often a species becomes extinct for a number of
different reasons.

CAUSE AND EFFECT **What is one way that humans
cause other species to become extinct?**

Express Lab

Activity Card 6
Create a Mountain Lion Habitat

Endangered Species

Today, many plant and animal species are in danger of becoming extinct. An **endangered species** (ehn DAYN jurd-SPEE sheez) is one that has so few members that the entire species is at risk of dying out.

Laws have been passed to protect endangered species. There have been some success stories. For example, bald eagles are returning to many states, including California, where they were once almost extinct.

CAUSE AND EFFECT What are two possible effects of an organism's habitat being destroyed?

California bighorn sheep

These animals became endangered because of hunting and habitat destruction. They must also compete for food with farm sheep.

Eurasian peregrine falcon

These birds were unable to reproduce because they ate poisons used for killing insects.

Queen Alexandra's birdwing butterfly

This is the largest butterfly known. Its wingspan can be as long as 30 cm (1 ft). It lives only in the rainforests of New Guinea, which are being cut down.

Visual Summary

A species becomes extinct when all members of the species die off and the species no longer exists.

A species can become extinct when its environment changes, either from natural or human causes.

A species is endangered when there are so few members left that the species is in danger of becoming extinct.

STANDARDS 3.d., 3.e.

Technology
Visit **www.eduplace.com/cascp** to find out more about extinct and endangered species.

Reading Review

① MAIN IDEA What can cause a species to become endangered or extinct?

② VOCABULARY Use the term *species* in a sentence.

③ READING SKILL What is an example of a human cause of extinction?

| Cause | ⇒ | Effect |

④ CRITICAL THINKING: Apply How could you save a species that is endangered because of hunting?

⑤ INQUIRY SKILL: Use Numbers Suppose one species becomes extinct for every 1,000 square meters of forest that are cut down. If 4,000 square meters of forest are cut, how many species become extinct?

✔ TEST PRACTICE

Which cause of extinction does NOT involve human activities?

A. hunting

B. habitat destruction

C. a volcanic eruption

D. new species introduction

STANDARDS
1–2: 3.d., 3.e., 3: 3.e., 4: 3.d., 5: 5.c., Test Practice: 3.e.

What Can Be Learned from Fossils?

Building Background

Parts of a long-dead animal are discovered in rock. Scientists try to answer questions about the discovery. What type of animal was it? When did it die? They study the remains of organisms that lived long ago. They hope to learn more about them. Often they look for ways in which these long-dead organisms resemble living things on Earth today.

PREPARE TO INVESTIGATE

Inquiry Skill

Hypothesize If you think you know why something that you observe happens, you can make a hypothesis, or an educated guess, about it.

Materials

- modeling clay
- small object (shell, leaf, twig)
- hand lens

Science and Math Toolbox

For step 3, review **Using a Hand Lens** on page H2.

STANDARDS

3.e. *Students know* that some kinds of organisms that once lived on Earth have completely disappeared and that some of those resembled others that are alive today.
5.b. Differentiate evidence from opinion and know that scientists do not rely on claims or conclusions unless they are backed by observations that can be confirmed.

Make a Fossil

Procedure

STEP 1

1. **Use Models** Make a model of a fossil (FAHS uhl). A **fossil** is the remains, or traces, of a living thing preserved in some way. Mold a piece of clay into a thick, flat layer. Press an object into the clay until the object makes an imprint. Carefully remove the object.

2. Exchange imprints with a partner. Do not let your partner see the object that you used to make the imprint.

STEP 2

3. **Record Data** Use a hand lens to look closely at your partner's imprint. Record your observations of the imprint.

4. **Hypothesize** Based on your observations, try to identify the object that was used to make your partner's imprint.

STEP 3

5. **Use Models** Now exchange objects with your partner. Record the similarities and differences between your partner's object and the imprint made from it.

Conclusion

1. **Infer** What clues about organisms can scientists learn from studying fossils?

2. **Infer** What cannot be learned from fossils? What other evidence can scientists use to study organisms of long ago?

Guided Inquiry

Experiment Collect other natural objects to make into fossils. **Hypothesize** which objects will make good fossils. Carry out an experiment to test your hypotheses.

VOCABULARY

era	p. 82
fossil	p. 80
paleontologist	p. 81

READING SKILL

Sequence

Use the chart below to show a simple version of the geologic time scale.

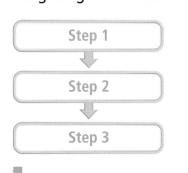

Step 1

↓

Step 2

↓

Step 3

STANDARDS

3.e. *Students know* that some kinds of organisms that once lived on Earth have completely disappeared and that some of those resembled others that are alive today.

This fossil is from a giant tree fern that lived about 300 million years ago. It looks much like ferns that exist today. ▶

Activity Card 7
Find Fossil Clues

Fossils

MAIN IDEA The remains of once living things can be preserved in rock. Scientists study these remains to find out about organisms that lived on Earth long ago.

Why Scientists Study Fossils

How do scientists know what Earth was like millions of years ago? Studying fossils (FAHS uhlz) gives them some clues. A **fossil** is the preserved remains of an organism that lived long ago. Fossils can include bones, teeth, shells, and imprints of organisms that were pressed into mud and sand.

Scientists study fossils to find out how organisms of long ago lived, what they looked like, and what they ate. For example, the shape of a dinosaur's teeth can tell scientists something about what food that dinosaur ate. What kind of food do you think a dinosaur with sharp teeth might have eaten?

modern fern

fossil tree fern

A scientist who studies fossils and forms of life that no longer exist is called a **paleontologist** (pay lee ahn TAHL uh-jihst). Paleontologists can learn many things by looking at fossils. Often, they can use what they learn to make hypotheses about how the organism lived and what its environment was like.

For example, suppose a paleontologist finds a fossil of a fish skeleton. The fossil provides information about the size and shape of the fish. The shape of the teeth give clues about what the fish ate. Scientists know that all fish must live in water. If they find many fish fossils in rock on dry land, they can hypothesize that the area was once underwater.

Fossils are often only part of the remains of an ancient organism. That is why studying a fossil does not always provide complete information about the organism that formed it.

SEQUENCE Describe how an organism becomes a fossil.

Most fossils form from hard parts of living things, such as bone, shell, and wood.

How Fossils Form

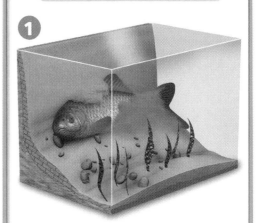
A living thing dies and is buried under layers of sand and soil.

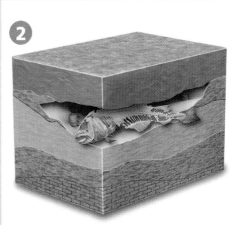
Over a long period of time, the sand and soil harden and turn into rock.

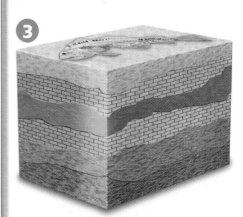
Over time, the rock covering the fossil wears away. The fossil appears on the surface.

65 million years ago to present

Cenozoic Era

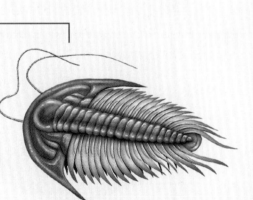

Saber-toothed cats were alive about 16,000 years ago. They lived during the current era, which is called the Cenozoic Era.

248–65 million years ago

Mesozoic Era

The velociraptor (vuh lahs ih-RAP tur) was a small dinosaur. It lived about 70 million years ago during the Mesozoic Era.

544–248 million years ago

Paleozoic Era

Trilobites (TRY luh byts) lived over 300 million years ago. They lived during the Paleozoic (pay lee oh ZOH ihk) Era.

Dating Fossils

Paleontologists find the age of fossils in different ways. In one method, scientists compare the ages of fossils by looking at how deeply the fossils are buried. Fossils in deeper layers of rock are likely older.

Scientists can also use materials in some fossils to find out how old the fossils are. They find the age of most fossils by measuring the ages of the rocks in which the fossils are found.

Scientists have made a timeline, called the geologic (jee uh LAH jihk) time scale. It shows important events in Earth's history. It also tells about the kinds of organisms that lived at different times. A simple version of this scale is shown.

The time scale is broken down into sections called eras (IHR-uhz). An **era** is a major division of time. Each era lasted many millions of years. An era is defined by the events that took place during that time.

SEQUENCE Look at the geologic time scale. Which era came before the Cenozoic Era?

Visual Summary

A fossil is the preserved remains of an organism that lived long ago. Fossils can include bones, teeth, shells, and imprints of organisms that were pressed into mud or sand.

Scientists study fossils to learn about organisms that were once alive.

Scientists have different methods of studying fossils to help them determine when a long-dead organism lived on Earth.

 STANDARDS 3.e.

 Technology
Visit **www.eduplace.com/cascp** to learn more about fossils.

Reading Review

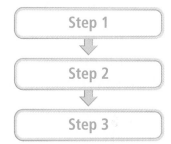

❶ MAIN IDEA What can scientists learn from fossils?

❷ VOCABULARY What is an era?

❸ READING SKILL What are three eras on the geologic time scale?

```
┌─────────────┐
│   Step 1    │
└─────────────┘
      ↓
┌─────────────┐
│   Step 2    │
└─────────────┘
      ↓
┌─────────────┐
│   Step 3    │
└─────────────┘
```

❹ CRITICAL THINKING: Analyze Can scientists tell what color an animal was by looking at a fossil? Why or why not?

❺ INQUIRY SKILL: Hypothesize Suppose you find a fossil that looks like a leaf. Hypothesize the type of environment that this fossil came from.

✔ TEST PRACTICE

A paleontologist studies ____.

A. endangered animals.

B. fossils.

C. fish.

D. leaves.

FOSSIL FIND

In ancient times when people found the skeletons of unusual animals, they thought they had found the bones of mythical creatures. In more recent times, scientists have learned about the true nature of the long-dead organisms that left fossil clues.

In the early 1800s, a girl named Mary Anning became a successful fossil hunter. She explored the cliffs near her house at the seashore in England. The fossils she found helped scientists learn about extinct species.

CHARACTERS

Mary Anning:
a young girl

Mrs. Anning:
Mary's mother

Joseph Anning:
Mary's brother

Thomas Birch:
a trained fossil collector

STANDARD

3.e. *Students know* that some kinds of organisms that once lived on Earth have completely disappeared and that some of those resembled others that are alive today.

READING LINK

Mrs. Anning: Thank you so much for coming all the way from London, Mr. Birch.

Thomas Birch: I heard that you had many unusual fossils to sell. They may be of great interest to scientists.

Joseph Anning: Scientists! But I thought these bones were just the remains of strange animals that people collected for fun.

Thomas Birch: Oh, no. These bones are actually fossils. That means that they were left by animals that lived long ago. One day, we may be able to tell what Earth was like millions of years ago. You deserve a lot of thanks for finding these fossils, Mrs. Anning.

Mrs. Anning: Actually, you should thank my daughter Mary. She found most of them.

Thomas Birch: Wonderful job, Mary. Why don't you show us your latest find?

Mary Anning: *(showing a fossil)* It's a strange sea creature that my brother and I found.

Joseph Anning: I found its head.

Mary Anning: And I dug it out of the cliff.

Thomas Birch: Wait a moment, how do you know that it's a sea creature?

Mary Anning: Well, its skull looks a bit like a crocodile. Plus, it has fins like a dolphin. Crocodiles and dolphins both live in water, so this creature probably did too.

Joseph Anning: They don't live around here, do they? They're scary looking.

Thomas Birch: Scientists think that they died out long ago.

Mrs. Anning: How did the bones come to be here?

Thomas Birch: Well, we're still not sure. We think the animals may have been buried in sand when they died. Over many years, the sand turned into rock. Then, as the ocean wore away the rock, it uncovered the creatures' bones.

Mary Anning: I've found another strange animal. It's much larger than the sea creature, and it has a neck like that of a snake.

Thomas Birch: I'd be very interested to see it.

Mary Anning: I've just begun to get it out of the cliff. You'll have to come down to see! *[Mary runs off.]*

◄ Mary found many fossils of plesiosaurs. These extinct reptiles lived in water, had four flippers, long necks, tiny heads, and wide bodies.

Thomas Birch: Your daughter is very brave and smart.

Joseph Anning: She always seems to know things about the bones she finds.

Mary Anning: [*reappearing*] Here's a fish I found the other day. It looks like a shark.

Thomas Birch: Mary, I have a feeling that you and your family are going to be a great help to scientists studying fossils.

Mary Anning uncovered the skeleton of an ichthyosaur. This extinct sea animal was a fishlike reptile. ▼

In 1828, Mary discovered the fossil of a pterodactyl. These ancient reptiles had large, featherless wings. ▼

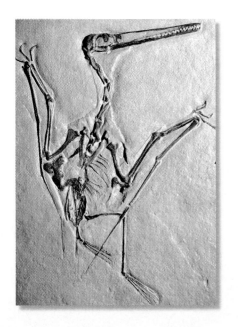

Sharing Ideas

1. **READING CHECK** How did fossil remains of sea animals come to be in the cliffs near Mary's house?

2. **WRITE ABOUT IT** What facts did Mary Anning use to hypothesize that the animal she found was a sea creature?

3. **TALK ABOUT IT** Discuss how Mary's discoveries could help scientists who did not yet understand what fossils were.

87

How Are Extinct and Living Things Alike?

Building Background

Most people would say a woolly mammoth looked like an elephant with thick fur. Scientists use similarities between modern and extinct species to learn about extinct species. Scientists believe that woolly mammoths, like modern-day elephants, ate plants and roamed in herds.

PREPARE TO INVESTIGATE

Inquiry Skill

Classify When you classify, you sort objects according to their properties.

Materials

- Extinct and Living Animal Species cards Support Master

STANDARDS

3.e. *Students know* that some kinds of organisms that once lived on Earth have completely disappeared and that some of those resembled others that are alive today.
5.b. Differentiate evidence from opinion and know that scientists do not rely on claims or conclusions unless they are backed by observations that can be confirmed.

Extinct and Living

Procedure

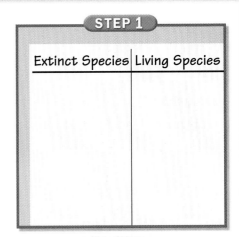

STEP 1

Extinct Species	Living Species

1. Make a chart like the one shown. Cut out the picture cards of extinct and living animal species. Arrange the cards in two sets—extinct species and living species.

2. **Observe** Look at the set of cards showing extinct species. Note the features of each species.

3. **Compare** Repeat step 2 for the cards showing living species. Compare the appearance of each extinct species with the appearance of each living species.

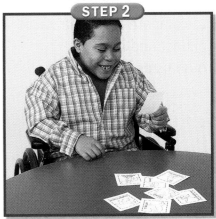

STEP 2

4. **Classify** Match each extinct species with the living species it most resembles. Then place each matched pair of cards on your chart in the correct columns.

5. **Hypothesize** Write a hypothesis about whether or not the species in each paired set might be related.

STEP 4

Conclusion

1. **Infer** What kind of information can you gather by comparing the appearance of extinct and living species?

2. What other evidence might scientists look for to determine whether an extinct species and living species are actually related?

Guided Inquiry

Ask Questions How was a _____ like a _____? Fill in the name of an extinct species in the first blank. Fill in the name of a living species in the second blank. **Research** the answer to your question.

VOCABULARY

ancestor	p. 90
relative	p. 91
trait	p. 91

READING SKILL

Compare and Contrast
Use the graphic organizer to compare and contrast extinct and living organisms.

Compare	Contrast

STANDARD

3.e. *Students know* that some kinds of organisms that once lived on Earth have completely disappeared and that some of those resembled others that are alive today.

Extinct and Modern Animals

MAIN IDEA Many extinct animals resemble animals that are alive today. Scientists use these similarities to help them understand what the extinct animals were like.

Elephant Ancestors

There are only two species of elephants alive today—African elephants and Asian elephants. And there are no other animals that look like elephants. Both these modern elephants share animal ancestors. An **ancestor** is a species or form of a species that lived long ago and to which modern species may be traced back.

Moeritherium
(50 million years ago)

Phiomia
(35 million years ago)

Elephants do not have any close living relatives. A **relative** is a species that shares a common ancestor with another species. A relative also shares many traits with that other species. A **trait** is a feature such as a body part or a behavior. For example, large ears are a trait of both African and Asian elephants.

Elephants have few living relatives, but they have many extinct ancestors and relatives. Some elephant ancestors looked a lot like modern elephants.

Other elephant ancestors looked very different from modern elephants. For example, Phiomia (fee-OH mee uh) had tusks but a very small trunk. The woolly mammoth was covered with fur.

Usually, ancestors that have very different traits from modern animals lived longer ago. Ancestors that have many of the same traits lived more recently.

COMPARE AND CONTRAST In what ways are modern elephants and their ancestors alike and different?

Deinotherium
(10 million years ago)

Elephants (alive today)

91

Animal Look-Alikes

Like the elephant, other modern species look similar to extinct species. However, not all of these look-alikes are related. For example, the emu is a large bird that cannot fly. It shares several traits with the extinct diatryma (dih AH trih mah). But fossils show that the birds are not related. The diatryma was a meat-eater. Emus eat seeds and insects.

Fossils show that the rhinoceros and the extinct indricothere (IHN druh koh-THIHR) are related. Rhinos, like the indricothere, are mammals, eat leaves, and have feet with three toes.

Diatryma

A diatryma was a large bird that is now extinct. It could not fly. It hunted small animals.

Indricothere

The indricothere was the largest land mammal ever known. It was 5.5 m (18 ft) tall.

▲ The emu is a large bird from Australia. It cannot fly.

◀ Although the modern rhinoceros looks fierce, it eats only leaves and grass.

▲ Crocodiles are reptiles that have changed very little over time.

Extinct Crocodile

This extinct crocodile species was similar to modern crocodiles. Its behavior was probably also similar.

The saber-toothed cat was a fierce-looking mammal. It had two 18-cm (7-in.) long teeth. It used its jaws to rip apart the animals it hunted. It was not a fast runner because its legs were short.

This animal is not closely related to modern wild cats. Bengal tigers are larger, have shorter teeth, and have longer legs than saber-toothed cats.

COMPARE AND CONTRAST How is a diatryma like an emu?

Saber-toothed Cat

Saber-toothed cats likely became extinct when the animals they ate died out.

◄ The Bengal tiger and saber-toothed cat share some traits, but they are not closely related.

◀ This animal, thought by some scientists to be one of the first birds, is called archaeopteryx (ark ee OP tuh riks). It was related to dinosaurs, had wings, and was covered with feathers.

▲ Modern birds look different from dinosaurs, but share some of their traits.

Dinosaur-Bird Connections

Dinosaurs became extinct about 65 million years ago. There are no modern species that have all of the traits of dinosaurs. But some modern species, such as birds, may have had dinosaurs as ancestors.

Recently, scientists have found fossils of dinosaurs that had wings and feathers. These small, winged, meat-eating dinosaurs share other traits with birds. The shape of their hips and the ways in which their hearts and lungs work are similar to those traits in birds. Many scientists believe that these dinosaurs are the ancestors of modern birds.

COMPARE AND CONTRAST In what ways are modern birds similar to their ancestors?

Express Lab

Activity Card 8
Classify Animals

Visual Summary

An ancestor is a species or form of a species that lived long ago and to which modern species can be traced back.

Some modern species resemble extinct species. These species may or may not be related.

Some modern animals, such as birds, share some traits with dinosaurs.

STANDARDS 3.e.

Technology
Visit www.eduplace.com/cascp to learn more about animal ancestors.

Reading Review

❶ MAIN IDEA How do scientists learn about extinct species?

❷ VOCABULARY Define the term *ancestor*.

❸ READING SKILL How are saber-toothed cats and Bengal tigers alike? How are they different?

Compare	Contrast

❹ CRITICAL THINKING: Evaluate You see a fossil that looks like the skeleton of a modern wolf. Can you conclude that the extinct animal is related to modern wolves? Explain.

❺ INQUIRY SKILL: Classify Why can the rhinoceros and the indricothere be classified as relatives?

✔ TEST PRACTICE
The fossil of an extinct ancestor of the pigeon has many of the same traits as the modern pigeon. This animal most likely lived _____ years ago.

A. 200   **C.** 200 million

B. 1 million   **D.** 3 billion

STANDARDS

1–5: 3.e., Test Practice: 3.e.

95

SuperCroc!

How big can crocodiles get? Modern crocodiles can reach about 5 m (16 ft) long and weigh almost a metric ton (about 2,000 pounds). Now imagine coming face-to-face with a creature that would make those crocs look puny. Meet SuperCroc—the largest crocodile that ever lived.

This huge animal's scientific name means "emperor of the flesh-eating crocodiles." But when paleontologists discovered its huge fossil in Africa, they called it "SuperCroc." You can see why. This beast could easily have eaten a 20-foot dinosaur. And it probably did!

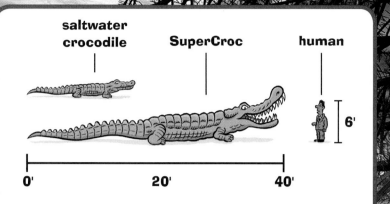

saltwater crocodile   SuperCroc   human

6'

0'   20'   40'

SuperCroc was 40 feet long — the length of a city bus. It weighed more than two large elephants!

Writing Journal

SuperCroc is extinct, but it must have been a fierce meat-eater. It lived around 110 million years ago. It hunted along the rivers in central Africa.

In your writing journal, tell why you think modern crocodiles are so much smaller than SuperCroc. Then, hypothesize why SuperCroc became extinct.

MATH Compare and Order Numbers

Draw a timeline to show the order of appearance of modern elephants and their ancestors on Earth. Use this sample timeline to help you get started. Then, place the elephant ancestors listed above the timeline in their correct order on your timeline.

Moeritherium (50 million years ago)
Deinotherium (10 million years ago)
Elephant (3 million years ago)
Phiomia (35 million years ago)

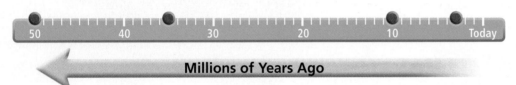

Use your timeline to answer the questions below.

1. What is the elephant's earliest ancestor?

2. Which two relatives of the elephant lived most recently?

3. Which relative lived closest in time to the modern elephant?

WRITING Letter

Some endangered species have been saved from extinction by the efforts of people. Choose a species on the endangered species list. Write a letter to a newspaper or a government official telling why it is important for that species to be saved. Be sure to include details about what can be done to save this species.

California

Dr. Carole Hickman

What was Earth like millions of years ago? One place to find out is the Museum of Paleontology of the University of California. The museum collects fossils of organisms that lived long ago.

Professor Carole Hickman is one of the scientists who run the museum. Can you guess which ancient living things she likes to research? She studies mollusks. These are animals that have soft bodies and usually have shells. Snails and clams are examples of mollusks.

▲ Dr. Carole Hickman studies mollusk fossils.

Professor Hickman knows what mollusks of long ago looked like and how they changed over time. She studies the fossils of mollusks to learn more about Earth's history.

Dr. Hickman at the University of California Museum of Paleontology where she does much of her work. ▼

Vocabulary

Complete each sentence with a term from the list.

1. A species or form of a species that lived long ago and to which modern species may be traced back is a/an _____.

2. The preserved remains of an organism is a/an _____.

3. A scientist who studies fossils is a/an _____.

4. A species that shares a common ancestor and has many traits in common with another species is a/an _____ of that species.

5. A group of the same type of living thing that can mate and produce living things of the same kind is a/an _____.

6. A major division of time is a/an _____.

7. A species that is at risk of dying out is a/an _____.

8. A feature, such as a body part or behavior, is a/an _____.

9. A species that has died off is called a/an _____.

ancestor p. 90
endangered species p. 76
era p. 82
extinct species p. 72
fossil p. 80
paleontologist p. 81
relative p. 91
species p. 72
trait p. 91

✔ Test Practice

Write the letter of the best answer choice.

10. A dodo is an example of a/an _____.

    A. ancestor of the elephant.
    B. endangered species.
    C. relative of the saber-toothed cat.
    D. extinct species.

11. A paleontologist would most likely study _____.

    A. why tigers have become endangered.
    B. whether dinosaurs are related to birds.
    C. how fish breathe with gills.
    D. what modern wolves eat.

12. Dinosaurs became extinct because of _____.

    A. natural causes and human activities.
    B. human activities.
    C. natural causes.
    D. water pollution.

13. The ancestors of the elephant _____.

    A. share no traits with modern elephants.
    B. share some traits with modern elephants.
    C. share all traits with modern elephants.
    D. are not related to modern elephants.

Inquiry Skills

14. **Classify** Look at the geologic time scale on page 82. An organism lived 300 million years ago. In which era did it live?

15. Suppose there are only 75 birds of a species left in the world. Because of over-hunting, the number of birds drops to 10. Is this species endangered or extinct? Explain.

Map the Concept

Use the terms from the list to fill in the concept map.

behavior   relatives
bones   shells
food sources   teeth

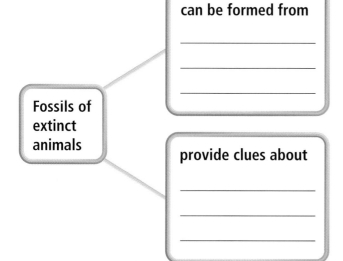

Fossils of extinct animals

can be formed from
_____
_____
_____

provide clues about
_____
_____
_____

Critical Thinking

16. **Analyze** A magazine article tells about an extinct ancestor of modern lions. What are some traits the extinct ancestor might have?

17. **Evaluate** Suppose a fossil is found on a mountain. The animal that formed the fossil had fins, a tail, and a flat body. What evidence is there to support the idea that the mountain was once under the ocean? Explain.

18. **Synthesize** Identify two human activities that might cause species to become extinct.

19. **Apply** What might people do to save a species that is endangered because of destruction of its habitat?

Performance Assessment

Make a Poster
Modern elephants have few living relatives. They include manatees and hyraxes. Research these animals and create a poster showing the traits they share with elephants.

Writing Journal

Review your answers to the Lesson Preview questions on page 67. Change your answers, as needed, based on what you learned.

STANDARDS

1–4: 3.e., 5: 3.d., 6: 3.e., 7–9: 3.d., 10–11: 3.e., 12: 3.d., 13–14: 3.e., 15: 3.e., 5.c.,
Map the Concept: 3.e., 16–17: 3.e., 18–19: 3.d., Performance Assessment: 3.e.

Write the letter of the best answer choice.

1. Which is an example of a population?

   A. all the soil in a grassland
   B. all the pebbles in a desert
   C. all the rabbits living in a forest
   D. all of the whales and sharks living in an ocean

2. Which environment is likely to have the fewest number of trees?

   A. forest
   B. tundra
   C. grassland
   D. wetland

3. Which of these organisms is most likely to compete with a coyote for food?

   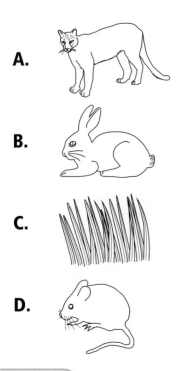

   A.

   B.

   C.

   D.

4. A plant growing near a tide pool most likely needs to be adapted

   to _____.

   A. long periods without rain.
   B. being covered with snow.
   C. being shaded by tall trees.
   D. being covered by salt water for short periods.

5. By looking at the geologic time scale,

   you can learn about _____.

   A. the best places to find fossils.
   B. organisms that lived in the past.
   C. food sources of extinct species.
   D. causes of species extinction.

6. Which species shares traits with the extinct woolly mammoth?

   A. rhinoceros
   B. emu
   C. elephant
   D. crocodile

7. Which habitat has been changed by human activities?

A.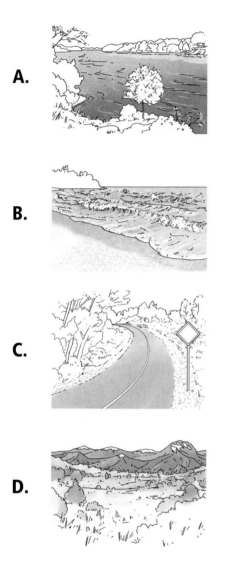

B.

C.

D.

8. Which of the following may happen when an environment changes?

A. organisms die.

B. organisms survive and reproduce.

C. organisms move to new locations.

D. all of the above

Answer the following in complete sentences.

9. The South American owl butterfly looks similar to an owl's face.

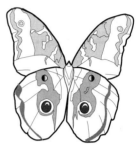

What kind of adaptation is this—structural or behavioral? How might this adaptation be helpful?

10. Explain all the ways that a tree might change the ecosystem around it.

STANDARDS

1–2: 3.b., 3: 3.c., 4: 3.a., 5–6: 3.e., 7: 3.c.,
8: 3.d., 9: 3.a., 10: 3.c., 3.d.

You Can...

Discover More

Polar bears are adapted to the cold, icy environment of the Arctic. Thick fur and a layer of fat keep them warm in freezing temperatures. Even their paws are adapted for their environment. These adaptations make it easy for polar bears to walk on ice without slipping.

Polar bears have four paws that can be over 25 cm (about 10 in.) wide. Each paw has five toes, and each toe has a long sharp claw. These claws help polar bears grip the ice.

Each polar bear paw has seven footpads. The footpads are made of a thick, black layer of skin and are covered with small bumps. The bumps on the bear's footpads are like the treads on a sport shoe. They grip the ice and keep the bear from slipping when it runs.

Long fur between the footpads and toes keeps polar bears from slipping, too. Webbing that is under the fur between the toes helps polar bears swim.

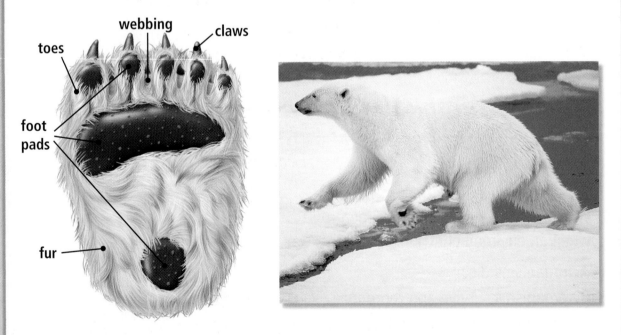

webbing
claws
toes
foot pads
fur

Simulations Go to www.eduplace.com/cascp to see how polar bears and other animals adapt to their environments.

Patterns in the Sky

California Connection

Visit www.eduplace.com/cascp
to find out about California
planetariums and observatories.

California Field Trip

Mount Palomar Observatory

The observatory has five telescopes that are used for astronomy research.

The Hale telescope is the second largest telescope in the world.

The California Nebula is made up of hydrogen gas and dust.

Patterns in the Sky

Earth from space

California Big Idea!

Objects in the sky
move in regular and
predictable patterns.

Chapter **4**

Our Solar System

Saturn and its rings

LESSON 1

They're on mountaintops, in backyards, and in outer space. How do telescopes help people study objects in space?

LESSON 2

Eight planets, dwarf planets, many moons, and other objects travel in paths around the Sun. What are Earth's neighbors in space?

LESSON 3

Mercury, Venus, and Mars have some things in common with Earth. What do scientists know about the planets closest to the Sun?

LESSON 4

Jupiter, Saturn, Uranus, and Neptune are the farthest planets from the Sun. What are these planets like?

Writing Journal

In your Writing Journal, show what you know by writing or drawing answers to each question.

Vocabulary Preview

Vocabulary

Vocabulary Skill

Homophones
Sun son

Homophones are words that sound the same but have different meanings. They may also be spelled differently. For example, the word *Sun* means "the nearest star to Earth." The homophone of *Sun*, the word *son*, means "a parent's male child." Both words are pronounced "suhn."

orbit
To move in a path around an object.

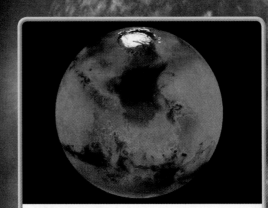

planet
A large body in space that orbits a star.

telescope
A tool that makes distant objects appear larger, brighter, and sharper.

Start with Your Standards

Standard Set 1. Physical Sciences (Energy and Matter)

1.a. *Students know* energy comes from the Sun to Earth in the form of light.

Standard Set 4. Earth Sciences

4.c. *Students know* telescopes magnify the appearance of some distant objects in the sky, including the Moon and the planets. The number of stars that can be seen through a telescope is dramatically greater than the number that can be seen by the unaided eye.

4.d. *Students know* that Earth is one of several planets that orbit the Sun and that the Moon orbits Earth.

Standard Set 5. Investigation and Experimentation covered in this chapter: 5.a., 5.c., 5.d., 5.e.

Sun
The nearest star to Earth.

How Do Scientists Use Telescopes?

Building Background

Stars and planets look like tiny points of light in the night sky. The Moon looks white and flat. How have scientists learned what distant objects in space really look like? They use telescopes to view these objects more clearly.

PREPARE TO INVESTIGATE

Inquiry Skill

Compare When you compare you describe how objects or events are alike and how they are different, often by using numbers.

Materials

- 2 cardboard tubes
- transparent tape
- convex lens A (15-cm focal length)
- convex lens B (5-cm focal length)

STANDARDS

4.c. *Students know* telescopes magnify the appearance of some distant objects in the sky, including the Moon and the planets. The number of stars that can be seen through telescopes is dramatically greater than the number that can be seen by the unaided eye.
5.a. Repeat observations to improve accuracy and know that the results of similar scientific investigations seldom turn out exactly the same because of differences in the things being investigated, methods being used, or uncertainty in the observations.

Making a Telescope

Procedure

STEP 1

1. Make a telescope. Slip a smaller tube inside a larger tube to make a telescope tube. Tape lens A, the larger, thinner lens, to the larger end of the telescope tube. Tape lens B, the smaller, thicker lens, to the smaller end of the tube.

STEP 1

2. **Observe** Without using the telescope, observe three objects that are across the room. In your *Science Notebook,* record how the objects look.

3. **Record Data** Use the telescope to observe the same three objects. Hold the smaller end of the telescope to your eye and look through the lens. Slowly slide the larger tube forward and back until you can see each object clearly. Record how the objects look.

STEP 3

4. **Compare** Exchange telescopes with a partner and repeat step 3.

Conclusion

1. **Compare** What differences did you notice when you viewed the objects with just your eyes, and then with the telescope? What differences did you notice when you viewed the objects with your partner's telescope?

2. **Infer** Why do you think telescopes are useful to scientists who study space?

Guided Inquiry

Experiment With an adult, take your telescope outside at night. **Observe** the Moon with just your eyes. Then use your telescope to observe the Moon.

VOCABULARY

magnify   p. 112
telescope   p. 112

READING SKILL

Problem-Solution
Use a chart like the one below. In the *Problem* column, write "Earth's atmosphere prevents people from having a clear view of the planets." In the *Solution* column, write a possible solution to the problem.

Problem	Solution

STANDARDS

4.c. *Students know* telescopes magnify the appearance of some distant objects in the sky, including the Moon and the planets. The number of stars that can be seen through telescopes is dramatically greater than the number that can be seen by the unaided eye.

Seeing Into Space

MAIN IDEA Telescopes help scientists study stars, the Moon, and the planets.

Telescopes

If you look up at the night sky, you can see the Moon. You can also see small points of light. Most of these points of light are stars. A few of them are planets. How can you see these objects more clearly?

A telescope can help you see details of objects in the sky. A **telescope** is a tool that makes distant objects appear larger, brighter, and sharper. When you make an object appear larger, you **magnify** it. The number of stars that can be seen through a telescope is much greater than the number that can be seen with just your eyes.

▲ This optical telescope is on Mount Palomar in California.

▲ This radio telescope in Arecibo, Puerto Rico, is the largest in the world.

It is dangerous to look directly at the Sun. Looking directly at the Sun can damage your eyes. People observing the Sun should never look straight at it, even with a telescope. It is safe to look directly at other stars, which are more distant.

There are different kinds of telescopes. One kind of telescope magnifies distant objects by collecting light. This is called an optical (AHP tihk uhl) telescope. A radio telescope collects radio waves instead of light. Computers use the radio waves to make pictures of space. As more powerful telescopes are invented, scientists learn more about objects in space.

PROBLEM AND SOLUTION What tool can you use to see objects in space more clearly?

The Hubble Space Telescope is an optical telescope. It travels around Earth 569 km (353 mi) above the surface. ▶

A Hubble Scrapbook

The Hubble Space Telescope is different from other telescopes because it is in space. It moves around Earth every 97 minutes. The Hubble was launched in 1990 from a space shuttle.

Earth's atmosphere, the blanket of air around the planet, contains clouds, dust, and water. The atmosphere blurs our view of objects in space. But the Hubble takes photographs of space from beyond Earth's atmosphere. It gives scientists a clearer view of distant regions of space.

PROBLEM AND SOLUTION **How is the Hubble able to help scientists see space more clearly?**

▲ Lagoon Nebula

▲ Pillars of Creation

Express Lab

Activity Card 9
Show What Magnification Does

Visual Summary

Telescopes are tools that make distant objects appear larger, brighter, and sharper so they can be seen more clearly.

Optical telescopes magnify distant objects, such as planets. Radio telescopes collect radio waves.

The Hubble Space Telescope is in space. It helps scientists to clearly see objects beyond Earth's atmosphere.

Technology
Visit **www.eduplace.com/cascp** to research more about telescopes.

Reading Review

❶ MAIN IDEA Why do scientists use telescopes?

❷ VOCABULARY Use the terms *telescope* and *magnify* in a sentence.

❸ READING SKILL Suggest a problem that could be solved by using a telescope.

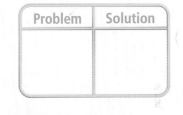

Problem	Solution

❹ CRITICAL THINKING: Evaluate Why do you think it is dangerous to look directly at the Sun?

❺ INQUIRY SKILL: Compare How is a radio telescope different from an optical telescope?

✔ TEST PRACTICE

The Hubble Space Telescope is _____.

A. a radio telescope.

B. above Earth's atmosphere.

C. on a mountaintop.

D. always in the same place.

DEEP IMPACT!

A comet is a small ball of dust, ice, and rock traveling around the Sun. Most comets are billions of kilometers from Earth. But some follow paths that bring them closer to Earth once every few thousand years. These objects can tell scientists many things about how the Sun and planets formed.

How can scientists learn a comet's secrets? In July of 2005, the spacecraft Deep Impact approached the comet Tempel 1. It fired a 370-kg object at the comet. The impact sent an explosion of dust and gases into space. It left behind a crater, or hole, in the comet's surface.

Telescopes all over Earth recorded the impact. Scientists in Goldstone, California, took photographs of the dust cloud and the crater. These photographs gave them many clues about the inside of the comet. Scientists can use these clues to learn about the comet's history.

A bright explosion of dust and gas flies off the Tempel 1 comet. This photograph was taken by the Deep Impact spacecraft.

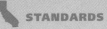
STANDARDS

4.c. *Students know* telescopes magnify the appearance of some distant objects in the sky, including the Moon and the planets. The number of stars that can be seen through telescopes is dramatically greater than the number that can be seen by the unaided eye.

READING

Large radio telescopes like this one in the Deep Space Network in Goldstone, California, recorded the comet impact. This radio telescope dish is 70 m (about 230 feet) across. But smaller telescopes could see the impact as well. People were encouraged to watch the impact through backyard telescopes and send scientists their observations. ▼

▲ Drawing of the Deep Impact spacecraft firing at the comet

Sharing Ideas

1. **READING CHECK** What two tools did scientists use to study the comet Tempel 1?

2. **WRITE ABOUT IT** Suppose you used a small telescope to observe the impact of Tempel 1. Write a descriptive paragraph telling what you might see.

3. **TALK ABOUT IT** Would scientists have been able to learn as much from Tempel 1 if they did not have telescopes? Why or why not?

What Is the Solar System?

Building Background

Earth is part of a group of objects including planets, moons, and one star—the Sun. The Sun is in the center of all these other objects. Each of eight planets, including Earth, moves in a path around the Sun.

STANDARDS

4.d. *Students know* that Earth is one of several planets that orbit the Sun and that the Moon orbits Earth.
5.e. Collect data in an investigation and analyze those data to develop a logical conclusion.

PREPARE TO INVESTIGATE

Inquiry Skill

Use Models You can use a model of an object, process, or idea to better understand or describe how it works.

Materials

- drinking straw
- scissors
- metric ruler
- string (1 m long)
- small plastic-foam ball
- metal washer
- tape
- goggles

Science and Math Toolbox

For step 1, review **Using a Tape Measure or Ruler** on page H6.

Planet Movements

Procedure

1. **Measure** Cut a drinking straw so that it is 12 cm long. Thread a piece of string that is 1 m long through the straw.

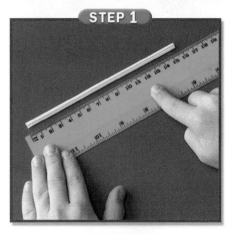
STEP 1

2. Tie one end of the string to a washer. Wrap the other end of the string around a plastic-foam ball and tie it tightly. Use tape to secure the string to the ball.

STEP 2

3. **Use Models** Hold the straw upright with one hand. Rest the washer in your other hand. Hold the washer so that there is 10 cm of string between the ball and the top of the straw. Stand away from your classmates. Move the straw in a circular motion above your head so the ball swings in a circle around the straw. In your *Science Notebook,* describe the motion of the ball. **Safety:** Wear goggles.

STEP 3

4. **Experiment** Repeat step 3, using 15 cm of string and then 60 cm of string.

Conclusion

1. **Use Models** What do you think the ball represents in the model?

2. **Infer** Venus is closer to the Sun than is Jupiter. Which planet travels farther around the Sun?

Guided Inquiry

Ask Questions Write a question about how a planet's distance from the Sun affects the time it takes to go around the Sun. Use the Internet to **compare** the lengths of a "year" on each planet.

The Solar System

MAIN IDEA The solar system is made up of the Sun, eight orbiting planets, their moons, dwarf planets, and other objects traveling around the Sun.

The Sun and Planets

Each day, the Sun fills our sky with light. The **Sun** is the nearest star to Earth. Like all stars, the Sun is a huge sphere of hot gases that gives off heat and light. We can see more distant stars at night.

Throughout time, people have also noticed starlike objects that move among the fixed patterns of stars. These objects came to be called "wanderers," or planets. A **planet** is a large body in space that moves around a star.

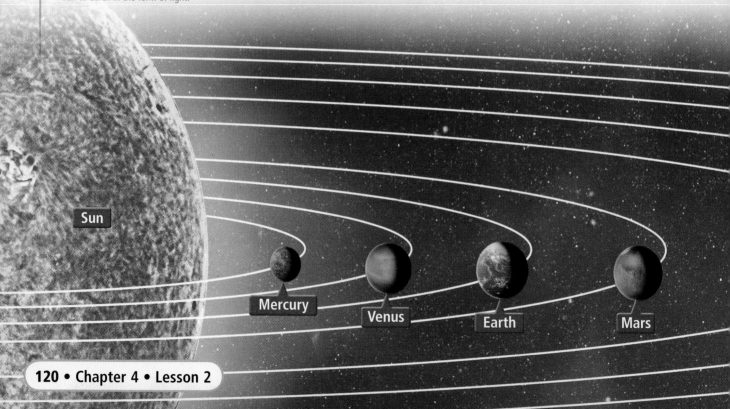

Sun

Mercury

Venus

Earth

Mars

A planet does not produce light of its own. We are able to see planets shining in the night sky when light from the Sun reflects, or bounces, off of them. Earth is one of eight planets that **orbit**, or move in a path, around the Sun.

You can also see Earth's moon in the night sky. A **moon** is a small, rounded body in orbit around a planet. A moon does not produce its own light. It reflects light from the Sun. Most planets have one or more moons. The Sun, planets, moons, and other objects that orbit the Sun make up the **solar system** (SOH lur SIHS tuhm). Planets and moons have oval-shaped orbits.

COMPARE AND CONTRAST **What is one way that planets and moons are similar?**

Eight planets orbit the Sun in the solar system. Pluto is classified as a dwarf planet.

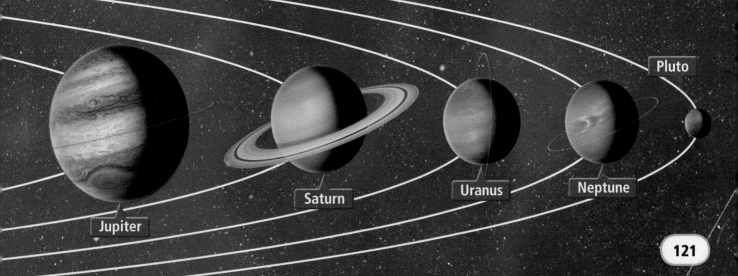

Jupiter

Saturn

Uranus

Neptune

Pluto

The Inner Planets

Mercury, Venus, Earth, and Mars are called the **inner planets**. These planets get a lot of heat and light because they are close to the Sun. The inner planets are small and are made of solid rock materials. Their surfaces have mountains and craters.

Venus (VEE nuhs) is the second planet from the Sun. It is covered by thick clouds of gas. The clouds trap heat and make the planet very hot.

Earth is the third planet from the Sun. It is the only planet known to support life. Earth has an atmosphere.

Mercury (MUR kyuh ree) is the closest planet to the Sun. Mercury is very hot during the day and very cold at night.

Mars (mahrz) is the fourth planet from the Sun. The surface of Mars has many craters, mountains, and volcanoes. Mars has the largest volcano ever discovered in the solar system.

Express Lab

Activity Card 10
Model Different Orbits

The Outer Planets

Jupiter, Saturn, Uranus, and Neptune are called the **outer planets**. They are cold and dark because they are far from the Sun. They are large, made of gases, and have many moons. Each also has a system of rings. Pluto is classified as a dwarf planet. Pluto is small and is made of rocks and frozen gases. It has no rings and only one moon.

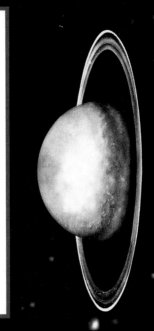

Uranus (YUR uh nuhs) is the seventh planet from the Sun. Unlike any other planet, Uranus spins on its side.

Jupiter (JOO pih tur) is the fifth planet from the Sun and is the largest planet. The Great Red Spot is a large storm.

Neptune (NEHP toon) is the eighth planet from the Sun. Methane in its atmosphere gives Neptune its blue color.

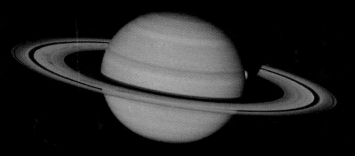

Saturn (SAT urn) is the sixth planet from the Sun. It has beautiful rings made of dust, ice, and rocks.

Pluto (PLOO toh) is a dwarf planet. It is smaller than the planets, and very far from the Sun.

Planets in Motion

As it orbits the Sun, each planet spins like a top. Earth's day, one full spin, is 24 hours long. Some planets spin more quickly than Earth, and some spin more slowly. Jupiter spins around about every 10 hours. Venus takes 243 Earth days to spin once.

The farther a planet is from the Sun, the longer it takes to orbit. The time it takes to complete one trip around the Sun is called a year. Earth's year is about 365 days long. Mercury makes a complete orbit in just 88 Earth days.

Because Earth spins and orbits, it is difficult to measure the orbits of the other planets. It has only been in the past few hundred years that people have figured out how Earth, the Moon, and the planets move.

A planet close to the Sun has a shorter distance to travel as it orbits. It moves faster and has a shorter year than planets farther from the Sun.

Mercury
1 year = 88 Earth days

Earth
1 year = 365 Earth days

Venus
1 year = 225 Earth days

A planet far from the Sun has a longer distance to travel as it orbits. It moves slower and has a longer year than planets closer to the Sun.

Lesson Wrap-Up

Visual Summary

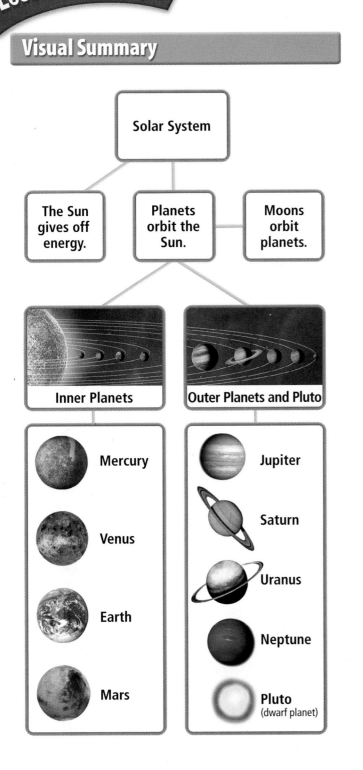

Solar System

The Sun gives off energy.

Planets orbit the Sun.

Moons orbit planets.

Inner Planets

Outer Planets and Pluto

Mercury

Venus

Earth

Mars

Jupiter

Saturn

Uranus

Neptune

Pluto
(dwarf planet)

STANDARDS 4.d., 1.a.

Technology
Visit **www.eduplace.com/cascp** to find out more about the solar system.

Reading Review

① MAIN IDEA Name the planets of the solar system in order of their distance from the Sun.

② VOCABULARY Write a sentence that uses the terms *planet* and *orbit*.

③ READING SKILL How are the inner planets and outer planets alike? How are they different?

Different | Alike | Different

④ CRITICAL THINKING: Analyze A planet has a very long year compared to Earth's year. Do you think that this planet is closer to or farther from the Sun than Earth?

⑤ INQUIRY SKILL: Use Models Suppose you want to use balls to make a model of the Sun and planets of the solar system. How many balls would you need?

TEST PRACTICE
Which statement about the Sun is true?

A. It gives off light.

B. It orbits the planets.

C. It is made of rock.

D. It has one moon.

STANDARDS

1–5: 4.d., Test Practice: 1.a.

What Are the Inner Planets?

Building Background

The inner planets—Mercury, Venus, Earth, and Mars—are alike in some ways. They are small, they are made of rock, and they have few moons. Within your lifetime, people may be traveling to other inner planets.

STANDARDS

4.d. *Students know* that Earth is one of several planets that orbit the Sun and that the Moon orbits Earth.
5.d. Predict the outcome of a simple investigation and compare the result with the prediction.

PREPARE TO INVESTIGATE

Inquiry Skill

Predict When you predict, you state what you think will happen based on observations and experiences.

Materials

- Signs labeled *Sun, Mercury, Venus, Earth*, and *Mars*
- masking tape
- tape measure
- stopwatch

Orbiting the Sun

Procedure

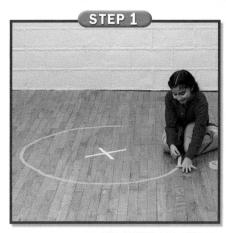
STEP 1

1. **Measure** Make a simple model of the solar system. Use masking tape to make an X on the floor to mark the Sun's position. Mark an orbit around the Sun by placing pieces of tape in a circle 1 m from the X. Make three more orbits with tape, each 1 m farther out from the X.

2. **Collaborate** Five students should hold signs to model the inner planets and the Sun. Use the data in the table to arrange the "planets" in their orbits.

STEP 2

Distance of Planets from Sun	
Planet	Average distance from Sun (millions of km)
Mercury	58
Venus	108
Earth	150
Mars	228

3. **Predict** Predict where each "planet" will be after walking for 5 seconds. Mercury should move most quickly. Venus should move slightly slower. Earth should move more slowly than Venus. Mars should move the slowest.

STEP 2

4. **Use Models** When a timekeeper says to start, the "planets" should walk in their own orbits as described in step 3. After 5 seconds, the timekeeper will tell the "planets" to stop. Draw the position of each "planet."

Conclusion

1. **Compare** Which planet has the greatest distance to travel to complete its orbit?

2. **Infer** What can you infer about how a planet's distance from the Sun and its speed affect the length of its year?

Guided Inquiry

Experiment Extend your model to include Jupiter. How should Jupiter move? **Infer** how the length of a year on Jupiter and a year on Mars differs.

The Inner Planets

VOCABULARY

space probe   p. 132

READING SKILL

Main Idea As you read, write down details that describe each of the inner planets.

STANDARDS

4.d. *Students know* that Earth is one of several planets that orbit the Sun and that the Moon orbits Earth.

MAIN IDEA The inner planets are Mercury, Venus, Earth, and Mars. They are small, ball-shaped, solid, and rocky.

Mercury

Mercury is the nearest planet to the Sun. It is a tiny planet not much larger than Earth's moon. Mercury is so close to the Sun that its surface gets broiling hot during its day. During its night, almost all of the heat escapes, and its surface becomes very cold.

Mercury moves very quickly through space. Its orbit is only 88 Earth days long. This is because Mercury's orbit is so close to the Sun.

Mercury orbits quickly, but spins slowly.

Mercury	
Length of day	59 Earth days
Length of year	88 Earth days
Distance from Sun	58 million km (36 million mi)
Average temperature	Day: 427°C (800°F); Night: −173°C (−279°F)
Diameter	4,878 km (3,029 mi)
Number of moons	none

Venus

Venus is the second planet from the Sun. Venus has been called Earth's twin. This is because Venus is about the same size as Earth and its orbit is next to Earth's orbit. Venus is a very bright planet in Earth's sky. Often Venus can be seen low in the sky, just after sunset.

Venus's motion is very different from Earth's. Venus spins in the opposite direction of most of the other planets. It also spins extremely slowly. In fact, a "day" on Venus is longer than its year. That means that Venus orbits all the way around the Sun before it completes a full spin.

MAIN IDEA Describe two types of motions of both Mercury and Venus.

Venus	
Length of day	243 Earth days
Length of year	225 Earth days
Distance from Sun	108 million km (67 million mi)
Average temperature	482°C (900°F)
Diameter	12,104 km (7,519 mi)
Number of moons	none

Venus's surface is covered by very thick clouds.

Earth

Earth, the third planet, is your home. It is the only planet in the solar system that is known to support life. Earth has both liquid water and oxygen, which most living things need. In addition, Earth's atmosphere keeps the planet from getting too hot or too cold.

Earth's motion causes many of the events you are familiar with from your daily life. Earth spins every 24 hours, causing day and night. It orbits around the Sun about every 365 days, or one year.

Earth

Length of day	24 hours
Length of year	about 365 Earth days
Distance from Sun	150 million km (93 million mi)
Average temperature	15°C (59°F)
Diameter	12,712 km (7,926 mi)
Number of moons	1

Earth's atmosphere and its distance from the Sun keep it at the right temperature to support life.

Mars

Mars, the fourth planet, is called the Red Planet. It is covered with red rocks and soil that contain rust. Canyons, craters, and valleys can be found on its surface. Many scientists believe that liquid water and perhaps life may have once existed on Mars. But no signs of life have yet been found.

Mars and Earth spin at similar speeds. A day on Mars is only slightly longer than a day on Earth. However, a year on Mars is almost twice as long as a year on Earth.

MAIN IDEA **In what way is Mars's motion similar to that of Earth?**

Mars	
Length of day	$24\frac{1}{2}$ hours
Length of year	687 Earth days
Distance from Sun	228 million km (141 million mi)
Average temperature	−63°C (−81°F)
Diameter	6,746 km (4,223 mi)
Number of moons	2

Mars's atmosphere is thinner than Earth's. Mars is also farther from the Sun than Earth is, so its temperature is colder.

Express Lab

Activity Card 11
Show the Spin of Venus

Exploring the Inner Planets

The planets of our solar system are difficult to study because they are so far away from Earth. Scientists were first able to study the planets in detail using telescopes. More recently, scientists have had the chance to see the planets up close using space probes. A **space probe** is a craft that helps scientists explore outer space. Space probes carry instruments, but not people.

Space probes carry cameras, lab equipment, and other tools to take pictures and collect data. They send the information back to Earth to be studied.

MAIN IDEA How do space probes help scientists to study other planets?

Mariner 10
Mariner 10 was the first space probe ever to collect data about two planets—Mercury and Venus.

Magellan
The Magellan probe was launched in 1989 to map the surface of Venus.

Mars Rovers
Two rovers, Spirit and Opportunity, landed on Mars in 2004. They studied rocks and soil. They also looked for signs that water was once on Mars.

Lesson Wrap-Up

Visual Summary

	Mercury is the planet closest to the Sun. It has the shortest orbit.
	Venus is between Earth and Mercury. It has the hottest surface of all the planets.
	Earth is the only planet known to have liquid water and life.
	Mars has red soil and rocks. Its day is almost the same length as Earth's.

STANDARDS 4.d.

Technology
Visit **www.eduplace.com/cascp** to learn more about the inner planets.

Reading Review

① MAIN IDEA What do the inner planets have in common?

② VOCABULARY What is a space probe?

③ READING SKILL What are four details that could be used to describe Mars?

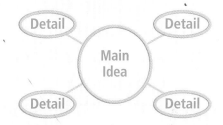

④ CRITICAL THINKING: Apply On Earth, the Sun rises in the east. If you were standing on Mars, where in the sky would the Sun rise?

⑤ INQUIRY SKILL: Predict Suppose the distance between Venus and the Sun increased. What might happen to the length of a year on Venus?

✔ TEST PRACTICE
The inner planet with the longest year is _____.

A. Venus.

B. Earth.

C. Mars.

D. Mercury.

STANDARDS

1–5: 4.d., Test Practice: 4.d.

133

What Are the Outer Planets?

Building Background

Using probes like this one, scientists have learned a lot about the planets farthest from the Sun. These planets are very different from Earth. They are huge and made mainly of gas. They have dozens of moons, and some have rings.

PREPARE TO INVESTIGATE

Inquiry Skill

Analyze Data When you analyze data, you look for patterns that can help you draw conclusions.

Materials

- 2 large sheets of construction paper
- metric ruler
- pencil
- scissors

Science and Math Toolbox

For step 1, review **Using a Tape Measure or Ruler** on page H6.

STANDARDS

4.d. *Students know* that Earth is one of several planets that orbit the Sun and that the Moon orbits Earth.
5.c. Use numerical data in describing and comparing objects, events, and measurements.

Outer Planets

Procedure

1) **Measure** For each measurement below, use a metric ruler to draw a line of that length on construction paper. Draw another line perpendicular to the first line. Connect the lines to make a circle, as shown. Label each circle with the name of the planet it represents.

Jupiter	23 cm
Saturn	19 cm
Uranus	8.2 cm
Neptune	7.6 cm
Pluto (dwarf planet)	0.4 cm (4 mm)

2) **Use Models** Cut out and label each planet. Put the model planets in the order they are in the solar system, as listed. Record this data in your *Science Notebook.*

3) **Compare** Now put your model planets in order from smallest to largest. Record the data. Now put your model planets in order from largest to smallest. Record the data.

Conclusion

1. **Analyze Data** Compare your data. Which two sets of data are similar?

2. **Infer** Refer to the data table on this page. What can you infer about the general relationship between planet size and distance from the Sun?

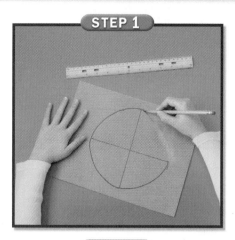

STEP 1

STEP 2

Data Table

Planet	Diameter (km)
Jupiter	142,980
Saturn	120,540
Uranus	51,120
Neptune	49,530
Pluto (dwarf planet)	2,390

Guided Inquiry

Experiment Predict the masses of each planet based on their diameters. Then use the Internet or the library to find the actual masses of the planets. **Compare** them to your predictions.

The Outer Planets

VOCABULARY

gas giant   p. 136

⊚ READING SKILL

Sequence Use a diagram like the one below to order the outer planets.

> Step 1
>
> ↓
>
> Step 2
>
> ↓
>
> Step 3

STANDARDS

4.d. *Students know* that Earth is one of several planets that orbit the Sun, and that the Moon orbits Earth.

MAIN IDEA The four planets farthest from the Sun are called the outer planets.

Jupiter

The four planets farthest from the Sun are called the outer planets. Jupiter is the largest planet. In fact, all the other planets could fit inside it! A huge storm in Jupiter's atmosphere, called the Great Red Spot, is more than twice the size of Earth. Jupiter rotates so quickly that its day is only about 10 hours long.

Jupiter is one of four gas giants. Saturn, Uranus, and Neptune are the others. A **gas giant** is a very large planet made up mostly of gases. Jupiter has a very deep atmosphere with high and low clouds. Jupiter has at least 63 moons. Scientists think that more moons will be discovered.

Jupiter	
Length of day	9.8 hours
Length of year	12 Earth years
Distance from Sun	780 million km (480 million mi)
Average temperature	–150°C (–101°F)
Diameter	142,980 km (88,844 mi)
Number of moons	63 discovered so far

The Great Red Spot has been observed from Earth through telescopes for more than 300 years.

Alphabet letters are used to name Saturn's rings. The A-ring was discovered in the 1600s when the first telescopes were made.

Saturn	
Length of day	$10\frac{1}{2}$ hours
Length of year	$29\frac{1}{2}$ Earth years
Distance from Sun	1.4 billion km (860 million mi)
Average temperature	−170°C (−274°F)
Diameter	120,540 km (74,900 mi)
Number of moons	47 discovered so far

Saturn

Saturn is the second-largest planet. Like the other gas giants, it is covered by thick clouds. Saturn has many moons. Like Jupiter, Saturn spins very quickly. A day on Saturn is about 11 hours long. Saturn spins so quickly that it has a slightly flattened shape.

In 2004, the Cassini spacecraft began sending close-up images of Saturn's bright, beautiful rings back to Earth. The rings are made of pieces of ice, dust, and rocks that orbit the planet. Most pieces are only a few centimeters across. Some are as large as a house.

SEQUENCE **Which two planets are next to Jupiter?**

Uranus

Uranus is the third-largest planet. It is only one-third the size of Jupiter. About 64 Earths could fit into Uranus. Although Uranus is much larger than Earth, it is not as dense as Earth. Methane, a gas in Uranus's atmosphere, gives the planet its beautiful blue-green color.

Uranus seems to rotate on its side. This unusual tilt may have been caused by a collision with another object in space.

Uranus	
Length of day	17 hours
Length of year	84 Earth years
Distance from Sun	3 billion km (1.8 billion mi)
Average temperature	–200°C (–328°F)
Diameter	51,120 km (31,764 mi)
Number of moons	27 discovered so far

Because Uranus is so tilted, each side of the planet has "day" for half the year and "night" for the other half.

Triton is Neptune's largest moon. The surface of Triton looks somewhat like a cantaloupe.

Neptune

Neptune	
Length of day	17 hours
Length of year	165 Earth years
Distance from Sun	$4\frac{1}{2}$ billion km (2.7 billion mi)
Average temperature	−210°C (−346°F)
Diameter	49,530 km (30,777 mi)
Number of moons	13 discovered so far

Neptune

Neptune is the fourth-largest planet in the solar system. It is the smallest of the four gas giants. Its diameter is four times larger than Earth's. Neptune is almost 5 billion kilometers (about 3 billion miles) from the Sun. Because it is so far from the Sun, Neptune takes 165 Earth years to orbit once.

Neptune is very cold, and has an extremely active atmosphere. Winds on Neptune can blow at 1,450 km per hour!

SEQUENCE List the gas giants in order from smallest to largest.

Express Lab

Activity Card 12
Compare the Outer Planets

Pluto

Pluto once was known as the ninth planet. Today it is classified as a dwarf planet. The **dwarf planets** are round, orbiting bodies much like planets, but smaller.

Pluto is rocky and icy. Its orbit is tilted compared with the orbits of the planets. In addition, its orbit is so stretched out that once every 248 years, Pluto moves inside of Neptune's orbit.

Scientists continue to discuss Pluto and the best way to classify it. Their decision may change.

SEQUENCE What is unusual about Pluto's position in the solar system?

Pluto	
Length of day	6 hours
Length of year	248 Earth years
Distance from Sun	6 billion km (3.7 billion mi)
Average temperature	−229°C (−380°F)
Diameter	2,390 km (1,485 mi)
Number of moons	3

Pluto

Neptune

Pluto

From 1979 to 1999, Pluto was inside the orbit of Neptune. This switch happened because their orbits cross.

Lesson Wrap-Up

Visual Summary

Outer Planets
- Larger than the inner planets
- Made up mostly of gases

Far from the Sun

Pluto
- A dwarf planet
- Rocky and icy
- Orbit more extreme oval and tilted

Jupiter

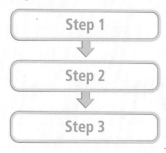
Pluto

Saturn

Uranus

Neptune

STANDARDS 4.d.

Technology
Visit **www.eduplace.com/cascp** to find out more about the outer planets.

Reading Review

❶ **MAIN IDEA** List the outer planets in order, starting with the planet nearest to the Sun.

❷ **VOCABULARY** What is a gas giant?

❸ **READING SKILL** List the outer planets in order from largest to smallest.

Step 1
↓
Step 2
↓
Step 3

❹ **CRITICAL THINKING: Synthesize** Based on its description, would you group Pluto with the outer planets or the inner planets? Why?

❺ **INQUIRY SKILL: Analyze Data** A year on Jupiter is 12 Earth years. What does this data tell about Jupiter's distance from the Sun as compared to Earth's?

✓ **TEST PRACTICE**
Which is an outer planet?

A. Mars

B. Earth

C. Saturn

D. Venus

STANDARDS

1–5: 4.d., Test Practice: 4.d.

141

EXTREME Science

STANDARDS 4.c. *Students know* telescopes magnify the appearance of some distant objects in the sky, including the Moon and the planets. The number of stars that can be seen through telescopes is dramatically greater than the number that can be seen by the unaided eye.

Eyes on the Skies

Look at those rings! The planet Saturn is a beautiful sight even in a small backyard telescope. How much more exciting would it be to look at Saturn through the biggest telescope in the world?

Compare these two images of Saturn. An amateur astronomer recorded the smaller image with his home telescope. The larger image comes from one of the mighty Keck telescopes on top of Mauna Kea in Hawaii. At the Keck Observatory, astronomers have not one, but two giant eyes on the sky. Each telescope is the largest of its type anywhere.

Here's how Saturn looks through a home telescope. Not bad!

Here's how Saturn looks through the mighty Keck telescope. What a difference!

▲

Each of the twin telescopes at the Keck Observatory has a mirror that is 10 meters across!

Writing Journal

In your writing journal, explain why you think being able to see and study an outer planet, like Saturn, is important.

Math Estimate Results

Two out of the four inner planets of our solar system have their own moons. Each of the four outer planets have their own moons. The number of known moons for each planet is listed in the chart shown.

1. Suppose you read in a book that the total number of known moons in our solar system is about 160. Is this estimate accurate? Show your work to explain why or why not.

2. Round the number of the outer planets' moons to the nearest ten. Is this number different from the estimated total number of moons in the solar system? Why or why not?

3. Round the total number of known moons in our solar system to the nearest hundred.

Number of Known Moons	
Planet	**Number of Moons**
Mercury	0
Venus	0
Earth	1
Mars	2
Jupiter	63
Saturn	47
Uranus	27
Neptune	13
Pluto (dwarf planet)	3

Writing Descriptive

Within your lifetime, people may be able to land on Mercury, Venus, or Mars. Imagine that you are able to travel to, and live on, one of those planets. Describe what living on the planet is like. Explain what type of home you live in. Do you need any special equipment to survive on this planet? How is living on this planet different from living on Earth?

Dr. Adriana Ocampo

Dr. Adriana Ocampo has been studying planets and the solar system since she was a teenager in Los Angeles, California. Today, she speaks about these subjects to scientists around the world.

Through her research, Dr. Ocampo has discovered some important facts about Earth's history. For many years, she studied the land over a buried crater in Central America. She helped show how an asteroid formed the crater. The asteroid, or piece of rock from space, hit Earth 65 million years ago.

Dr. Ocampo also works with NASA, the government agency that explores space. One of her goals is to join the crew of a Space Shuttle mission.

Vocabulary

Complete each sentence with a term from the list.

1. When you make an object look larger, you _____ the object.

2. The Sun and the objects that orbit it make up the _____.

3. When planets move around the Sun, they _____ it.

4. A small, rounded body that orbits a planet is a/an _____.

5. A craft that carries instruments to explore space is a/an _____.

6. Mercury, Venus, Earth, and Mars are called the _____.

7. Jupiter, Saturn, Uranus, and Neptune are each a/an _____ because of their size and makeup.

8. A tool that makes distant objects appear larger is a/an _____.

9. Jupiter, Saturn, Uranus, and Neptune make up the _____.

10. A body that orbits the Sun and does not produce light is a/an _____.

gas giant p. 136
inner planets p. 122
magnify p. 112
moon p. 121
orbit p. 121
outer planets p. 123
planet p. 120
solar system p. 121
space probe p. 132
Sun p. 120
telescope p. 112

✓ Test Practice

Write the letter of the best answer choice.

11. The Hubble Space Telescope helps scientists view space from _____.

    A. the surface of Mars.
    B. a mountaintop.
    C. within Earth's atmosphere.
    D. beyond Earth's atmosphere.

12. The body in the solar system from which Earth gets light is _____.

    A. the Moon   **C.** Mars
    B. Jupiter   **D.** the Sun

13. Which is true of all of the inner planets?

    A. They are made of frozen gases.
    B. They are made of rocky materials.
    C. They have no moons.
    D. They orbit a planet.

14. The time it takes a planet to orbit the Sun exactly once is called a _____.

    A. day   **C.** year
    B. season   **D.** decade

Inquiry Skills

15. Use Models Suppose you want to make a model of the solar system with planets and moons that move. How will the motion of the moons compare with the motion of the planets?

16. Suppose you look through a telescope at Jupiter and see its Great Red Spot facing Earth. Predict whether or not you would see the Great Red Spot in the same position each time you looked at Jupiter.

Map the Concept

Complete the concept map using the following terms:

Mercury	Jupiter	Neptune
Mars	Outer	Uranus
Inner	Venus	

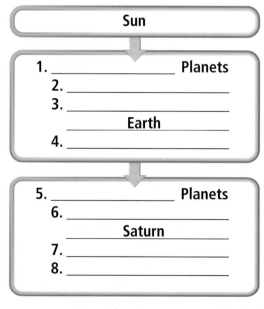

```
┌─────────────────────────────┐
│            Sun              │
└─────────────────────────────┘
              ↓
┌─────────────────────────────┐
│ 1. _____ Planets  │
│ 2. _____          │
│ 3. _____          │
│        Earth                │
│ 4. _____          │
└─────────────────────────────┘
              ↓
┌─────────────────────────────┐
│ 5. _____ Planets  │
│ 6. _____          │
│        Saturn               │
│ 7. _____          │
│ 8. _____          │
└─────────────────────────────┘
```

Critical Thinking

17. Apply In 2006, scientists decided to classify Pluto as a dwarf planet. How is Pluto different from the eight planets?

18. Synthesize You have learned about the advantages that the Hubble telescope offers to scientists. What disadvantages might it offer?

19. Evaluate Someone tells you that Earth's moon produces its own light. They say that the proof of this is that the Moon is very bright at night. Evaluate this statement.

20. Analyze Venus turns on its axis every 243 Earth days. What does this tell you about the speed at which Venus spins compared to the speed at which Earth spins?

Performance Assessment

Write an Advertisement
Suppose you have been asked to write an advertisement for land on Mars that is for sale. Describe the land and some of its features. Describe the motion of Mars. Try to make the planet sound attractive so that someone will want to buy the land.

Review your answers to the questions on page 107 at the beginning of this chapter. Change your answers as needed, based on what you have learned.

STANDARDS

1: 4.c., 2–7: 4.d., 8: 4.c., 9–10: 4.d., 11: 4.c., 12: 1.a., 13–14: 4.d., 15: 4.d., 16: 5.d., Map the Concept: 4.d., 17: 4.d., 18: 4.c., 19–20: 4.d., Performance Assessment: 4.d.

Chapter 5

Cycles and Patterns in Space

Star paths in the night sky

LESSON 1

The Sun seems to rise in the east, travel across the sky, and set in the west. Where is the Sun at night?

LESSON 2

Temperatures can be scorching hot in summer and icy cold in winter. What causes the seasons to change?

LESSON 3

The Moon seems to change from a thin sliver of light to a glowing circle. What different shapes of the Moon have you seen during the month?

LESSON 4

On a clear night, the sky may be filled with stars. What do you know about stars and star patterns?

Writing Journal

In your Writing Journal, show what you know by writing or drawing answers to each question.

Vocabulary Preview

Vocabulary

Glossary
English-Spanish p. H24

Vocabulary Skill

Prefix/Suffix
constellation

Knowing prefixes can help you understand word meanings. The word *constellation* contains the prefix *con-*, which means "together." It also contains the word part *-stella-*, which means "star" in Latin. So part of the meaning of *constellation* is "a group of stars."

full moon
The phase of the Moon when the side of the Moon facing Earth is in sunlight.

rotate
To turn on an axis.

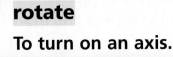

star
A ball of hot gases that gives off light and other forms of energy.

constellation

A group of stars that forms a pattern in the sky shaped like an animal, person, or object.

California

Start with Your Standards

Standard Set 1. Physical Sciences (Energy and Matter)

1.a. *Students know* energy comes from the Sun to Earth in the form of light.

Standard Set 2. Physical Sciences (Light)

2.a. *Students know* sunlight can be blocked to create shadows.

2.b. *Students know* light is reflected from mirrors and other surfaces.

Standard Set 4. Earth Sciences

4.a. *Students know* the patterns of stars stay the same, although they appear to move across the sky nightly, and different stars can be seen in different seasons.

4.b. *Students know* the way in which the Moon's appearance changes during the four-week lunar cycle.

4.d. *Students know* that Earth is one of several planets that orbit the Sun and that the Moon orbits Earth.

4.e. *Students know* the position of the Sun in the sky changes during the course of the day and from season to season.

Standard Set 5. Investigation and Experimentation covered in this chapter: 5.c., 5.d., 5.e.

What Causes Day and Night?

Building Background

In early morning, the Sun comes up in the east. During the day, it travels across the sky, giving light and warming Earth. In the evening, it sets in the west. But the Sun doesn't actually move. The Sun appears to move because Earth is slowly spinning.

STANDARDS

4.e. *Students know* the position of the Sun in the sky changes during the course of the day and from season to season.
5.c. Use numerical data in describing and comparing objects, events, and measurements.

PREPARE TO INVESTIGATE

Inquiry Skill

Measure When you measure, you use tools to find distance, mass, or other information about an object.

Materials

- large square sheet of paper
- 2 metric rulers
- modeling clay
- watch or clock

Science and Math Toolbox

For step 3, review **Using a Tape Measure or Ruler** on page H6.

Shadows in the Sun

Procedure

1. **Collaborate** Work with a partner. Place a square sheet of paper outdoors in a sunny area. Hold a ruler in the center of the paper while your partner molds the clay around the base, as shown. The clay should keep the ruler standing upright.

2. In your *Science Notebook,* make a two-column chart. Title one column *Time* and the other column *Shadow Length (cm).*

3. **Measure** Trace the shadow made by the ruler on the paper. Use a metric ruler to measure the length of the shadow. Have your partner record the time of day and the shadow length in the chart.

4. **Observe** Repeat step 3 once each hour for the rest of the school day.

5. **Use Numbers** In your *Science Notebook,* make a bar graph like the one shown to display the data you collected.

STEP 1

STEP 3

STEP 5

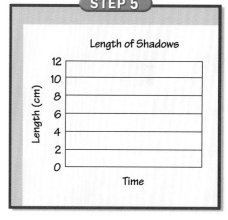

Length of Shadows

Length (cm): 12, 10, 8, 6, 4, 2, 0

Time

Conclusion

1. **Draw Conclusions** In what ways did the shadow change during the day?

2. **Analyze Data** Did the shadow's length change by the same amount each hour?

3. **Predict** What do you think the length of the shadow will be two hours after the last time you measured?

Guided Inquiry

Experiment Take the ruler setup indoors. Use a flashlight to produce the same shadows as the Sun did. **Observe** the position of the "Sun" for each shadow.

Day and Night

READING SKILL

Cause and Effect
Use the chart below to explain what causes day and night.

Cause → Effect

STANDARDS

4.e. *Students know* the position of the Sun in the sky changes during the course of the day and from season to season.
1.a. *Students know* energy comes from the Sun to Earth in the form of light.

MAIN IDEA The position of the Sun in the sky changes during the day because Earth rotates on its axis. As Earth rotates, the Sun appears to rise, move across the sky, and then set.

Rotating Earth

While you are enjoying breakfast in California, it is the middle of the night in China. How can this be?

You have learned about one of the ways Earth and the other planets move. They orbit, or move in a path, around the Sun.

Los Angeles, California

Athens, Greece

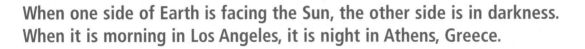

When one side of Earth is facing the Sun, the other side is in darkness. When it is morning in Los Angeles, it is night in Athens, Greece.

axis

As the planets orbit, they also rotate (ROH tayt). To **rotate** is to turn on an axis (AK sihs). An **axis** is an imaginary line through the center of an object. Earth's axis goes through the North and South Poles.

Imagine it is sunrise where you live. As Earth rotates, the side of Earth where you live turns to face the Sun. Only the side of Earth facing the Sun has daylight. Your day begins as the Sun appears to rise in the east.

During the day, your side of Earth receives light and heat from the Sun. As the day goes on, the Sun appears to move across the sky. But it is not the Sun that is moving. It is Earth that is actually turning, causing the Sun to look like it is moving.

As Earth continues to rotate, your side of Earth turns away from the Sun's light. The Sun appears to set in the west. It becomes dark, and night begins for your side of Earth. Now it is daytime on the other side of Earth.

▲ What time of day is it for the part of Earth marked by the flag? Is it morning, afternoon, or late evening?

CAUSE AND EFFECT What causes the Sun to appear to move across the sky?

Express Lab

Activity Card 13
Model Day and Night

Changing Shadow Length

sunlight

sunlight

sunlight

early morning

noon

late afternoon

▲ As the Sun appears to move across the sky from east to west, shadows grow shorter and then grow longer again.

Sunrise and Sunset

Which room of your home gets the most sunlight when you wake up in the morning? Which room gets the most when you come home from school? It is probably not the same room.

In the morning, the Sun rises in the east. As Earth turns, the Sun seems to move west and rise higher in the sky. At noon, the Sun seems to be at its highest point. Earth continues to turn, and the Sun seems to move west until it sets in the west.

As Earth turns, the position of the Sun in the sky changes. This causes the angle at which sunlight strikes your part of Earth to change. The changing angle of sunlight causes shadows to change throughout the day. When the Sun is low in the sky, shadows are long. When the Sun is high in the sky, shadows are short.

CAUSE AND EFFECT What causes shadows to change in length during the day?

Visual Summary

Earth rotates on its axis one full turn each day. It is daytime for the side of Earth facing toward the Sun. Night comes for that side of Earth when it turns away from the Sun.

As Earth rotates, the position of the Sun in the sky appears to change. The Sun rises in the east, moves across the sky, and sets in the west.

As the Sun appears to move across the sky, sunlight strikes Earth at different angles. This causes the length and angle of shadows to change throughout the day.

STANDARDS 4.e., 1.a.

Technology
Visit **www.eduplace.com/cascp** to find out more about day and night.

Reading Review

① **MAIN IDEA** What causes day and night?

② **VOCABULARY** What is an axis?

③ **READING SKILL** What effect does the Sun have on the side of Earth where it is daytime?

Cause → Effect

④ **CRITICAL THINKING: Apply** Suppose you called a friend in Athens right after you eat dinner. Is it likely that your friend just finished eating dinner also? Explain.

⑤ **INQUIRY SKILL: Measure** What can you measure to tell whether it is morning or noon where you live? Explain.

✓ TEST PRACTICE
The Sun appears to move from _____ across the sky.

A. north to south

B. east to west

C. west to east

D. south to north

STANDARDS

1–2: 4.e., 3: 1.a., 4: 4.e., 5: 5.c., Test Practice: 4.e

What Causes the Seasons?

Building Background

Why do the days grow shorter and cooler as summer changes to fall? The seasons change because Earth is tilted on its axis as it moves around the Sun. When your part of Earth begins to tilt away from the Sun, sunlight strikes your area less directly. Less daylight and less warmth mean that it is fall and that winter is on the way.

PREPARE TO INVESTIGATE

Inquiry Skill

Use Models You can use a model of an object, process, or idea to better understand or describe how it works.

Materials

- globe
- modeling clay
- toothpicks
- lamp

STANDARDS

4.e. *Students know* the position of the Sun in the sky changes during the course of the day and from season to season.
5.e. Collect data in an investigation and analyze those data to develop a logical conclusion.

Earth's Tilt

Procedure

1. Work with a partner. As shown, place a lump of clay with a toothpick on each pole of a globe. The toothpicks represent Earth's axis.

2. **Observe** Hold the globe so the North Pole points at a drawing of Polaris your teacher taped to a wall.

3. **Use Models** Use a lamp as a model of the Sun. As you hold the globe, have your partner place the lamp so that it shines on the globe. **Safety:** Do not touch the bulb. It will get hot.

4. **Record Data** Draw your Earth-Sun model. Mark *X* on the part of Earth that is getting the most direct light.

5. **Use Models** While holding the globe so the axis stays pointed at Polaris, walk around the lamp to the opposite side. Draw the model again. Mark *O* on the drawing to show the part of the globe that is now receiving the most direct light.

STEP 1

STEP 2

STEP 5

Conclusion

1. **Use Models** Describe how Earth's motion changes the amount of direct light received by different parts of Earth.

2. **Draw Conclusions** What season would it be for the place marked *X*? *O*?

Guided Inquiry

Experiment Rotate the globe as you hold it next to the lamp. **Predict** whether California gets more hours of sunlight on a summer day or on a winter day. Experiment to find out.

VOCABULARY

equator	p. 161
revolve	p. 160
season	p. 161

READING SKILL

Sequence Fill in the chart to relate Earth's motion to the changing seasons.

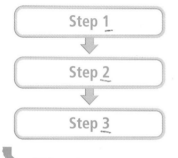

Step 1

Step 2

Step 3

STANDARDS

4.e. *Students know* the position of the Sun in the sky changes during the course of the day and from season to season.
4.d. *Students know* Earth is one of several planets that orbit the Sun, and that the Moon orbits Earth.

Seasons

MAIN IDEA As Earth orbits the Sun, the tilt of Earth's axis causes changes in the seasons and in the Sun's position in the sky.

Revolving Earth

You have learned that Earth and the other planets orbit, or move in paths, around the Sun. To move in a path around another object is to **revolve** (rih VAHLV). It takes one year for Earth to revolve around the Sun one time. The path it takes is in the shape of an ellipse (ee LIHPS). An ellipse is a circle that is flattened and slightly stretched out.

The Seasons

Because Earth's axis is tilted, parts of Earth have four different seasons.

Summer

Summer When the Northern Hemisphere tilts toward the Sun, it is summer here.

As Earth revolves, its axis is tilted. So the Sun's rays strike Earth's surface at a different angle at different times of the year. The tilt is what causes Earth's seasons to change. A **season** (SEE zuhn) is one of the four parts of the year— spring, summer, fall, and winter.

The **equator** (ee KWAY tur) is an imaginary line that circles Earth halfway between the North and South Poles. It divides Earth into two halves called hemispheres.

In June, Earth's Northern Hemisphere, where you live, is tilted toward the Sun. It receives strong, direct sunlight, so it is summer here. In December, the Northern Hemisphere tilts away from the Sun. It receives weak, indirect sunlight. It is winter here. At the same time the Southern Hemisphere tilts toward the Sun, so it is summer there.

 SEQUENCE In December the Southern Hemisphere is tilted toward the Sun. What season is it there in March?

Spring

Winter

Fall

Winter When the Northern Hemisphere tilts away from the Sun, it is winter here.

Changing Position of the Sun

You know that the Sun changes position in the sky during the day. It appears to rise in the east and set in the west. But have you ever noticed another way the position of the Sun changes? This change occurs from season to season.

Suppose that it is noon in June, and you are outside playing. The Sun appears very high in the sky. It is very hot, and soon you are looking for some shade. Now suppose that it is noon in December, and you are outside at recess. The Sun appears much lower in the sky. Even if you are sitting in sunlight, you might feel chilly. What causes this difference?

June 21

In the Northern Hemispere on June 21 at noon, a person looking south would see the Sun high in the sky. Summer temperatures tend to be warm.

December 21

In the Northern Hemisphere on December 21 at noon, a person looking south would see the Sun low in the sky. Winter temperatures tend to be cool.

In June, the Northern Hemisphere tilts toward the Sun. This makes the Sun appear high in the sky. The Sun's rays shine more directly on the Northern Hemisphere. For this reason, the land and water are heated more in June than in December.

In December, the Northern Hemisphere tilts away from the Sun. Then the Sun appears lower in the sky. The Sun's rays are less direct, so the land and water are heated less. This is part of the reason that summers tend to be hot and winters tend to be cold.

Express Lab

Activity Card 14
Model Earth's Tilt

Length of Day and Night Changes

The length of day and night changes throughout the year. This is also caused by the tilt of Earth's axis.

As Earth revolves around the Sun, different parts of Earth are tilted toward the Sun. In June, the North Pole is tilted toward the Sun. So places north of the equator face the Sun for more hours than they face away from it. They have more hours of daylight and fewer hours of darkness.

In December, the Northern Hemisphere tilts away from the Sun. This means that places north of the equator face away from the Sun for more hours than they face toward it. So, in these places, there are more hours of darkness than daylight. The different amounts of daylight also help make summer warmer than winter.

SEQUENCE **In what season do the days have the fewest hours of daylight?**

7:00 P.M. in June in Santa Monica, California

7:00 P.M. in December in Santa Monica, California

Visual Summary

It takes one year for Earth to revolve around the Sun one time. Earth's axis is tilted, so each hemisphere leans toward the Sun for part of the year and away from the Sun for the other part of the year.

During winter in the Northern Hemisphere, the Sun appears lower in the sky than it does during summer.

As one hemisphere tilts toward the Sun, it has more hours of daylight and the Sun's rays are more direct there.

As that hemisphere tilts away from the Sun, it has fewer hours of daylight and the Sun's rays are less direct. These differences cause Earth's seasons.

STANDARDS 4.e., 4.d.

Technology
Visit **www.eduplace.com/cascp** to find out more about Earth's motion.

Reading Review

❶ MAIN IDEA Why is the Sun lower in the sky in winter?

❷ VOCABULARY Describe the location of the equator.

❸ READING SKILL In the Southern Hemisphere, does the Sun appear lower in the sky in June or in December?

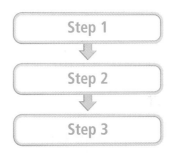

> Step 1
>
> Step 2
>
> Step 3

❹ CRITICAL THINKING: Evaluate Seasons would occur even if Earth were not tilted on its axis. Is this statement correct? Explain.

❺ INQUIRY SKILL: Use Models How would you tilt Earth's axis in an Earth–Sun model in December?

✔ TEST PRACTICE

Which does NOT affect seasons?

A. Earth's revolution

B. whether it is day or night

C. Earth's tilted axis

D. the angle at which sunlight strikes Earth

STANDARDS

1–3: 4.e., 4–5: 4.d., 4.e., Test Practice: 4.e.

Lesson 3

What Are the Phases of the Moon?

Building Background

One evening, you notice the Moon in the sky. It appears to be a thin sliver. Several nights later, you look for the Moon and see a half-circle. After another few days, you notice the full moon shining through your window. These changes in the way the Moon appears are caused by its motion around Earth.

PREPARE TO INVESTIGATE

Inquiry Skill

Communicate When you communicate, you share information using words, actions, sketches, graphs, charts, or diagrams.

Materials

- lamp
- plastic-foam ball with craft-stick handle

STANDARDS

4.b. *Students know* the way in which the Moon's appearance changes during the four-week lunar cycle.
5.e. Collect data in an investigation and analyze those data to develop a logical conclusion.

Moon Motion

Procedure

1. Use a ball with a stick handle to stand for the Moon. Use a lamp or other light to stand for the Sun. You will be an observer on Earth. **Safety:** Do not touch the bulb. It will get hot.

STEP 2

2. **Use Models** Stand in front of the Sun model with your back to it. Hold the Moon model at arm's length in front of you and above your head. Look at the shape the light makes on the Moon.

STEP 3

3. **Observe** Slowly make a quarter turn in place and stop, keeping the Moon model in front of you.

4. **Record Data** In your *Science Notebook*, draw the shapes of light and dark that you observed on the Moon model in steps 2 and 3.

STEP 4

5. **Use Models** Repeat step 3 two more times. Face a different direction each time. Draw the shapes of light and dark you observe.

Conclusion

1. **Communicate** Write three sentences explaining why the shapes in your drawings are alike or different.

2. **Infer** If you look at the Moon on different nights, do you think it will look the same? Explain.

Guided Inquiry

Ask Questions Write a question about how the Moon appears to move each night. With an adult, observe the Moon. **Record** where you see it every hour for three hours.

Moon Phases

READING SKILL

Compare and Contrast
Use the chart to compare a full moon and a new moon.

Compare	Contrast

STANDARDS

4.b. *Students know* the way in which the Moon's appearance changes during the four-week lunar cycle.
2.b. *Students know* light is reflected from mirrors and other surfaces.

MAIN IDEA The Moon's shape appears to change from a crescent to a half circle, to a whole circle, and back again. These changes are caused by the way sunlight strikes the Moon as it revolves around Earth.

Earth's Moon

The Moon is a ball-shaped object made of rock that revolves around Earth once every $27\frac{1}{3}$ Earth days. As it revolves, the Moon also rotates once on its axis in the same amount of time. As a result, the same side of the Moon, the near side, always faces Earth.

The Moon does not make its own light. "Moonlight" is really sunlight reflecting from, or bouncing off, the Moon's surface. This reflected sunlight makes the side of the Moon facing the Sun look bright. The other side is dark, so you cannot see it.

If the same side of the Moon always faces Earth, why does the Moon appear to change shape? As it revolves around Earth, the Moon's near side receives different amounts of sunlight. At one point during the Moon's revolution around Earth, the Moon's near side receives no sunlight. The near side of the Moon is dark, and you cannot see it. This is called a **new moon**.

As the Moon revolves around Earth, a small part of the near side is sunlit and can be seen from Earth. This thin shape is called the **crescent** (KREHS uhnt) **moon**.

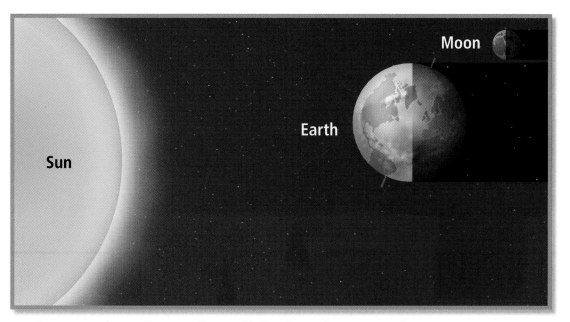

▲ The Moon's surface reflects light, but the Moon does not make its own light.

When the Moon has revolved one quarter of its orbit around Earth, half the Moon's near side is sunlit. This is called a **quarter moon**, because you see one quarter of the entire Moon. When the Moon has revolved halfway around Earth, the Moon's entire near side is sunlit. This is the **full moon**.

Following a new moon, an increasing amount of the Moon's near side is sunlit. This is called a **waxing moon**. Following a full moon, a decreasing amount of the near side is sunlit. This is called a **waning moon**. After about a month, the Moon reaches the point in its orbit where none of its near side is sunlit. This is a new moon again.

COMPARE AND CONTRAST What are two different ways that the Moon moves?

Express Lab

Activity Card 15
Show Phases of the Moon

The Moon in Motion

The different ways the Moon looks throughout the month are called the **phases of the Moon**. The diagram below shows the Moon's position at each phase. The photos on the next page show how each Moon phase looks as seen from Earth.

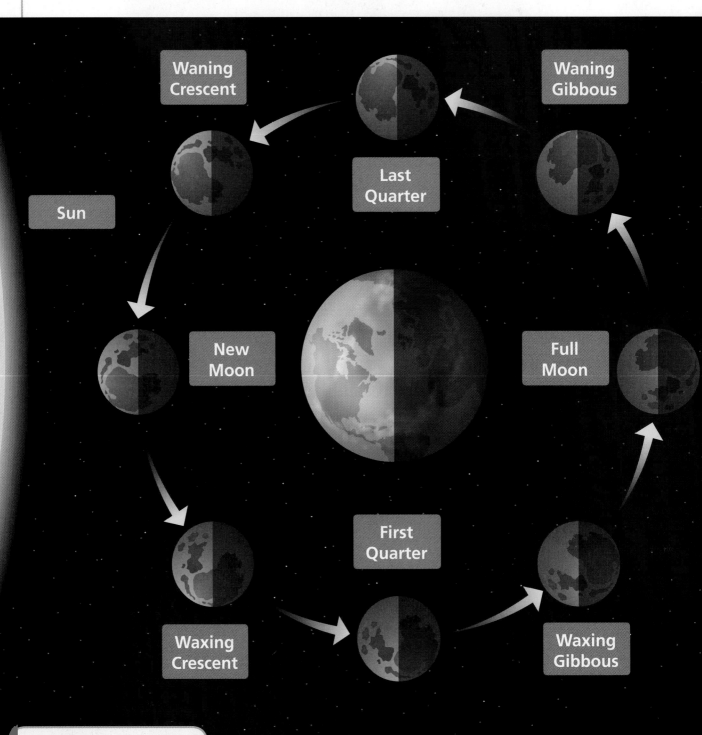

Last Quarter
Half of the Moon's near side is sunlit.

Waning Crescent
The Moon looks like a thin sliver.

Waning Gibbous
The Moon looks almost full.

New Moon
None of the Moon's near side is sunlit.

Full Moon
All of the Moon's near side is sunlit.

Waxing Crescent
The Moon looks like a thin sliver.

Waxing Gibbous
The Moon looks almost full.

First Quarter
Half of the Moon's near side is sunlit.

A Closer Look at the Moon

The rocky surface of the Moon is covered with mountains, flat plains, and craters.

A crater is a bowl-shaped dent. It is caused by an object from space striking the surface of a planet or moon. There is no air or liquid water on the Moon, and there are no living things. Daytime temperatures on the Moon are much hotter than on Earth. Nighttime temperatures are much colder.

The Moon's diameter is only about one-fourth of Earth's diameter. Because the Moon is smaller, its gravity is weaker than Earth's gravity. So things weigh less on the Moon than they do on Earth.

COMPARE AND CONTRAST **Compare the daytime temperatures on the Moon with those on Earth.**

Moon

Temperature	day: 123°C (253°F) night: −233°C (−387°F)
Diameter	3,476 km (2,086 mi)
Distance from Earth	384,400 km (230,600 mi)
Length of day	about 29$\frac{1}{2}$ Earth days

The Moon's surface is made of dark volcanic rock, large boulders, and powdery dust.

Lesson Wrap-Up

Visual Summary

The Moon is a ball-shaped object made of rock that revolves around Earth once every $27\frac{1}{3}$ days. The Moon reflects light from the Sun.

As the Moon revolves around Earth, different amounts of its near side are sunlit. This causes the shape of the Moon to appear to change in a cycle each month.

The Moon's shape appears to change from a dark new moon, to a thin crescent, to a half-circle, to a full circle and back again as it revolves around Earth.

Technology
Visit **www.eduplace.com/cascp** to find out more about the Moon.

Reading Review

❶ **MAIN IDEA** Why does the Moon's shape look different on different nights?

❷ **VOCABULARY** Make a sketch of a quarter moon.

❸ **READING SKILL** How does a full moon compare with a quarter moon?

Compare	Contrast

❹ **CRITICAL THINKING:**
Evaluate Suppose you look up at the sky and see a waxing gibbous moon. Your friend says that that new moon will be the next phase you can see. Is your friend correct? Explain why or why not.

❺ **INQUIRY SKILL:**
Communicate Draw a diagram to show what causes moonlight.

✓ **TEST PRACTICE**
If the near side of the Moon receives no sunlight, it is a _____ moon.

A. crescent   **C.** new

B. waning   **D.** waxing

STANDARDS
1–4: 4.b., 5: 2.b., Test Practice: 4.b.

173

Primary Source

Drawing the Moon

In ancient times, artists usually drew the Moon as a circle or a sliver in the sky. They drew the Moon's surface as if it were perfectly smooth because they thought it was.

The invention of the telescope allowed astronomers to see and draw the features of the Moon more accurately and in more detail. They saw that dark areas on the Moon were low plains and shadows in craters. Telescopes also helped them learn why the Moon seemed to change shape.

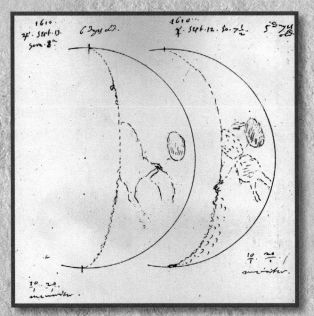

▲ Thomas Harriot was the first astronomer to draw the Moon while looking through a telescope. He made sketches over a period of weeks in 1609 and 1610 showing different Moon phases.

◄ Harriot also drew this "map" of the Moon that showed its surface features, including craters.

 **STANDARDS**

4.b. *Students know* the way in which the Moon's appearance changes during the four-week lunar cycle.

READING

◀ Galileo Galilei was a skilled artist as well as a famous scientist. He made these watercolor paintings of the Moon's phases in 1609 while looking through a telescope.

Galileo Galilei

Sharing Ideas

1. **READING CHECK** How did the invention of the telescope change the way scientists drew the Moon?

2. **WRITE ABOUT IT** Compare Galileo's paintings with the drawings by Harriot.

3. **TALK ABOUT IT** Discuss how photos of the Moon compare with Galileo's paintings.

175

What Is a Star?

Building Background

A star map is a guide to the stars and the patterns they form in the night sky. You can use a star map any time of the year, because star patterns do not change. As Earth rotates and revolves, those patterns appear to move in the sky. But the shapes formed by groups of stars stay the same.

PREPARE TO INVESTIGATE

Inquiry Skill

Predict When you predict, you state what you think will happen based on observations and experiences.

Materials

- cardboard
- black construction paper
- Star Pattern Support Master
- sharp pencil
- cardboard tube
- scissors
- tape

STANDARDS

4.a. *Students know* the patterns of stars stay the same, although they appear to move across the sky nightly, and different stars can be seen in different seasons.
5.d. Predict the outcome of a simple investigation and compare the result with the prediction.

Star Gazing

Procedure

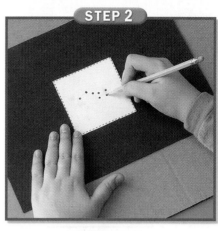
STEP 2

1. Place a sheet of black paper over a sheet of cardboard. Place a star pattern sheet on top.

2. **Use Models** Make a star pattern. Use a pencil to poke a hole in each dot on the star pattern sheet and the black paper. Then remove the star pattern sheet.

STEP 3

3. **Use Models** Place one end of a tube over the star pattern you made. Use the tube to trace a circle on the black paper around the star pattern. Make sure that all of the star pattern is within the circle. Cut out a circle that is slightly larger than the one you traced. Tape it onto one end of the tube.

4. **Use Models** While holding the tube up to a light, look through the open end. Draw the star pattern you see.

STEP 4

Conclusion

1. **Infer** What might cause a real star pattern to change position in the sky during one night?

2. **Predict** Do you think the position of a star pattern would change from season to season? Explain.

Guided Inquiry

Experiment Bring your star pattern home with you. On a clear night, look for your star pattern in the sky. **Observe** it again several hours later. Record how the star pattern has moved.

Stars

VOCABULARY

constellation   p. 180

star   p. 178

READING SKILL

Draw Conclusions Earth gets heat from the Sun but not from other stars. The Sun looks like the largest star when viewed from Earth. Use the chart to show conclusions that can be drawn from these facts.

STANDARDS

4.a. *Students know* the patterns of stars stay the same, although they appear to move across the sky nightly, and different stars can be seen in different seasons.

MAIN IDEA A star is a huge ball of hot gases. When seen from Earth most stars appear as small points of light because they are very far away. They form fixed patterns that change position in the sky as Earth rotates and revolves.

The Night Sky

When you look up at stars in the night sky, they look like tiny dots of light. But really, they are not tiny. They only look that way because they are very far away. A **star** is a ball of hot gases that gives off light and other forms of energy.

Stars come in different sizes. The smallest stars are only about 20 km (about 12 mi) across. White dwarf stars are about the size of Earth. Supergiant stars can be more than 500 million km (about 300 million mi) across. That is more than 1,000 times the distance from Earth to the Moon!

Stars look small in the night sky because they are far from Earth.

The Sun is the closest star to Earth.

The Sun

The Sun is a star. It is the largest object in the solar system. More than 1 million Earths would fit inside the Sun. Even so, the Sun is just a medium-sized star. The Sun looks much larger than the stars you see at night because it is so much closer to Earth than any other star. Living things on Earth depend on the Sun for heat and light.

Even though the Sun is the closest star to Earth, it is still very far away. The Sun is about 150 million km (about 93 million mi) from Earth.

DRAW CONCLUSIONS Why does the Sun look larger than the other stars you can see?

Express Lab

Activity Card 16
Make a Constellation

Constellations

Have you ever seen a bear in the sky? How about a lion or a dog? Of course not! But if you look closely, you might see a constellation (kahn stuh LAY shuhn) shaped like one of these animals. A **constellation** is a group of stars that forms a pattern shaped like an animal, person, or object. There are 88 constellations recognized by scientists.

There are always stars in the sky, even during the day. You just cannot see them during the day because the sky is so bright.

You have learned that the Sun appears to move across the sky each day. Each night, the stars appear to move across the sky. Both these effects are caused by the rotation of Earth.

The Big Dipper is part of the Great Bear Constellation. ▼

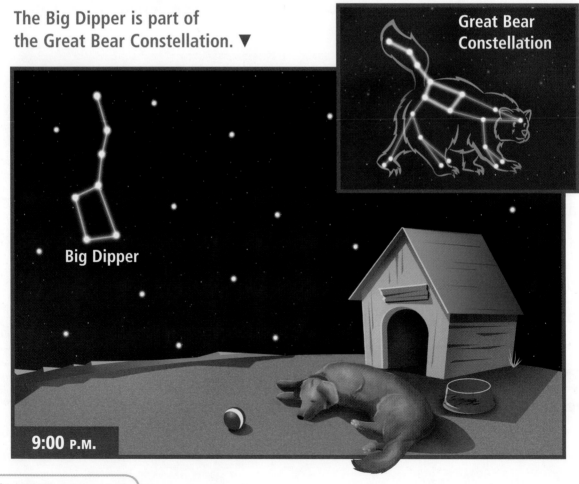

Great Bear Constellation

Big Dipper

9:00 P.M.

As Earth rotates on its axis, the part of the sky you see changes. For this reason, the constellations change position in the sky during the night. But the shape of each constellation does not change. The stars in each constellation stay in their fixed places in the pattern. This is because the stars are trillions of kilometers away, far outside the solar system.

There are some points of light in the sky that do appear to move among the fixed patterns of stars. These points of light are not stars. They are the planets of our solar system—Earth's nearest neighbors in space.

DRAW CONCLUSIONS **Why do the stars appear to move during the night?**

Notice that the Big Dipper looks like it has moved. ▼

Big Dipper

2:00 A.M.

Seasonal Constellations

A few constellations, such as the Small Bear, can be seen from the United States all year round. But usually the night sky in any one place looks different throughout the year.

Some constellations can be seen only on a summer night. Others can be seen only on a winter night. This is because Earth revolves around the Sun. As it does, the part of the night sky that is visible from any one place changes. So you see different constellations at different times of year.

One constellation commonly seen in the summertime is Scorpius (SKAWR pee uhs). Long ago, people looked at this group of stars and saw the claws and curved tail of a scorpion. In winter, people in North America can observe the Big Dog. This constellation contains Sirius (SIHR ee uhs), the brightest star in the night sky.

DRAW CONCLUSIONS **If you see a constellation in the sky in November, would you expect to see the same constellation in May? Explain.**

The Scorpius Constellation

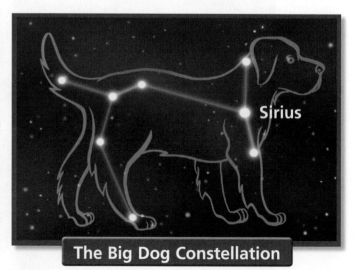
Sirius

The Big Dog Constellation

Visual Summary

A star is a large ball of hot gases that gives off light and other forms of energy. The stars in the night sky look small because they are far away. The Sun is the closest star to Earth.

The stars in the night sky form patterns called constellations. Constellations appear to move across the sky as Earth rotates, but the patterns stay the same.

Different constellations are visible at different times of the year. This is because Earth revolves around the Sun. As it does, the part of the sky that is overhead at night changes.

STANDARDS 4.a.

Technology
Visit **www.eduplace.com/cascp** to find out more about constellations.

Reading Review

❶ MAIN IDEA What is a star?

❷ VOCABULARY Use the term *constellation* in a sentence.

❸ READING SKILL If Earth did not rotate, would the position of a constellation change during the night? Explain.

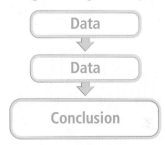

Data

↓

Data

↓

Conclusion

❹ CRITICAL THINKING: Analyze The constellation Lyra is called a "summer constellation" in North America. What do you think this means?

❺ INQUIRY SKILL: Predict In the evening, a constellation is in the eastern sky. Where will it be just before morning?

✔ **TEST PRACTICE**
Which of the following is true of a constellation?

A. It orbits the Sun.

B. It changes shape.

C. It is a pattern of stars.

D. It is close to Earth.

STANDARDS
1–4: 4.a., 5: 5.d., Test Practice: 4.a.

EXTREME Science

Orion's Surprise

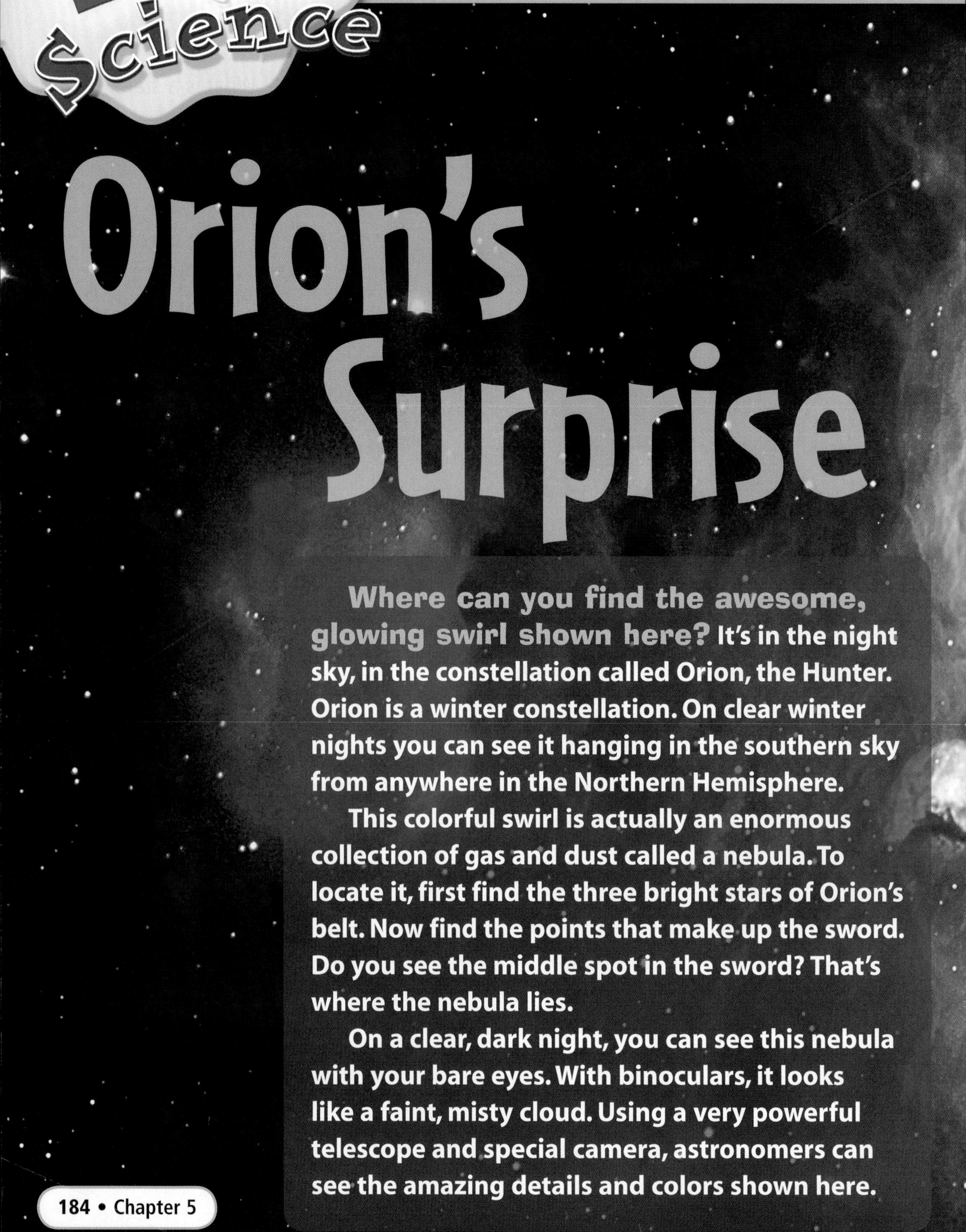

Where can you find the awesome, glowing swirl shown here? It's in the night sky, in the constellation called Orion, the Hunter. Orion is a winter constellation. On clear winter nights you can see it hanging in the southern sky from anywhere in the Northern Hemisphere.

This colorful swirl is actually an enormous collection of gas and dust called a nebula. To locate it, first find the three bright stars of Orion's belt. Now find the points that make up the sword. Do you see the middle spot in the sword? That's where the nebula lies.

On a clear, dark night, you can see this nebula with your bare eyes. With binoculars, it looks like a faint, misty cloud. Using a very powerful telescope and special camera, astronomers can see the amazing details and colors shown here.

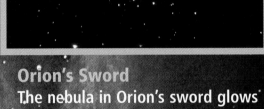
Orion's Sword
The nebula in Orion's sword glows bright with the light of hot young stars that have formed there.

Writing Journal

In your writing journal, tell why Orion is called a winter constellation. Then explain why it is possible to recognize Orion each winter, year after year.

185

Math Number Sense

A day is 24 hours long everywhere on Earth. There are more hours of sunlight during some days of the year than others. In North America, June 21 or June 22 is usually the day with the most hours of sunlight. But on any given day, the number of hours of sunlight varies from place to place.

Sunlight on June 21

Anchorage, AK
19 h 22 min

Portland, OR
15 h 41 min

Cleveland, OH
15 h 11 min

San Diego, CA
14 h 19 min

Savannah, GA
14 h 15 min

1. Which city has the most daylight time on June 21? The least?

2. What is the difference, in minutes, between the city with the most daylight and the city with the least daylight?

3. What do you notice about the daylight times shown on the map as you look from North to South?

Writing Narrative

The Inuit people of Greenland told a story that explains why the Moon has different phases. In the story, Brother Moon is always chasing his sister across the sky. He forgets to eat and gets very thin. Finally, he disappears to find some food and then returns full.

Write your own myth to explain the phases of the Moon. Tell details that will make the reader think about how the Moon looks in the sky.

Planetarium Director

A planetarium is a kind of theater. Instead of showing a movie, a planetarium has a star show. The planetarium director is in charge of the planetarium and the people who work there. One of the best parts of the job is sharing knowledge about stars and planets, and developing shows.

What It Takes!

• A degree in astronomy

• The ability to manage other workers and to make presentations

Satellite Systems Technician

Satellite systems include small home TV satellite dishes and huge communication satellites that orbit Earth. The people who build and take care of this equipment are called satellite systems technicians. Some satellite systems technicians have their own companies. Others work for companies involved in cable television, cellular phones, or broadcasting.

What It Takes!

• A high-school diploma

• Courses in electronics or electrical engineering

Vocabulary

Complete each sentence with a word from the list.

1. The ways the Moon looks when seen from Earth are the _____.

2. An imaginary line through the center of an object is called a/an _____.

3. When all of the Moon's near side is sunlit, it is a/an _____.

4. A ball of hot gases that gives off light and other forms of energy is a/an _____.

5. When the Moon's near side receives no sunlight, it is a/an _____.

6. To move in a path around another object is to _____.

7. When the Moon becomes visible again and appears as a thin shape, the phase is called a/an _____.

8. When half of the Moon's near side is sunlit it is a/an _____.

9. Spring, summer, fall, and winter are each a/an _____.

10. A group of stars that form a pattern is called a/an _____.

axis p. 155
constellation p. 180
crescent moon p. 168
equator p. 161
full moon p. 169
new moon p. 168
phases of the Moon p. 170
quarter moon p. 169
revolve p. 160
rotate p. 155
season p. 161
star p. 178
waning moon p. 169
waxing moon p. 169

Test Practice

Write the letter of the best answer choice.

11. A waning moon occurs _____.

    A. between a first-quarter moon and a new moon.
    B. when none of the Moon's near side is sunlit.
    C. right after a full moon.
    D. right after a crescent moon.

12. The position of the Sun changes during the day because Earth is _____.

    A. revolving.   C. rotating.
    B. waxing.   D. waning.

13. The equator is _____.

    A. an imaginary line on which Earth rotates.
    B. an imaginary line that divides Earth.
    C. an imaginary line between Earth and the Moon.
    D. a constellation.

14. The phase of the Moon that directly follows a new moon is a _____.

    A. last-quarter moon.   C. waxing crescent.
    B. waning crescent.   D. full moon.

Inquiry Skills

15. Use Models Suppose the Moon stopped rotating on its axis. Would you still see the phases of the Moon? Would you still see only one side of the Moon? How could you use a model to test your predictions?

16. How is thinking about what the sky looked like last night helpful when making a prediction about what the sky will look like tonight?

Map the Concept

Complete the concept map using the following terms:

revolves
rotates
phases of the Moon
pattern of day and night

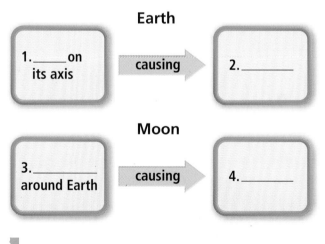

Earth

1. _____ on its axis

causing →

2. _____

Moon

3. _____ around Earth

causing →

4. _____

STANDARDS

1: 4.b., 2: 4.e., 3: 4.b., 4: 4.a., 5: 4.b., 6: 4.d.,
7–8: 4.b., 9: 4.e., 10: 4.a., 11: 4.b., 12: 4.e., 13: 4.e., 14: 4.b., 15: 5.d.,
16: 5.d., 4.a., 4.b., 17: 4.e., 18: 4.d., 19: 4.e., 20: 4.d., Map the Concept: 4.b.,
4.e., Performance Assessment: 5.b.

Critical Thinking

17. Apply Your family calls a relative who lives in a different country. It is 1:00 in the afternoon where you live. Is it possible that your relative will be in bed for the night? Explain.

18. Synthesize The Moon is much smaller than the Sun. But they look about the same size when viewed from Earth. Explain why this is.

19. Evaluate You hear someone say that the Sun rises in the morning, moves across the sky, and sets at night. How would you evaluate this statement?

20. Analyze How is the movement of the Moon similar to that of Earth?

Performance Assessment

Write a Dialogue
Suppose you are an astronaut walking on the Moon. Write a radio dialogue between yourself and scientists back on Earth. What information can you report about the Moon? What data are you collecting? What conclusions do the scientists make based on your observations?

Writing Journal

Review your answers to the questions on page 149 at the beginning of this chapter. Change your answers as needed, based on what you have learned.

Write the letter of the best answer choice.

1. At noon in California, when the Northern Hemisphere is tilted toward the Sun, it is _____.

   A. winter and the Sun appears low in the sky.

   B. summer and the Sun appears low in the sky.

   C. winter and the Sun appears high in the sky.

   D. summer and the Sun appears high in the sky.

2. The diagram shows Earth in orbit around the Sun.

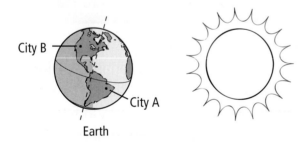

City B

City A

Earth

   Which explains why it is daytime in City A now but will later be night?

   A. Earth's axis is tilted.

   B. Earth rotates on its axis.

   C. City A is north of the equator.

   D. Earth revolves around the Sun.

3. Earth's moon _____.

   A. is a star.

   B. does not revolve.

   C. orbits around another moon.

   D. orbits around Earth.

4. A gibbous moon occurs just before and just after a full moon. Which shows a gibbous moon?

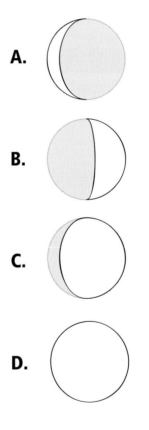

   A.

   B.

   C.

   D.

5. Earth gets light from _____.

    A. the Moon.

    B. the Sun.

    C. Venus.

    D. itself.

6. The illustration below most likely shows which planet?

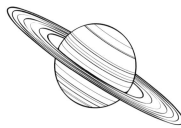

    A. Mars

    B. Pluto

    C. Saturn

    D. Venus

7. The Moon can be seen from Earth because it _____.

    A. produces its own light.

    B. reflects sunlight.

    C. has a rocky surface.

    D. is smaller than Earth.

8. Telescopes are tools that make distant objects appear _____.

    A. dimmer and larger.

    B. smaller and dimmer.

    C. smaller, brighter, and sharper.

    D. larger, brighter, and sharper.

Answer the following in complete sentences.

9. Explain why we can see certain star patterns in summer and other star patterns in winter.

10. The length of shadows change throughout the day. Describe how and why shadows change as the Sun appears to move from east to west in the sky.

STANDARDS

1–2: 4.e., 3: 4.d., 4: 4.b., 5: 1.a., 6: 4.d.,
7: 2.b., 8: 4.c., 9: 4.a., 10: 4.e., 2.a.

You Can...

Discover More

The largest volcano in the solar system, Olympus Mons, is on Mars. It rises up from the surface of Mars about 26 km (16 mi). The base of the volcano is about 602 km (374 mi) wide.

Olympus Mons is much bigger than Mauna Loa in Hawaii, one of the largest volcanoes on Earth. Mauna Loa is about 10 km (6 mi) high and about 121 km (75 mi) wide.

Volcanoes on Mars may become so large because the crust of Mars does not move. Lava erupts over and over again in the same place. As the lava builds up, the volcanoes grow higher.

Olympus Mons does not appear to be an active volcano. Scientists believe that it stopped erupting millions of years ago.

Olympus Mons
80 km
26 km
602 km

Mauna Loa
2 km
10 km
121 km

Simulations Go to **www.eduplace.com/cascp** to visit the volcanoes on Mars and other places in the solar system.

PHYSICAL UNIT C SCIENCE

Matter

California Connection

Visit www.eduplace.com/cascp to find out about materials used to build bridges, such as the Golden Gate in San Francisco, and other structures.

Lava Beds National Monument

Over 500,000 years ago, volcanic eruptions created this rugged landscape.

Sulfur flowers get their name because their yellow color is similar to the element sulfur.

Fern Cave was formed by hot lava flowing through underground cracks in the rocks.

PHYSICAL UNIT C SCIENCE

Matter

Golden Gate Bridge
San Francisco, California

Energy and matter have
multiple forms and can be
changed from one form
to another.

Chapter 6

Properties of Matter

An ice sculpture

LESSON

1

Like a toy made of small blocks, matter is made up of tiny units. They are too small to be seen without special tools. What are these tiny units that make up all matter?

LESSON

2

Ice, water, and invisible water vapor are three different forms of the same kind of matter— water. What are the three basic forms, or states, of matter?

LESSON

3

In a furnace, iron bars become molten iron. Water becomes ice in a freezer. What changes can occur when matter is heated or cooled?

Writing Journal

In your Writing Journal, show what you know by writing or drawing answers to each question.

Vocabulary Preview

Vocabulary

Glossary

Vocabulary Skill

Antonyms/Synonyms

Antonyms are words that mean the opposite, or nearly opposite. Knowing antonyms can help you learn and remember the meaning of words. *Evaporate* means to change from a liquid to a gas. The word *condense* is an antonym of *evaporate.* If you know this, you can figure out that *condense* means to change from a gas to a liquid.

melt

To change form from solid to liquid.

atom

The smallest particle of some kinds of matter that has the properties of that kind of matter.

liquid

Matter that takes the shape of its container and takes up a definite amount of space.

freeze

To change form from liquid to solid.

Start with Your Standards

Standard Set 1. Physical Sciences (Energy and Matter)

1.e. *Students know* matter has three forms: solid, liquid, and gas.

1.f. *Students know* evaporation and melting are changes that occur when the objects are heated.

1.h. *Students know* all matter is made of small particles called atoms, too small to see with the naked eye.

Standard Set 5. Investigation and Experimentation standards covered in this chapter: 5.b., 5.d., 5.e.

What Is Matter?

Building Background

Look at the objects in the room around you. Feel and smell the air. Every object you see and feel around you is matter. The air around you is matter. All of that matter is made of particles that are too small to see.

⬛ **STANDARDS**

1.h. *Students know* all matter is made of small particles called atoms, too small to see with the naked eye.
5.e. Collect data in an investigation and analyze those data to develop a logical conclusion.

PREPARE TO INVESTIGATE

Inquiry Skill

Compare When you compare, you describe how objects or events are alike and how they are different, often by using numbers.

Materials

- wood block
- sandpaper
- magazine photo
- chalk
- 2 sheets of black construction paper
- hand lens
- illuminated microscope
- goggles

Science and Math Toolbox

For step 1, review **Using a Hand Lens** on page H2.

Smaller and Smaller

Procedure

1. **Observe** Use a hand lens to observe chalk, wood, sandpaper, and a magazine photo. In your *Science Notebook*, record the appearance of each material.

STEP 1

2. **Observe** Gently rub the chalk on the sandpaper, over a sheet of black construction paper. Use the hand lens to observe the appearance of the particles of chalk on the paper. Record your observations. Set aside the black paper with the chalk particles. **Safety:** Wear goggles while using the sandpaper.

STEP 2

3. Repeat step 2, rubbing the wood on clean sandpaper over a clean sheet of black construction paper.

4. **Compare** Use a microscope to observe the chalk particles, wood particles, and magazine photo. Draw the smallest details you can see of each material.

STEP 4

5. **Communicate** Share your observations with classmates. Talk about why your drawings might look different.

Conclusion

1. **Compare** How did the materials look under the hand lens as compared with the microscope?

2. **Infer** If you could magnify the materials more, what do you think you would see?

Guided Inquiry

Experiment Find other materials to observe with a hand lens and microscope. After viewing with a hand lens, **predict** how each material will look under a microscope. Test your predictions.

199

Matter

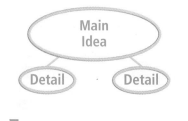
Identify five things in this kitchen that are matter.

MAIN IDEA All material around you is made up of matter. All matter is made up of atoms, which are tiny particles too small to see.

Properties of Matter

What do you like to do in the kitchen? You might like to help with the cooking, or maybe you just like to eat. Whether you're cooking or eating, you're using matter. **Matter** is anything that has mass and takes up space. Everything in this kitchen is matter. And even though you can't see it, the air in the kitchen is matter, too.

A trait of matter that can be measured or observed with the senses is a **physical property**. Physical properties include size, shape, color, texture, hardness, flavor, and temperature.

Air, which is invisible, fills the room.

The countertop is hard and smooth.

You observe the physical properties of matter using your senses—sight, touch, taste, smell, and hearing. Look for the melon on the countertop. What physical properties of the melon did you use to find it? Perhaps you looked for its color and shape.

There are many different ways to describe matter using its physical properties. The countertop shown is heavy and hard. The knife is long, thin, and sharp. The boy's shirt is soft and yellow. The ice cubes are smooth and cold.

Another way to describe matter is to measure it. How heavy matter is depends on its mass. Mass is the amount of matter in an object. An orange and a strawberry have different masses. They also have different volumes. Volume is the amount of space that matter takes up. Mass and volume are both physical properties.

MAIN IDEA AND DETAILS What is matter?

The melon is soft and sweet.

The ice cubes are cold.

Atoms

What is matter made of? A brick wall is made up of many individual bricks. A beach is made up of countless grains of sand. Bricks, sand, and all other matter are made up of smaller parts.

The metal that makes up these copper objects is matter. Like all matter, it is made up of tiny particles called atoms (AT uhms). An **atom** is the smallest particle of some kinds of matter that has the properties of that kind of matter. You can compare the copper atoms that make up these objects to the bricks in a brick wall. Other kinds of matter are made of more than one kind of atom joined together.

Copper atoms make up all of these objects.

Platinum is often used to make jewelry and wires. ▼

▲ This photo of platinum atoms was taken by an extremely powerful microscope.

Because atoms are so tiny, it takes a great many of them to make up an object. In fact, there are more atoms in a single grain of sand than there are people on Earth!

Atoms are far too small to see without extremely powerful microscopes. Long before they could see atoms, scientists guessed that all matter was made of atoms. Scientists tested their hypothesis by looking at how different kinds of matter behaved.

MAIN IDEA AND DETAILS What is all matter made of?

Express Lab

Activity Card 17
Classify Physical Properties

Physical Changes

How do you make a paper airplane? You fold a sheet of paper in a certain way. When you do this, you are changing the shape of the paper. You are also making a physical change to matter. A **physical change** is a change in the size, shape, or form, of matter. Physical changes do not change the makeup of matter.

You make physical changes to matter every day. Sharpening pencils and tying shoelaces are physical changes. Mixing chopped celery into tuna fish is a physical change. You can taste both the celery and the tuna. That's because mixing does not change the celery or the tuna into new kinds of matter.

MAIN IDEA AND DETAILS **Give two examples of a physical change.**

You make many physical changes while molding clay and folding paper.

Visual Summary

Matter is anything that has mass and takes up space. Everything you can sense around you is made of matter.

All matter is made of atoms, which are tiny particles that are too small to see without powerful microscopes.

A physical change is a change in the size, shape, or form of matter.

STANDARDS 1.e., 1.h.

Technology
Visit **www.eduplace.com/cascp** to find out more about matter.

Reading Review

❶ **MAIN IDEA** What is matter?

❷ **VOCABULARY** What is a physical change?

❸ **READING SKILL** Give two examples of physical changes in matter. Tell what kind of changes they are.

❹ **CRITICAL THINKING: Evaluate** If you looked at a piece of wood through a hand lens, would you be able to see its atoms? Explain.

❺ **INQUIRY SKILL: Compare** Suppose you crumple a large sheet of paper into a small ball. Describe what physical properties of the paper are changed.

✔ **TEST PRACTICE**
A physical change does NOT affect _____.

A. the size of matter.

B. the makeup of matter.

C. the shape of matter.

D. the form of matter.

STANDARDS
1–5: 1.h., Test Practice: 1.e.

STANDARDS **1.h.** *Students know* all matter is made of small particles called atoms, too small to see with the naked eye.

Atom Sized

Just how small is an atom? A million atoms side by side would barely cover the period at the end of this sentence. That's so small, it's hard to visualize! So try this comparison.

Imagine that you could magnify an atom to the size of a period. How big would a 2 mm grain of sea salt become if all of its atoms were magnified to period size? Would you believe the grain of salt would grow to a cube over 1,800 m tall, or over a mile high?

Each grain of salt contains more atoms than the number of stars in ten million Milky Way galaxies!

▲ Compared to an atom, a grain of sea salt is an enormous mountain higher than four Empire State Buildings. No wonder you can't see an atom with the naked eye!

Writing Journal

Imagine that you could shrink yourself to the size of an atom. Write in your journal how everyday objects might look.

What Are the Forms of Matter?

Building Background

Ice sparkles on an evergreen tree. A river flows nearby. There is invisible water vapor in the air. Ice, water, and water vapor are all alike in one important way—they are different forms of the same kind of matter.

PREPARE TO INVESTIGATE

Inquiry Skill

Predict When you predict, you state what you think will happen based on observations and experiences.

Materials

- clear plastic cup
- clear plastic container
- paper towel
- water

STANDARDS

1.e. *Students know* matter has three forms: solid, liquid, and gas.
5.d. Predict the outcome of a simple investigation and compare the result with the prediction.

States of Matter

Procedure

STEP 1

1. **Observe** Fill a large, clear container with water. Observe the shape of the water in the container.

2. Crumple a paper towel into the bottom of a clear plastic cup. Turn the cup over, as shown, to make sure the paper towel stays in the cup.

STEP 2

3. **Predict** Think about what will happen to the paper towel if you push the overturned cup straight down into the container of water. Record your prediction in your *Science Notebook*.

4. **Experiment** Carefully push the cup straight down into the container as shown. Remove the cup and look at the paper towel to see if it is wet or dry. Record your observations.

STEP 4

Conclusion

1. **Predict** Did your observations match your prediction? Explain.

2. **Hypothesize** Did the paper towel get wet or remain dry? Make a hypothesis about why you obtained these results.

3. **Draw Conclusions** How do your results help support the idea that air is matter?

Guided Inquiry

Experiment Add two marbles to a clear cup of water. Describe what happens to the water level. **Predict** what would happen if you added two more marbles to the water.

Forms of Matter

VOCABULARY

gas	p. 214
liquid	p. 213
solid	p. 211

READING SKILL

Classify Use the chart below to classify different substances as solid, liquid, or gas.

Group	Group	Group

STANDARDS

1.e. *Students know* matter has three forms: solid, liquid, and gas.

MAIN IDEA Matter can exist in three forms, or states, which are solid, liquid, and gas. Each state has its own physical properties.

Classifying Matter

Matter can be grouped by its physical properties. Think about your desk. Compare its properties with the properties of water in a drinking fountain. Then compare the properties of both the desk and water with the properties of air. The three kinds of matter you compared have different states, or forms.

Scientists use physical properties to classify matter into one of three forms. These forms of matter are solid, liquid, and gas.

Solids can be almost any texture, color, weight, or shape.

Solids

A **solid** is matter that has a definite shape. Solids also have a definite volume (VAHL yoom). This means solids take up a definite amount of space.

The particles of a solid are packed close together. They vibrate, or move back and forth, in place. They do not move past each other. That's the reason a solid keeps its shape.

CLASSIFY What form of matter is ice?

The particles in a solid are packed close together. Because their particles vibrate but do not move about, solids have a definite shape.

Liquids

To observe one physical property of a liquid, fill a glass with water. You'll see that the water takes the shape of the glass. If you pour the water into a bowl, you'll observe the water takes the shape of the bowl.

To observe another physical property of a liquid, measure the volume of the water in the glass. Then compare this volume with the volume of the water in the bowl. You'll find the volume is the same in each container.

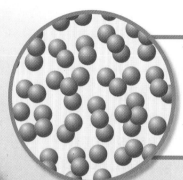

The particles in a liquid slide past each other. This movement allows a liquid to change shape and flow.

A **liquid** is matter that takes the shape of its container and has a definite volume. The particles of a liquid have more space between them than those of a solid.

The particles in a liquid are in contact, but they can slide past each other as they move. This movement is the reason that liquids can change shape and flow. It is also why liquids do not have a definite shape, but take the shape of their container.

CLASSIFY **Honey is very thick, but it takes the shape of its container. Is honey a solid or a liquid?**

Each container has the same amount of water in it.
What two properties of liquids does the photo show?

Express Lab

Activity Card 18
Model How a Liquid Moves

The particles in a gas move about freely and will spread out to fill their container.

Gases

Most of the gases you know about are invisible. Air is made up of several gases, including oxygen and carbon dioxide. Helium that fills some balloons is also a gas that cannot be seen. Although many gases are invisible, all gases are matter and have certain physical properties.

A **gas** is matter that has no definite shape and no definite volume. The particles in a gas move around freely and rapidly. Because of this movement, a gas takes the shape of its container. But unlike a liquid, the particles in a gas will spread out to fill the entire space. If a gas in a large space is squeezed, it can be made to fit in a smaller space.

CLASSIFY How are the particles in a gas spaced?

Visual Summary

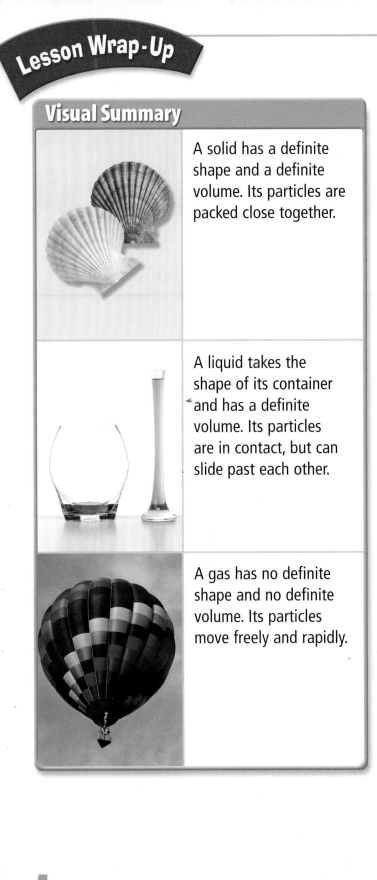

A solid has a definite shape and a definite volume. Its particles are packed close together.

A liquid takes the shape of its container and has a definite volume. Its particles are in contact, but can slide past each other.

A gas has no definite shape and no definite volume. Its particles move freely and rapidly.

Reading Review

❶ MAIN IDEA What are the three forms of matter?

❷ VOCABULARY What is a liquid?

❸ READING SKILL You find a clear substance that has a definite shape. What form of matter is the substance?

Group	Group	Group

❹ CRITICAL THINKING: **Analyze** Explain how the particles of a liquid allow the liquid to change shape and flow.

❺ INQUIRY SKILL: Predict If you open a container of gas, what will happen to the gas?

✔ TEST PRACTICE

Particles of matter are spread farthest apart in a _____.

A. solid.

B. liquid.

C. piece of ice.

D. gas.

STANDARDS 1.e.

Technology
Visit **www.eduplace.com/cascp** to learn more about forms of matter.

STANDARDS
1–5: 1.e., Test Practice: 1.e.

How Does Heat Change Matter?

Building Background

A solid iceberg floats in liquid water. Slowly, the ice melts into the ocean. Over time, the iceberg disappears. A change in form can occur when matter is heated.

STANDARDS

1.f. *Students know* evaporation and melting are changes that occur when the objects are heated.
5.b. Differentiate evidence from opinion and know that scientists do not rely on claims or conclusions unless they are backed by observations that can be confirmed.

PREPARE TO INVESTIGATE

Inquiry Skill

Hypothesize If you think you know why something that you observe happens, you can make a hypothesis, or an educated guess, about it.

Materials

- pat of butter (room temperature)
- dropper
- vanilla extract
- plastic dish
- disposable gloves
- clock or watch

Science and Math Toolbox

For step 1, review **Measuring Elapsed Time** on pages H12–H13.

Changing Matter

Procedure

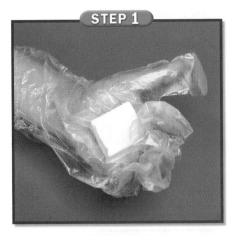

STEP 1

1. Put on a pair of disposable gloves. In one hand, hold a pat of room-temperature butter over a dish. Observe the butter. Then close your hand loosely around the butter. Keep your hand this way for 5 minutes. **Safety:** Do not eat any of the food materials.

STEP 2

2. **Observe** After 5 minutes, open your hand and observe the butter. Remove the gloves. In your *Science Notebook*, record any changes.

3. Put one drop of vanilla extract on a clean dish. Place the dish on a sunny windowsill where it won't be disturbed. Record the appearance of the vanilla extract.

STEP 3

4. **Record Data** The next day, observe the vanilla extract and record any changes.

Conclusion

1. **Hypothesize** What caused the change in the butter?

2. **Hypothesize** What caused the change in the vanilla extract?

3. How could you make sure that your ideas are correct?

Guided Inquiry

Experiment Repeat steps 3 and 4. This time, cover the dish tightly with plastic wrap. **Predict** what will happen to the vanilla extract. Check the dish the next day to see if your prediction was correct.

Thermal Energy

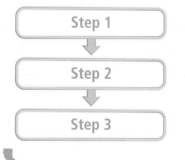
MAIN IDEA When matter is heated or cooled, it can expand, contract, or change form.

Heating Matter

Recall that matter is made up of tiny particles that are always moving. Particles in solids move back and forth in a small space. In liquids, particles slide past each other. Particles in gases move quickly and freely. The energy of moving particles in all matter is called **thermal energy** (THUR muhl EHN-ur jee). Adding or taking away thermal energy can cause changes in matter.

The particles in the cool metal lid are close together. Thermal energy from the warm water causes the particles in the lid to move farther apart. The metal expands.

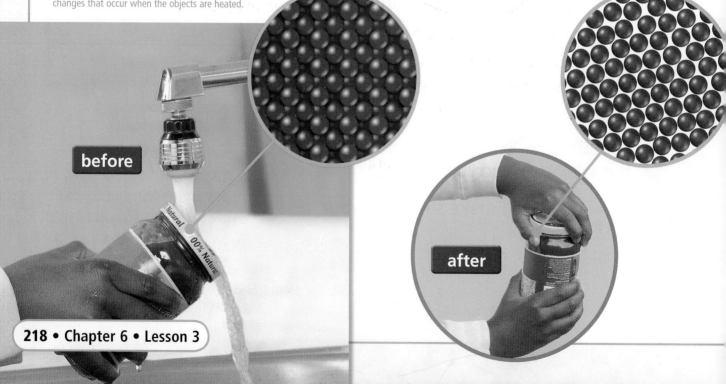

before

after

Why do engineers need to leave spaces between the metal parts of a bridge?

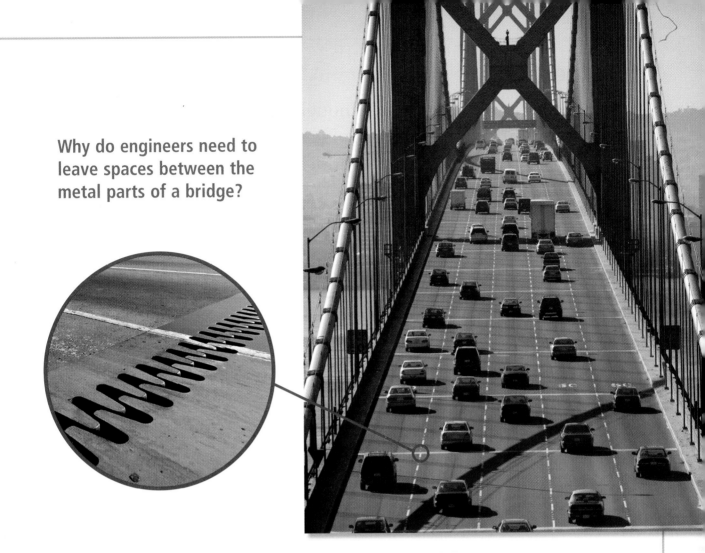

What happens when you heat matter, or add thermal energy to matter? Look at the example on page 218. Thermal energy from hot water is added to a metal jar lid that is too tight to turn. The increased energy causes the particles of matter that make up the lid to move more and farther apart. This makes the lid expand, or get larger. The expanded lid is easier to turn.

Thermal energy can also be removed from matter. When thermal energy is removed, particles slow down and move closer together. This causes most kinds of matter to get smaller, or contract.

SEQUENCE What causes matter to expand when you add thermal energy?

Melting

You have learned that although the particles of a solid cannot move around, they do have thermal energy. If thermal energy is added to the particles of a solid, the particles vibrate more.

As the particles move more, they are able to slide past each other. The solid no longer has a definite shape. The matter that was solid is now liquid. Adding thermal energy has caused a change in form from solid to liquid.

Particles in solid iron are tightly packed together. They vibrate in a small space.

As thermal energy is added to solid iron, the solid changes to a liquid. The particles in the liquid iron slide past each other.

Melting Point of Some Common Metals

Metal		Melting Point (°C)	Melting Point (°F)
tin		232	450
lead		327	621
aluminum		660	1,220
iron		1,539	2,802

To change form from a solid to a liquid is to **melt**. Melting occurs when enough thermal energy is added to solid matter. Melting is a physical change. Melted iron has different physical properties from solid iron. But both solid and liquid iron are made of the same particles of matter.

The temperature at which a solid changes to a liquid is called its melting point. The table shows the melting point of some common metals.

SEQUENCE What must be added to a solid before it will melt?

Express Lab

Activity Card 19
Time a Change of State

Evaporation

Adding enough thermal energy to a solid causes it to melt and become a liquid. What happens if you continue to add thermal energy to the liquid? The particles in the liquid move faster and farther apart. Finally, they move so fast and so far apart that the liquid changes form and becomes a gas.

To change form from a liquid to a gas is to **evaporate** (ih vap uh RAYT). Like melting, evaporation is a physical change in matter. The particles of matter do not change.

◀ Thermal energy from the Sun causes the water from the girl's skin and swimsuit to evaporate.

Evaporation occurs when wet clothes are hung outdoors on a clothesline to dry. If it is sunny, evaporation will occur more quickly because the sunlight provides added thermal energy. When wet clothes are put in a clothes dryer, added thermal energy causes even more rapid evaporation.

The change from a liquid to a gas can occur very quickly if a pot of water is put on a hot burner. After a few minutes, the water will boil. Boiling is the rapid change from a liquid to a gas.

SEQUENCE **What change of form takes place when you add thermal energy to a liquid?**

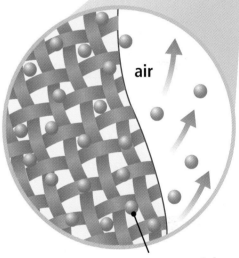

air

water particle

▲ As the liquid water evaporates from the dress, water particles enter the air as water vapor, which is a gas.

▲ In summer, this lake is liquid. Winter temperatures can remove enough thermal energy to permit ice skating.

Cooling Matter

When thermal energy is removed from matter, cooling results. The particles of matter slow down and move closer together. If enough thermal energy is removed, matter will change form. If a gas is cooled enough, the particles will move so close together that they will be in contact with each other. When this happens, the matter is said to **condense**, or change from a gas to a liquid.

If enough thermal energy is removed from a liquid, the particles of the liquid will slow down until they vibrate in place. When this happens, the matter is said to **freeze**, or change from a liquid to a solid. Condensing and freezing are both physical changes. Both processes can be reversed by adding thermal energy to matter.

SEQUENCE What must happen to a gas before it can condense?

Visual Summary

solid

melt

freeze

liquid

evaporate

condense

gas

STANDARDS 1.f., 1.e.

Technology
Visit **www.eduplace.com/cascp** to learn
more about changing forms of matter.

Reading Review

1 **MAIN IDEA** What two changes of form can occur when thermal energy is added to matter?

2 **VOCABULARY** Write a sentence using the term *condense*.

3 **READING SKILL** List the steps needed to change a solid to a gas.

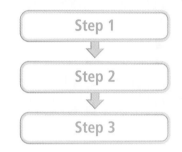

Step 1

Step 2

Step 3

4 **CRITICAL THINKING: Evaluate** A classmate says that when ice melts, it becomes a new kind of matter. Evaluate this statement.

5 **INQUIRY SKILL: Hypothesize** Why do large puddles disappear more slowly than small puddles?

✔ **TEST PRACTICE**
When matter freezes, its particles _____.

A. speed up.   **C.** evaporate.

B. slow down.   **D.** condense.

STANDARDS
1–5: 1.e., 1.f., Test Practice: 1.f., 1.h.

225

Cooling Off

Have you ever heard someone call a refrigerator an *icebox?* One hundred years ago, people kept their food in a wooden cabinet. The cabinet had a large block of ice inside that kept the food cool. It was a box of ice, or an icebox. But because the ice would melt, the icebox could not freeze food.

Today, a refrigerator can keep food cool or even frozen. It does this by removing thermal energy from the food. Because thermal energy is removed, the particles of the food slow down, and the food cools.

Ice was once very valuable. People cut blocks of ice from frozen lakes and stored them for the summertime. Some of the ice was shipped to warm places.

STANDARDS

1.e. *Students know* matter has three forms: solid, liquid, and gas.
1.f. *Students know* evaporation and melting are changes that occur when the objects are heated.

READING LINK

A Modern Refrigerator

1 Refrigerators use changes in form to cool food. A compressor squeezes a gas called a coolant until it changes to a liquid.

2 The liquid coolant moves into a new container where it begins to evaporate. As it evaporates it gives off thermal energy and becomes cold.

3 The cold gas moves through tubes inside the refrigerator, keeping the food cold.

Sharing Ideas

1. **READING CHECK** Describe how a refrigerator keeps food cold.

2. **WRITE ABOUT IT** Compare a refrigerator to an old-fashioned icebox.

3. **TALK ABOUT IT** How do you think refrigerators have changed the kinds of foods people eat?

Math **Measurement**

The physical properties of matter include size, volume, and mass. Scientists use different tools to measure the physical properties of solids. A ruler can be used to measure length, width, and height. Multiplication can be used to find volume. A balance can be used to measure mass.

Physical Properties of a Solid				
Length	Width	Height	Volume	Mass

1. Find a small box such as a shoebox. Use a ruler to measure its length, width, and height.

2. Find the volume of the box by multiplying the length times the width times the height.

3. Use a balance to find the mass of the box. Record your data in a chart like the one shown.

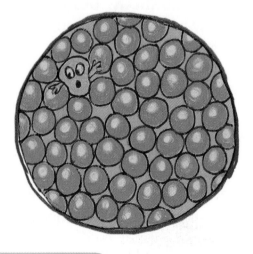

Writing **Narrative**

Imagine you are a particle in a solid. You are surrounded on all sides by your neighbors. You can move around a little, but you can't get past anyone. What would happen if thermal energy were added to your solid? Write a short story from the point of view of an atom. Include at least two changes of state in your story.

Metallurgists

What do bicycles, toasters, and cars have in common? They are all made from metal. Metallurgists are scientists who work with metals, usually at companies that make metal products. They know how to use changes in state to get metals out of rocks and minerals, and how to use physical changes to make the metals into objects.

What It Takes!

- A degree in metallurgical engineering, materials science, or materials engineering
- Strong problem-solving skills

Jewelry Designer

Creating jewelry is part art and part science. Jewelry designers use artistic abilities to craft pieces that will attract customers' attention. They use science knowledge to work with all sorts of precious metals and gems. For example, to shape rings into different sizes, jewelry designers must have an understanding of the properties of metals such as gold and silver.

What It Takes!

- A high-school diploma
- Courses in gemology, jewelry manufacturing, and jewelry design

Vocabulary

Complete each sentence with a term from the list.

1. A state of matter that has no definite shape and no definite volume is a/an _____.

2. A change in the size, shape, or form of matter is a/an _____.

3. To change from a gas to a liquid is to _____.

4. Anything that has mass and takes up space is _____.

5. The smallest particle of some kinds of matter that has the properties of that kind of matter is called a/an _____.

6. Matter that has a definite shape and a definite volume is a/an _____.

7. When liquids change to gas, they _____.

8. To change form from a solid to a liquid is to _____.

9. The energy of moving particles in all matter is called _____.

10. When liquids change state to become solids, they _____.

atom p. 202
condense p. 224
evaporate p. 222
freeze p. 224
gas p. 214
liquid p. 213
matter p. 200
melt p. 221
physical change p. 204
physical property p. 200
solid p. 211
thermal energy p. 218

✔ Test Practice

Write the letter of the best answer choice.

11. In the liquid state, particles _____.

A. are in constant contact, but can move.
B. are tightly packed together.
C. are not in constant contact.
D. are not moving.

12. A trait of matter that can be measured or observed is called a/an _____.

A. thermal energy.   C. physical property.
B. atom.   D. physical change.

13. Adding thermal energy to matter causes its particles to _____.

A. speed up and move closer together.
B. speed up and move farther apart.
C. slow down and move farther apart.
D. slow down and move closer together.

14. The amount of space an object takes up is called _____.

A. mass.   C. length.
B. weight.   D. volume.

15. **Compare** Suppose you heat an ice cube until it melts into water. Compare how the particles in the ice move to how the particles in the water move.

16. You fill a bowl of water outside for birds to drink from. The next day, you see that the bowl is empty. Do you have enough information to conclude what happened to the water? Explain.

Map the Concept

Use the terms below to fill in the concept map.

evaporation

melting

liquid

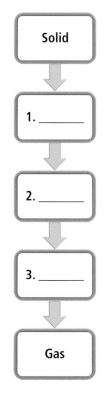

Solid

1. _____

2. _____

3. _____

Gas

Critical Thinking

17. **Analyze** When you arrive at school on a rainy day, your hat is covered with water drops. At the end of the day, your hat is dry. What kind of change has taken place? Explain.

18. **Evaluate** Suppose you look at a piece of metal through a hand lens. The metal looks very smooth. Can you draw the conclusion that the metal is not made of smaller parts? Explain.

19. **Synthesize** How could you demonstrate that air has mass and takes up space?

20. **Apply** Suppose a recycling center grinds cardboard into pulp. What kind of change has occurred? Have the particles of the cardboard changed?

Performance Assessment

Draw a Diagram
Read about volcanoes on the Internet or in a book. Draw a diagram that explains the changing states of matter that occur during and after an eruption.

Writing Journal

Review the answers you wrote to the Lesson Preview questions on page 195. Change your answers, as needed, based on what you learned.

STANDARDS

1–2: 1.e., 3: 1.f., 4–5: 1.h., 6: 1.e., 7–10: 1.f., 11: 1.e., 12: 1.h., 13–14: 1.f.,
15: 1.f., 1.h.,16: 1.f., 5.b., Map the Concept: 1.e., 1.f., 17: 1.f., 18–19: 1.h.,
20: 1.f., Performance Assessment: 1.e., 1.f.

Chapter 7

Chemical Changes

Fireworks are chemical changes in matter.

LESSON 1

A silver bowl, oxygen in air, and an aluminum bat are all made of atoms. What are some different types of atoms?

LESSON 2

Fire turns a wooden log into ash. Oxygen in air changes iron into rust. How does matter change from one kind to another?

Writing Journal

In your Writing Journal, show what you know by writing or drawing answers to each question.

233

Vocabulary Preview

Vocabulary

Glossary

Vocabulary Skill

Related Words
compound
element

Some words are related because of their meanings. For example, the words *compound* and *element* have related meanings. A compound is made up of parts called elements. Knowing the definition of *element* can help you understand the definition of *compound*. In turn, knowing the definition of *compound* can help you understand the definition of *element*.

element
A pure form of matter in which all the atoms are the same kind.

chemical change
A change in which one or more new kinds of matter are formed.

periodic table
A chart that shows an arrangement of the elements and information about their atoms and properties.

mixture

A combination of two or more substances or materials that are physically combined.

Start with Your Standards

Standard Set 1. Physical Sciences (Energy and Matter)

1.g. *Students know* that when two or more substances are combined, a new substance may be formed with properties that are different from those of the original materials.

1.h. *Students know* all matter is made of small particles called atoms, too small to see with the naked eye.

1.i. *Students know* people once thought that earth, wind, fire, and water were the basic elements that made up all matter. Science experiments show that there are more than 100 different types of atoms, which are presented on the periodic table of the elements.

Standard Set 5 Investigation and Experimentation standards covered in this chapter: 5.b., 5.e.

What Are Elements?

Building Background

The surface of an iron sculpture combines with oxygen to make rust. But what is the iron made of? What is the oxygen made of? Iron and oxygen are examples of pure substances called elements. Different combinations of elements make up all matter.

PREPARE TO INVESTIGATE

Inquiry Skill

Classify When you classify, you sort objects according to their properties.

Materials

- copper wire in sealed plastic bag
- charcoal in sealed plastic bag
- aluminum foil in sealed plastic bag
- sulfur in sealed plastic bag
- hand lens

Science and Math Toolbox

For step 2, review **Using a Hand Lens** on page H2.

STANDARDS

1.i. *Students know* people once thought that earth, wind, fire, and water were the basic elements that made up all matter. Science experiments show that there are more than 100 different types of atoms, which are presented on the periodic table of the elements.
5.e. Collect data in an investigation and analyze those data to develop a logical conclusion.

Periodic Table

Procedure

① Read the data table showing the physical properties of substances that are metals and substances that are nonmetals.

② **Record Data** Work with a partner. Use a hand lens to observe the color, shape, and texture of a copper wire. With the wire inside the sealed bag, try to bend the wire. Record your observations in your *Science Notebook*.

③ **Classify** Use the data table and your observations to classify the copper as a metal or nonmetal.

④ **Experiment** Repeat steps 2 and 3 for the aluminum foil, sulfur, and charcoal, which is mostly carbon. Classify each substance as a metal or nonmetal.

Conclusion

1. **Compare** Which substances did you classify as metals? What data did you use to reach your conclusion?

2. **Analyze Data** Look at the periodic table on pages 240–241. Were your classifications correct?

Metals and Nonmetals	
Group	**Properties**
Metals	usually shiny; can be formed into sheets or wire; can be bent; good conductors of heat; usually solid at room temperature
Non metals	usually dull; not easily shaped; brittle; poor conductors of heat; solid, liquid, or gas at room temperature

STEP 2

STEP 4

Guided Inquiry

Ask Questions Write a question about other ways to classify materials. Then look in books and on the Internet to answer your question. **Classify** two other materials using this information.

Elements

MAIN IDEA All matter is made up of one or more elements. In an element, all of the atoms are of the same kind.

Types of Atoms

Today, scientists know that there are over 100 different elements. You are familiar with some common elements such as copper, helium, gold, silver, carbon, oxygen, and aluminum.

An **element** is a pure form of matter in which all of the atoms are the same kind. All matter is made up of one or more of these different elements. Elements combine in different ways to form different materials.

Gold is an element. All of the atoms in a nugget of gold are the same.

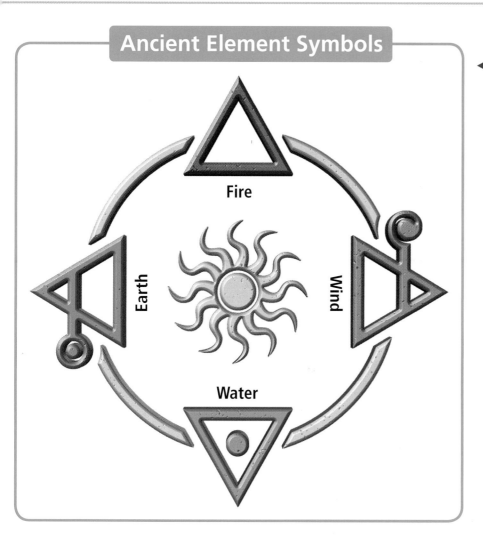

Ancient Element Symbols

Fire

Earth

Wind

Water

◀ In ancient times, scientists thought all matter was made from just four elements: earth, water, wind, and fire. The symbols shown were used to represent these elements.

Each element has its own kind of atom. For example, a pure silver ring is made up of silver atoms. Atoms of silver are different from the atoms of any other element.

You have learned that atoms are very small. Within an atom there are even smaller particles called protons. Atoms of different elements have different numbers of protons. For example, an atom of silver has 47 protons. An atom of gold has 79 protons. One way scientists group elements is by the number of protons in one atom of that element.

COMPARE AND CONTRAST Contrast the type of atoms that make up a silver ring with those that make up a gold ring.

Express Lab

Activity Card 20
Classify Elements

Arranging Elements

Scientists group all the elements in a chart called the periodic table of the elements. The **periodic table** is an arrangement of the elements that gives information about their atoms and properties. Each box shows the name and symbol for one element. The number at the top of the box tells how many protons are in an atom of that element.

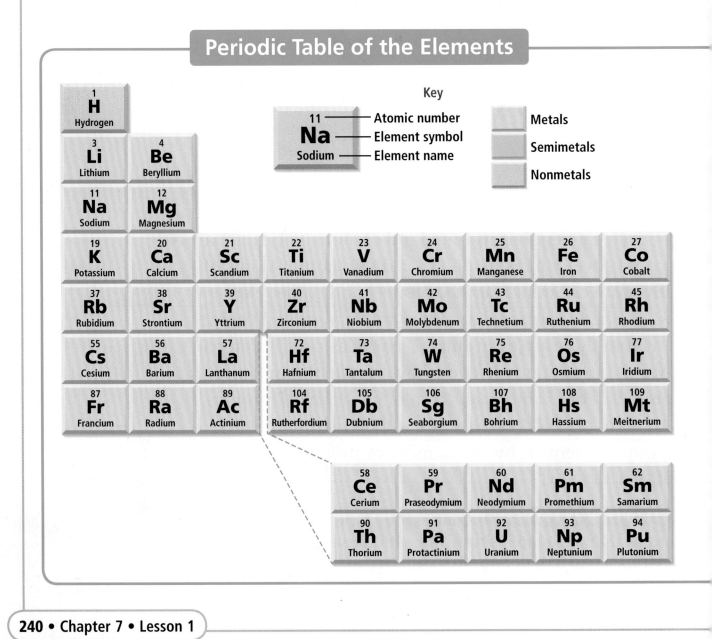

Periodic Table of the Elements

Key

11 — Atomic number
Na — Element symbol
Sodium — Element name

Metals
Semimetals
Nonmetals

An element's position in the periodic table gives information about properties of that element. For example, gold and silver have many similar properties. They are both heavy and shiny. They can both be shaped, and neither one rusts or burns.

Look at the periodic table. Notice that gold and silver appear in the same column. They are together with a group of elements called metals. Other element groups include nonmetals, such as chlorine, and semimetals, such as silicon.

COMPARE AND CONTRAST **Use the periodic table to tell how aluminum and silicon are different.**

								2 **He** Helium
			5 **B** Boron	6 **C** Carbon	7 **N** Nitrogen	8 **O** Oxygen	9 **F** Fluorine	10 **Ne** Neon
			13 **Al** Aluminum	14 **Si** Silicon	15 **P** Phosphorus	16 **S** Sulfur	17 **Cl** Chlorine	18 **Ar** Argon
28 **Ni** Nickel	29 **Cu** Copper	30 **Zn** Zinc	31 **Ga** Gallium	32 **Ge** Germanium	33 **As** Arsenic	34 **Se** Selenium	35 **Br** Bromine	36 **Kr** Krypton
46 **Pd** Palladium	47 **Ag** Silver	48 **Cd** Cadmium	49 **In** Indium	50 **Sn** Tin	51 **Sb** Antimony	52 **Te** Tellurium	53 **I** Iodine	54 **Xe** Xenon
78 **Pt** Platinum	79 **Au** Gold	80 **Hg** Mercury	81 **Tl** Thallium	82 **Pb** Lead	83 **Bi** Bismuth	84 **Po** Polonium	85 **At** Astatine	86 **Rn** Radon

63 **Eu** Europium	64 **Gd** Gadolinium	65 **Tb** Terbium	66 **Dy** Dysprosium	67 **Ho** Holmium	68 **Er** Erbium	69 **Tm** Thulium	70 **Yb** Ytterbium	71 **Lu** Lutetium
95 **Am** Americium	96 **Cm** Curium	97 **Bk** Berkelium	98 **Cf** Californium	99 **Es** Einsteinium	100 **Fm** Fermium	101 **Md** Mendelevium	102 **No** Nobelium	103 **Lr** Lawrencium

Compounds

You may have noticed that many common materials, such as water, sugar, and salt, are not included in the periodic table. These substances are not pure elements. They are made up of two or more elements. A substance made of two or more elements that are joined together is called a **compound**.

Compounds can have very different properties than the elements of which they are made. For example, water is a compound made up of the elements hydrogen and oxygen. As you know, water is a liquid at room temperature. However, both the elements hydrogen and oxygen are colorless gases. The gas hydrogen can burn.

Another example of a compound is table salt. Salt, or sodium chloride, is a compound. It is made from the elements sodium and chlorine. Sodium is a silvery metal. Chlorine is a poisonous green gas. You wouldn't want either of these separate elements on your dinner table. But you may use the compound sodium chloride to flavor your food.

calcium carbonate   Many hard substances produced by animals, such as bones and eggshells, contain calcium carbonate.

silicon dioxide Glass is made from the compound silicon dioxide, which is found in common sand.

sugar This common compound is fuel that plants and animals use for energy.

citric acid This common compound found in orange juice makes foods taste sour.

water This common compound is made of the gases hydrogen and oxygen.

sodium chloride Table salt is made of the elements sodium and chlorine. Combined as salt, these elements form a compound you can put on food.

Mixtures

There are many kinds of matter that are neither elements nor compounds. In fact, most kinds of matter are mixtures. A **mixture** is matter made up of two or more substances that are physically combined, or mixed. Unlike a compound, the substances in a mixture keep their own properties. They are not joined together.

The nachos mixture in the photo includes chips, beans, olives, tomatoes, and cheese. The properties of the materials in the mixture have not changed by being physically mixed together. For example, the tomatoes are still tomatoes and the olives are still olives.

COMPARE AND CONTRAST How are mixtures and compounds different?

Unlike compounds, mixtures can be separated by physical means. You can take the olives out of the nacho mixture by hand.

Visual Summary

All matter is made up of one or more elements. In ancient times, scientists thought that the elements that made up all matter were earth, wind, fire, and water.

Over 100 elements are listed in the periodic table. Each element in the periodic table is made up of one type of atom.

Compounds are substances made up of two or more elements. They have different properties from the elements that make them up.

Mixtures are combinations of two or more substances that are physically combined. The substances in mixtures keep their properties.

 STANDARDS 1.h., 1.i.

 Technology
Visit **www.eduplace.com/cascp** to learn more about elements.

Reading Review

❶ MAIN IDEA What is an element?

❷ VOCABULARY What is the periodic table?

❸ READING SKILL Use the chart to compare and contrast a compound and a mixture.

Compare	Contrast

❹ CRITICAL THINKING: Analyze The elements calcium and argon are on opposite sides of the periodic table. Would you expect these elements to be very similar? Explain.

❺ INQUIRY SKILL: Classify You make a salad out of lettuce, tomatoes, and carrots. Would you classify the salad as a compound or a mixture?

✓ TEST PRACTICE

Which of the following is NOT an element?

A. water   **C.** gold

B. calcium   **D.** aluminum

STANDARDS
1–5: 1.i., 1.h, Test Practice: 1.i.

245

Naming the Elements

How did scientists name over 100 elements? The names for some elements, such as gold and mercury, have been around since ancient times. But in the last seventy years, scientists have produced new elements that do not exist in nature. These artificial elements needed new names.

Often an element is named to honor a scientist. An element can also be named for the place where it was first produced.

◀ Dr. Glenn T. Seaborg was a famous scientist who helped discover several elements, including plutonium. Here he points to the element seaborgium, which was named in his honor.

STANDARDS

1.i. *Students know* people once thought that earth, wind, fire, and water were the basic elements that made up all matter. Science experiments show that there are more than 100 different types of atoms, which are presented on the periodic table of the elements.

READING LINK

The element gold has been used for thousands of years. It was named in ancient times. ▶

Two of the new elements, berkelium and californium, were named for Berkeley, California. The University of California at Berkeley is home to many scientists who study elements. One of those scientists was Dr. Glenn T. Seaborg, for whom the element seaborgium was named. The lab at the University of California at Berkeley continues to search for new elements.

Another element, curium, was named for the French chemist Marie Curie. Einsteinium was named for the American scientist Albert Einstein.

▲ In 1946 Dr. Seaborg named a new element, americium. It is element 95 on the periodic table.

95	97	98	106
Am	**Bk**	**Cf**	**Sg**
Americium	Berkelium	Californium	Seaborgium

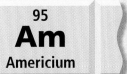

▲ It has been said that Dr. Glenn T. Seaborg could almost write his address using the names of four elements: seaborgium, berkelium, californium, americium (Dr. Seaborg, Berkeley, California, America).

Sharing Ideas

1. **READING CHECK** What is berkelium named after?

2. **WRITE ABOUT IT** Suppose you discovered a new element. Create a name for your element using your own name or the place where you live.

3. **TALK ABOUT IT** Discuss why scientists might want to create new elements.

What Is a Chemical Change in Matter?

Building Background

As strawberries ripen they change color. They also get larger. Changes in color and size are physical changes. But they result from chemical changes that occur in the fruit. Some of the matter that makes up the strawberries is changing to other kinds of matter.

STANDARDS

1.g. *Students know* that when two or more substances are combined, a new substance may be formed with properties that are different from those of the original materials.
5.b. Differentiate evidence from opinion and know that scientists do not rely on claims or conclusions unless they are backed by observations that can be confirmed.

PREPARE TO INVESTIGATE

Inquiry Skill

Record Data You can record and display the data you collect in the form of charts, graphs, and labeled diagrams. You can construct graphs in order to record measurements.

Materials

- water
- hand lens
- goggles
- scissors
- magnet
- toothpick
- 2 pieces of steel wool
- 2 white paper plates
- plastic bag, self-sealing
- small plastic bowl
- disposable gloves

Science and Math Toolbox

For step 3, review **Using a Hand Lens** on page H2.

A Rusty Change

Procedure

1. **Experiment** In your *Science Notebook,* make a chart like the one shown. Place a dry piece of steel wool in a plastic bag and seal the bag. Put a piece of wet steel wool in a plastic bowl. **Safety:** Wear goggles and disposable gloves.

2. **Observe** The next day, use scissors to snip some of the dry steel wool fibers onto a paper plate. Over another paper plate, use a toothpick to tap on the parts of the wet steel wool that show a change in color. Tap until you have a pile of colored pieces.

3. **Record Data** Use a hand lens to carefully observe the dry fibers and colored pieces from the steel wool. Record the properties of each.

4. **Compare** Hold a magnet close to the fibers of steel wool, and then close to the colored pieces. Compare and record what happens.

STEP 1

Material	Color	Feel	Magnetic
Fibers (dry)			
Fibers (wet)			

STEP 2

STEP 4

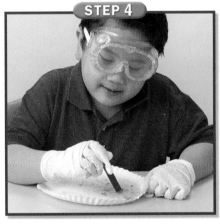

Conclusion

1. **Compare** The color change is due to rust. How is the rust similar to the original steel wool? How is it different?

2. **Infer** Are rust and steel wool the same material? What observations support your conclusion?

Guided Inquiry

Experiment When metal rusts, its properties change. **Hypothesize** about a way to keep metal from rusting. Experiment to test your hypothesis.

Chemical Changes

VOCABULARY

chemical change p. 251
chemical property p. 250

READING SKILL

Sequence List the properties of a wooden match before it has burned. Then list the properties of the match after it has burned.

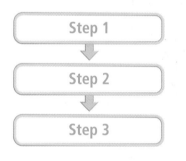

Step 1

↓

Step 2

↓

Step 3

STANDARDS

1.g. *Students know* that when two or more substances are combined, a new substance may be formed with properties that are different from those of the original materials.

MAIN IDEA In a chemical change, a new compound with different properties is created.

Chemical Reactions

Compare the tarnished silver candleholder with the candleholder after it was cleaned. Before cleaning, the silver is dull and has a dark coating. After cleaning, the silver is bright and shiny.

Silver reacts with sulfur, an element in air. A new compound is formed that has different properties from the original silver. The ability to react with sulfur to form new matter is a chemical (KEHM ih kuhl) property of silver. A **chemical property** is a property that describes how one kind of matter can react with other kinds of matter. Chemical properties of matter include the ability to burn, rust, and explode.

Before

When sulfur in air combines with silver, a new compound forms.

After

Cleaning the tarnished silver removes the new matter.

▲ The properties of the yellow compound differ from the properties of the two clear compounds that formed it.

A piece of wood cannot rust, but it can burn. The ability to burn is a chemical property of wood, paper, and some other kinds of matter. Compare the wooden match before and after it has burned. Burning has changed physical and chemical properties of the wood.

The burned part of the match is no longer wood. It is a different kind of matter. A chemical change has taken place. A **chemical change** is a change in matter in which one or more new kinds of matter form.

A chemical change is different from a physical change. In a chemical change, the original matter and the new matter have different properties. Rusting is a chemical change. Iron rusts when it comes in contact with air and water. The new matter that forms is softer than iron and is orange-colored.

▲ When a wooden match burns, new matter forms. It has different properties than wood.

SEQUENCE What happens to a wooden match after it has burned?

Physical and Chemical Changes

In a physical change, no new matter is formed. Although matter might look different, the atoms that make up the matter have not changed.

A chemical change always produces a new kind of matter. The new matter looks different and has different physical properties.

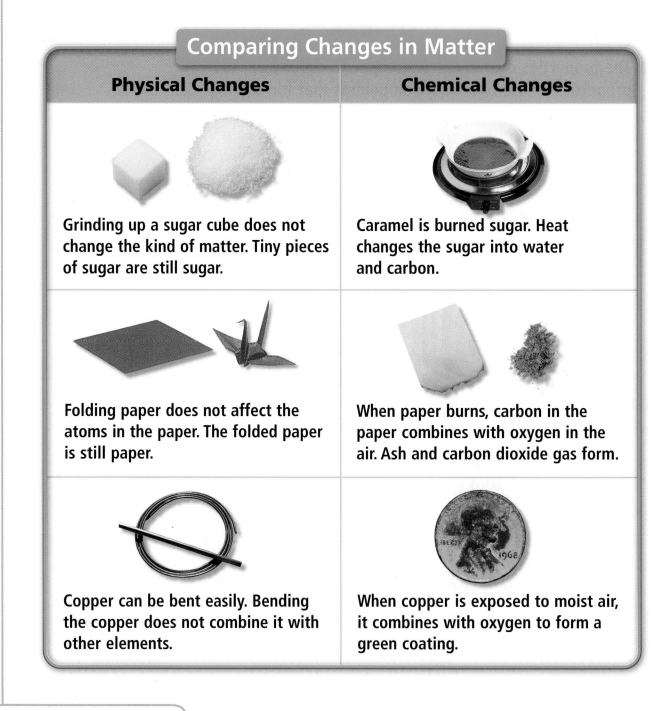

Comparing Changes in Matter

Physical Changes	Chemical Changes
Grinding up a sugar cube does not change the kind of matter. Tiny pieces of sugar are still sugar.	Caramel is burned sugar. Heat changes the sugar into water and carbon.
Folding paper does not affect the atoms in the paper. The folded paper is still paper.	When paper burns, carbon in the paper combines with oxygen in the air. Ash and carbon dioxide gas form.
Copper can be bent easily. Bending the copper does not combine it with other elements.	When copper is exposed to moist air, it combines with oxygen to form a green coating.

Sugar is a common compound. When sugar is heated to very high temperatures, a chemical change takes place. You can see this chemical change when you toast a marshmallow.

Toasting a marshmallow starts as a physical change. The solid marshmallow begins to melt. At a certain temperature, the sugar begins to change to other substances. One of these substances is the element carbon. When this chemical change occurs, carbon becomes visible as a dark material. Hydrogen and oxygen are other elements that result from the chemical change.

SEQUENCE **Describe the changes that occur when you toast a marshmallow.**

The carbon on this toasted marshmallow indicates that a chemical change has taken place. ▼

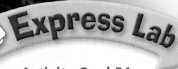

Express Lab

Activity Card 21
See Chemical and Physical Changes

253

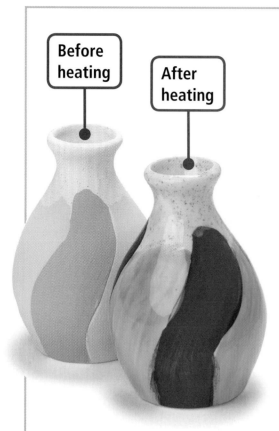

Before heating

After heating

▲ Heating clay causes a chemical change. After heating, the vase is strong, shiny, and waterproof.

Useful Chemical Changes

Chemical changes are an important part of life. Many take place in your body. You could not stay alive without them. For example, when you eat, a series of chemical changes begins. Inside your body, food is changed chemically into new matter that your body can use for energy and growth. Cooking food also causes chemical changes.

A series of chemical changes in plants produces food from energy in sunlight. Chemical changes that take place in a battery are used to produce electricity. Cars and buses move because of chemical changes. When gasoline is burned in the engine, chemical changes release energy. Colorful displays of exploding fireworks also come from chemical changes.

SEQUENCE **What happens to food in the body after it is eaten and before it is used for energy and growth?**

During cooking, pancake batter undergoes a chemical change. The cooked pancakes have different properties than the batter. ▼

Visual Summary

A chemical property is a property that describes how matter can react with other kinds of matter.

Chemical changes produce new kinds of matter. The new kinds of matter have different properties than the original matter.

In a physical change, such as the bending of copper wire, no new matter is formed. In a chemical change, such as when copper combines with oxygen in air, new matter is formed.

STANDARDS 1.g.

Technology

Visit **www.eduplace.com/cascp** to learn more about chemical changes.

Reading Review

❶ MAIN IDEA What happens during a chemical change?

❷ VOCABULARY Define *chemical property.*

❸ READING SKILL Sequence the steps of a nail rusting.

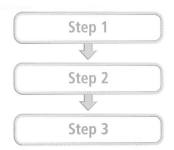

Step 1

Step 2

Step 3

❹ CRITICAL THINKING: Evaluate Your friend says that paper, wood, and gasoline share the ability to burn. Evaluate this statement.

❺ INQUIRY SKILL: Record Data Count the examples of chemical changes in this lesson. Make a table to record what causes each type of chemical change.

✓ TEST PRACTICE

Which is NOT an example of a chemical change?

A. food cooking

B. water freezing

C. a match burning

D. iron rusting

STANDARDS

1–5: 1.g., Test Practice: 1.g.

255

STANDARDS **1.g.** *Students know* that when two or more substances are combined, a new substance may be formed with properties that are different from those of the original materials.

Vanishing Bottles

Why are these bottles falling apart? Actually, they were designed to fall apart! Why? So they don't become a permanent part of the mountains of trash produced every day.

These bottles are made of a kind of plastic that is biodegradable (BY oh dee-GRAYD uh buhl). Biodegradable means that a substance can be broken down by small living things called bacteria and molds.

The bacteria and molds actually eat and digest the plastic. This causes a chemical change in the plastic. Before, the plastic was hard and tough. But the new materials formed by the chemical reactions are soft. The physical properties of the bottles have changed, and the bottles fall apart.

Day 1

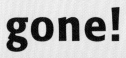

Going, going, gone!

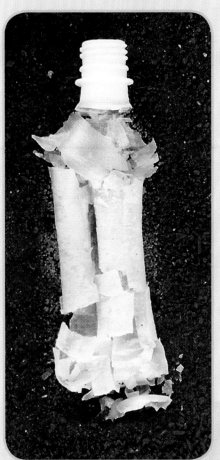

Day 30

Day 50

Day 64

Most plastic is not biodegradable. If an ancient Egyptian Pharaoh had drunk from a plastic bottle, that bottle might last as long as the stone pyramids—thousands of years!

Writing Journal

In your writing journal, tell about what might happen if none of the products we used were biodegradable.

257

Math Inequalities

There are more than 100 elements in the periodic table. They are all classified according to their type.

Key

11 — Atomic number
Na — Element symbol
Sodium — Element name

Metals

Semimetals

Nonmetals

Refer to the key and the color outline of the periodic table above. Use the symbols < or > to complete the following exercises.

1. Compare the number of metals and semimetals.

2. Compare the number of semimetals and nonmetals.

3. Compare the number of metals and nonmetals.

Writing Descriptive

Make a log of all of the chemical changes you use or see in a typical day. Describe each change, and tell how you know that this change is a chemical change and not a physical change.

Dr. Wilson Ho

In Irvine, California, scientist Wilson Ho builds some of the most powerful microscopes in the world! A microscope is a tool that makes small objects appear larger. Dr. Ho uses his microscopes to study and take pictures of atoms. He is researching how to take pictures of even smaller things, such as the parts of atoms.

By using new knowledge of atoms, scientists might find ways to make computers smaller and faster. They might make metals stronger, or find new medicines. Maybe you will use such things in the future or invent them yourself!

◀ Atoms of silicon

Vocabulary

Complete each sentence with a term from the list.

1. A form of matter in which substances are combined chemically is a/an _____.

2. All of the elements are arranged in the _____, which shows information about their atoms and properties.

3. A combination of two or more substances that are physically combined is a/an _____.

4. A property that describes how matter reacts with other matter is a/an _____.

5. One or more new kinds of matter are formed during a/an _____.

6. All of the atoms are of the same kind in a/an _____.

chemical change p. 251
chemical property p. 250
compound p. 242
element p. 238
mixture p. 244
periodic table p. 240

Test Practice

Write the letter of the best answer choice.

7. Which of the following is NOT a mixture?

   A. peanut butter and jelly sandwich
   B. water
   C. nachos
   D. a salad

8. A compound is made up of _____.

   A. two or more elements combined chemically.
   B. one pure element.
   C. two or more mixtures.
   D. two or more elements combined physically, but not chemically.

9. Which of the following is a chemical property of iron?

   A. It melts at a high temperature.
   B. It combines with oxygen to form rust.
   C. It is gray.
   D. It is very strong.

10. What is probably true if two elements are close to each other in the periodic table?

   A. One is a gas and one is a solid.
   B. They have similar properties.
   C. They have very different properties.
   D. Neither one is a solid.

Inquiry Skills

11. Classify Suppose you are unable to separate an unknown substance using physical changes. Is the unknown substance a mixture or a compound? Explain.

12. Suppose your teacher burned a candle for the class. What observations might you make while the candle burned? after it is put out? What data would lead you to conclude that a chemical change took place?

Map the Concept

Fill in the concept map with terms from the list. You may use one of the terms more than once.

element
compound
chemical reaction

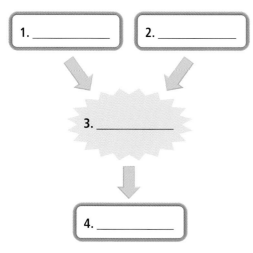

1. _____   2. _____

3. _____

4. _____

Critical Thinking

13. Analyze The elements sodium and chlorine combine to form sodium chloride. Are the properties of sodium chloride similar to those of sodium and chlorine? Explain.

14. Apply Suppose you build a metal spacecraft to visit the planet Neptune. The air around Neptune contains methane. What chemical properties should the metal you use have?

15. Evaluate Your friend says that toasting a marshmallow causes only a physical change. Evaluate this statement.

16. Synthesize An artist creates a sculpture and displays it outdoors. Soon, the sculpture begins to rust. What can you conclude about the materials from which the sculpture was made?

Performance Assessment

Bake Pumpkin Bread
Find a simple recipe for pumpkin bread. List the steps needed to make it. Identify each step as a physical or chemical change.

Writing Journal

Review your answers to the questions on page 233 at the beginning of this chapter. Change your answers as needed, based on what you have learned.

STANDARDS

1: 1.g., 2: 1.i., 3–5: 1.g., 6: 1.i., 7–9: 1.g., 10: 1.i., 11: 1.g.,
12: 5.e., Map the Concept: 1.g.,13: 1.g., 14–16: 1.g.,
Performance Assessment: 1.g.

Write the letter of the best answer choice.

1. About how many elements have scientists discovered?

   A. four
   B. twenty
   C. one
   D. one hundred

2. Which is an example of a physical change?

   A.

   B.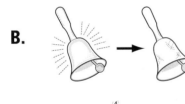

   C.

   D.

3. Which change happens when energy is taken away from a gas?

   A. freezing
   B. condensing
   C. evaporating
   D. melting

4. Whis is true of matter?

   A. It is made up of atoms.
   B. It can always be seen.
   C. It is always a solid.
   D. It has no mass.

5. A substance made up of two or more elements joined together is a/an

   _____.

   A. compound.
   B. atom.
   C. mixture.
   D. proton.

6. Which is a chemical property of matter?

   A. texture
   B. ability to change state
   C. ability to burn
   D. temperature

7. Which diagram most likely represents atoms in a solid?

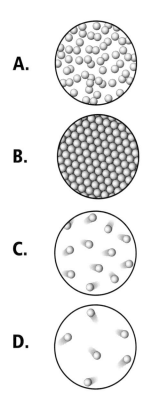

A.

B.

C.

D.

8. When two or more elements combine, _____.

A. melting occurs.
B. a new element forms.
C. no new matter forms.
D. a compound forms.

Answer the following in complete sentences.

9. Identify the three states, or forms, of matter. Explain the differences among the three forms, using water as an example.

10. Use the periodic table on pages 240–241 to answer the following.

- Identify three elements that are metals.
- Identify three elements that are nonmetals.
- What does the number 7 at the top of the box for nitrogen mean?
- What elements are numbers 13 and 14?

You Can...

Discover More

When it was built over 120 years ago, the Statue of Liberty had a bright, shiny copper surface. Today, the surface is a light green color. What caused this change?

The Statue of Liberty has welcomed people to the United States for more than 120 years. In that time, the statue has been exposed to rain, snow, pollution, and salty ocean air. Substances in the environment have caused changes to the statue's copper surface. The elements sulfur and oxygen in the air caused changes to the statue's copper surface.

The statue had a bright copper surface when it was built in France in the 1800s. Copper is a pinkish-brown metal.	The statue was put on an island in New York Harbor in 1886. By that time, the shiny copper surface had turned dark brown.	Substances in the environment caused more chemical changes. The dark brown copper started to turn green.	Today, the statue is light green. A new compound, copper sulfate, now covers its surface.

Simulations Go to www.eduplace.com/cascp to play a timeline of important events in the statue's history.

PHYSICAL

SCIENCE

UNIT
D

Energy

California Connection

Visit **www.eduplace.com/cascp** to find out about energy and its changes in California.

Roaring Camp

Today in the United States, steam locomotives are used only in museums to teach people about the history of the railroads.

Diesel engines use less energy and cost less money to run than steam engines.

A worker loads coal from a coal silo into this steam locomotive. The coal must be heated to over 1800 degrees Fahrenheit in order to produce enough steam to move the train.

PHYSICAL UNIT D SCIENCE

Energy

Energy changes during a roller-coaster ride.

Standard Sets 1., 2.
Physical Sciences

Energy and matter have multiple forms
and can be changed from one form
to another.

Light has a source and travels
in a direction.

Chapter 8

Forms of Energy

An ocean wave has energy.

LESSON 1

Energy comes from the Sun to Earth in the form of light. How is this energy stored?

LESSON 2

An electric stove heats food and runners race around a track. How do machines and living things change stored energy into motion?

LESSON 3

Music travels through the air. Waves move through the oceans. How is energy carried from place to place?

LESSON 4

Electricity powers the lights of the U.S. Capitol Building. How does an electric current carry energy?

Writing Journal

In your Writing Journal, show what you know by writing or drawing answers to each question.

Vocabulary Preview

Vocabulary

Glossary

Vocabulary Skill

Multiple-Meaning Words

crest

Science The crest of a wave is its highest point. A wave with a lot of energy has a high crest.

Science A crest is the showy growth of feathers on the head of a bird. The California valley quail has a large, curved crest.

electric circuit

A path around which electric current can flow.

friction

A force that occurs when one object rubs against another object.

vibrate

To move back and forth quickly.

Start with Your Standards

kinetic energy

Energy of motion.

What Is Energy?

Building Background

In warm weather, people go to beaches and parks to enjoy activities in the Sun. The Sun provides light, which is one form of energy. Light energy allows you to see the world around you.

PREPARE TO INVESTIGATE

Inquiry Skill

Measure When you measure, you use tools and units to find distance, mass, or other information about an object.

Materials

- masking tape
- ruler
- clay
- clock
- thermometer
- pizza box with flap cut in the top
- shallow bowl of water
- aluminum foil
- black construction paper
- heavy-duty plastic wrap

Science and Math Toolbox

For steps 1 and 5, review **Using a Thermometer** on page H8.

STANDARDS

1.a. *Students know* energy comes from the Sun to Earth in the form of light.
5.c. Use numerical data in describing and comparing objects, events, and measurements.

Solar Heater

Procedure

① **Measure** Put the bulb of a thermometer into a bowl of water. Record the water temperature.

② Make a solar heater. Use aluminum foil to cover the inside of the flap cut in a pizza box. Make sure the shinier side of the foil is showing. Tape the foil in place.

③ Open the box and cover the inside bottom with foil. Tape the foil in place. Tape sheets of black paper over the foil bottom so the foil is covered.

④ Tape plastic wrap across the inside of the pizza box lid so it forms a tight seal.

⑤ **Measure** Put the solar heater outdoors. Place the bowl of water in the box. Adjust the flap so that it reflects sunlight onto the water. Use a ruler with clay on both ends to prop open the flap. After 2 hours, again record the temperature of the water. **Safety:** Do not touch the aluminum foil.

STEP 3

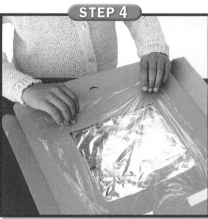
STEP 4

STEP 5

Conclusion

1. **Compare** In which step did you record the higher temperature?

2. **Predict** What would happen to the water if you left it in your solar heater for another 2 hours?

Guided Inquiry

Ask Questions Think about your results. What questions do you have about solar energy? Choose a question to investigate. **Collaborate** on a plan to find the answer.

Energy

MAIN IDEA Energy is the ability to cause motion or other changes in matter. There are many forms of energy.

Forms of Energy

You use energy to ride a bike. A stove uses energy to cook food. Your eyes use energy from the Sun to see. How can energy do all these things? **Energy** is the ability to cause movement or to cause matter to change in other ways.

There are many forms of energy. Each form of energy changes matter, but in a different way. For example, a bike is matter. The energy you use to ride a bike causes that matter to move. Food is matter. The energy used to cook food causes that matter to heat up.

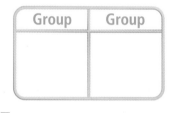
Which form of energy are these children using to play leapfrog? Look at the chart on the next page. ▶

Express Lab

Activity Card 22
Measure Solar Energy

Forms of Energy

Chemical Energy Chemical energy is energy that is stored in substances. It is found in food, fuel, and batteries.

Light Energy Light energy is energy you can see. It moves as waves through space or clear matter. Earth receives light energy from the Sun.

Electrical Energy Electrical (ih LEHK trih-kuhl) energy is the energy of charged particles. It is used to run appliances and other machines.

Mechanical Energy Mechanical (mih KAN-ih kuhl) energy is the energy of moving objects. It is used to move people and objects from place to place.

Sound Energy Sound energy is energy you can hear. It moves as waves through air or other matter. It is used to hear music.

Thermal Energy Thermal energy is the energy of tiny moving particles of matter. It is used to heat food and warm homes. Heat is the flow of thermal energy from warmer objects to cooler objects.

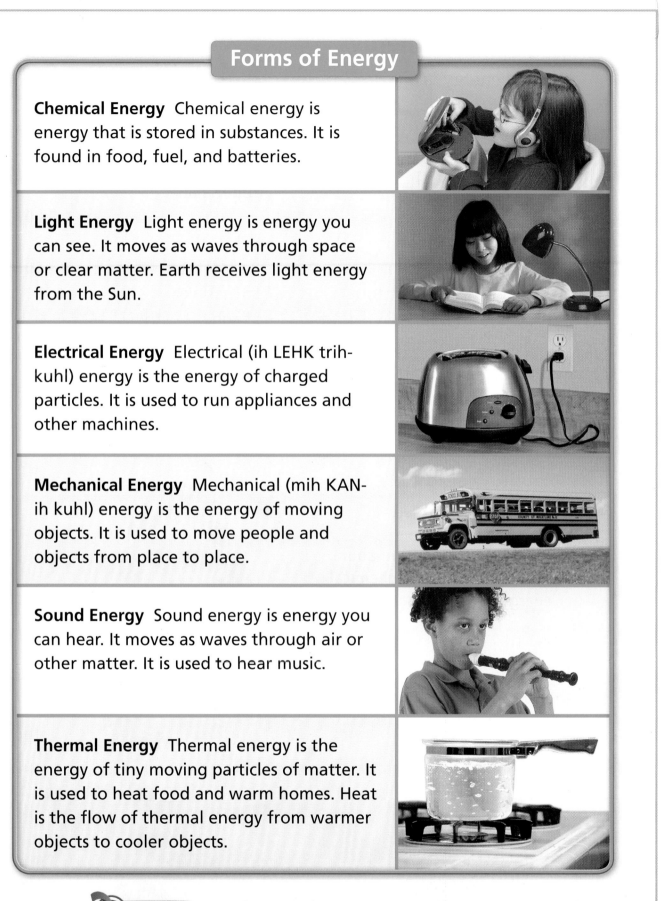

CLASSIFY What form of energy does a moving guitar string produce?

Useful Chemical Energy

Chemical energy is energy that is stored in different sources, such as food, gasoline, and batteries. It comes in many forms and can be used for all sorts of activities. For example, you use chemical energy when you play basketball, go to school, or use a flashlight.

The chemical energy in food is needed for you to live, move, and grow. In one day you might eat food containing 1,500 Calories. This is about the same amount of chemical energy as in a cup of gasoline or in two car batteries.

Energy from Food

Food	Calories
Cereal with milk	225
Banana	200
Orange juice	110
Tuna salad sandwich	300
Baby carrots	50
Baked potato chips	150
Soft drink	150
Spaghetti with tomato sauce	295
Zucchini	20
TOTAL	**1,500**

Two car batteries have about the same amount of chemical energy as this food.

car battery

car battery

=

Visual Summary

Energy is the ability to cause motion or other changes in matter.

There are many forms of energy. They include chemical, light, electrical, mechanical, sound, and thermal energy.

Sources of stored chemical energy include food, fuel, and batteries.

 STANDARDS 1.a., 1.b.

Technology
Visit **www.eduplace.com/cascp** to find out more about forms of energy.

Reading Review

❶ **MAIN IDEA** What is energy?

❷ **VOCABULARY** Use the words *energy* and *Sun* in a sentence.

❸ **READING SKILL** Classify the energy stored in gasoline as either mechanical energy or chemical energy.

Group	Group

❹ **CRITICAL THINKING: Apply** The Sun is the main source of light energy during the day. What are some sources of light energy you can use at night?

❺ **INQUIRY SKILL: Measure** The amount of chemical energy stored in batteries affects how long you can listen to a portable radio. How could you evaluate the amount of chemical energy stored in two AA batteries?

✔ **TEST PRACTICE**
Light energy comes from _____.

A. trees.

B. oceans.

C. clouds.

D. the Sun.

STANDARDS

1: 1.b., 2: 1.a., 3: 1.b., 4: 1.a., 5: 1.b., Test Practice: 1.a.

How Is Energy Converted?

Building Background

A swimmer jumps into the water and hits the surface with a loud splash! Water sprays everywhere! The sound and motion caused by the swimmer's jump are forms of energy. Everything you do, see, or hear involves energy.

PREPARE TO INVESTIGATE

Inquiry Skill

Measure When you measure, you use tools and units to find distance, mass, or other information about an object.

Materials

- thin dowel
- plastic-foam ball
- spring
- tape
- metric tape measure
- goggles

Science and Math Toolbox

For steps 3 and 4, review **Using a Tape Measure or Ruler** on page H6.

STANDARDS

1.c. *Students know* machines and living things convert stored energy to motion and heat.
5.a. Repeat observations to improve accuracy and know that the results of similar scientific investigations seldom turn out exactly the same because of differences in the things being investigated, methods being used, or uncertainty in the observation.

Launch It!

Procedure

STEP 2

1. **Collaborate** Work with a partner. Tape one end of a thin dowel to the surface of a table as shown. Half of the dowel should stick out past the edge of the table. Slide a spring onto the dowel. **Safety:** Wear goggles.

2. Push a plastic-foam ball onto the end of the dowel. Slide the ball back and forth until it can move freely.

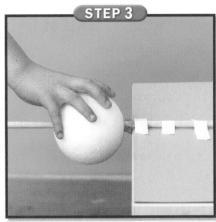

STEP 3

3. **Measure** Push the ball toward the desk until the coils of the spring are squeezed tightly together. Let go of the ball. After the ball stops rolling, use a tape measure to find out how far the ball traveled. Do this five times. Record each distance in your *Science Notebook.* **Safety:** Aim the ball away from people.

4. **Use Variables** Repeat step 3, but squeeze the spring only halfway. Predict how far the ball will travel. Release the ball. Then measure and record the distance. Do this five times.

STEP 4

Conclusion

1. **Infer** The spring stored energy when squeezed. What happened to this stored energy when you let go of the ball?

2. **Hypothesize** Explain why squeezing the spring halfway affects the distance that the ball travels.

Guided Inquiry

Experiment Find a tool or toy that uses the stored energy of a spring to make an object move. Try to make the object move in different ways. Record your data and **compare** the results.

VOCABULARY

friction p. 282
kinetic energy p. 278
potential energy p. 278

READING SKILL

Cause and Effect Use a graphic organizer to list some possible effects of chemical energy.

Cause → Effect

STANDARDS

1.b. *Students know* sources of stored energy take many forms, such as food, fuel, and batteries.
1.c. *Students know* machines and living things convert stored energy to motion and heat.

Energy, Motion, and Heat

MAIN IDEA Machines and living things change stored energy to motion and heat.

Kinetic and Potential Energy

Some energy involves motion. For example, a bowling ball rolling down an alley has energy of motion. Energy of motion is also called **kinetic energy** (kuh NEHT ihk-EHN ur jee).

Other energy does not involve motion. For example, chemical energy is a form of stored energy. Objects or living things can have stored energy based on their positions. The energy of position is called **potential energy** (puh TEHN shuhl EHN ur jee). A diver standing on a diving board above a pool has potential energy because of his or her position.

◄ The children at the top of the hill have **potential energy** because of their position.

◄ As the boy slides down the hill, he has **kinetic energy** because of his motion.

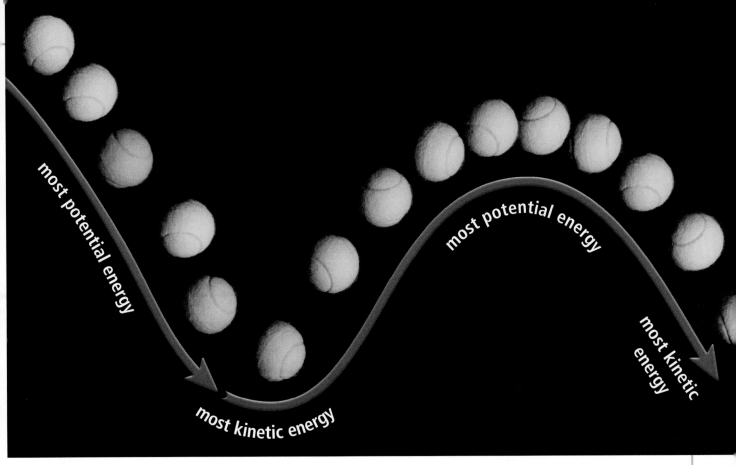

most potential energy

most kinetic energy

most potential energy

most kinetic energy

▲ When a ball is held above the ground, it has potential energy. As the ball falls, it gains kinetic energy.

Storing and Releasing Energy

Potential energy can change to kinetic energy. When you hold a ball above the ground, it has potential energy because of its position. When you drop the ball, it falls to the ground because of gravity. As the ball falls, its potential energy changes to kinetic energy.

Kinetic energy can also change to potential energy. As the ball falls, it has kinetic energy. When it bounces off the ground, it still has kinetic energy. As the ball moves upward, it slows down because its kinetic energy is changing back to potential energy.

CAUSE AND EFFECT Driving up a steep hill will cause a truck to lose kinetic energy and slow down. What kind of energy does the truck gain?

Express Lab

Activity Card 23
Store and Release Energy

279

Changing Forms of Energy

You have learned that kinetic and potential energy can change back and forth. Energy can also change from one form to another. For example, when you move around, chemical energy stored in the food you ate changes, or converts, to mechanical and thermal energy. When a car engine runs, chemical energy in gasoline converts to mechanical and thermal energy.

Whenever you use energy, it is almost always converted to another form. When you switch on a light to do your homework, electrical energy is converted to light energy. When you use a calculator, the chemical energy stored in its battery is converted to electrical energy.

CAUSE AND EFFECT **What effect does running have on chemical energy stored in your body?**

◄ Stored energy in gasoline changes to motion and heat in a car's engine.

Cells in your body change chemical energy in food to heat energy and motion. ▶

▲ The heat lamp changes electrical energy to thermal energy that keeps the chicks warm. The lamp also gives off light energy.

Producing Thermal Energy

Most forms of energy can change to thermal energy. You have probably noticed that you feel warm when you stand in sunlight. That is because the Sun gives off energy. Some of that energy becomes thermal energy. Electrical appliances, such as toasters and hair dryers, use electrical energy to produce thermal energy.

Another way to produce thermal energy is by converting chemical energy to thermal energy. When wood is burned, chemical energy stored in the wood is converted to thermal energy. That's why you feel heat from a campfire.

CAUSE AND EFFECT Give an example of how thermal energy can be produced from another form of energy.

Friction

You have learned that your body converts chemical energy in food to thermal energy. But you can also use your body to produce thermal energy in another way.

You have probably noticed that when you rub your hands together, they get warm. This happens because friction (FRIHK shuhn) between your moving hands produces thermal energy. **Friction** is a force that occurs when one object rubs against another object. Friction slows down and stops motion between two surfaces that touch.

CAUSE AND EFFECT What causes your hands to get warm when you rub them together?

1 The rubber on the brakes rubs against the moving tire, producing friction.

2 The brakes and the tire heat up, and the tire slows down.

Lesson Wrap-Up

Visual Summary

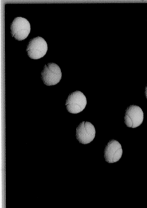

Kinetic energy is energy of motion. Potential energy is stored energy. Energy can be stored in food, fuel, and batteries.

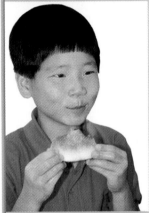

Energy can change from one form to another. Machines and living things convert stored energy to motion and heat.

Friction is a force caused by objects rubbing together. Thermal energy is produced by friction.

STANDARDS 1.b., 1.c.

Technology
Visit **www.eduplace.com/cascp** to find out more about how energy changes form.

Reading Review

① MAIN IDEA What is stored energy converted to in machines and living things?

② VOCABULARY What is kinetic energy?

③ READING SKILL Suppose you are at the top of a hill wearing roller skates. If you convert your potential energy to kinetic energy, what is the effect?

Cause → Effect

④ CRITICAL THINKING: Evaluate Your classmate says the food he ate for lunch gave him stored energy to run during recess. Is his statement true? Explain.

⑤ INQUIRY SKILL: Measure Using a meterstick, how could you compare the kinetic energy of a ball that is dropped from different heights?

✓ TEST PRACTICE

The type of energy stored in batteries is _____.

A. kinetic.

B. sound.

C. chemical.

D. electrical.

STANDARDS
1–3: 1.c., 4: 1.b., 1.c., 5: 1.c., Test Practice: 1.b.

EXTREME Science

HIGH FLYER!

No pilot, no fuel tanks, no engine pollution! Meet Helios, one of the lightest and highest-flying airplanes ever made. Steered by remote control and powered by the Sun, Helios (named after the Greek Sun god) could fly three times higher than most jet planes.

Thousands of solar cells covered the top of Helios's single, giant wing. Solar cells collect solar energy and convert it to electrical energy. This electrical energy was converted to mechanical energy that powered the aircraft's propellers. The solar energy collected during the day could also be stored as chemical energy in onboard batteries for night flights.

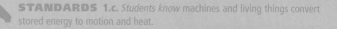

	Helios	Boeing 747
Wingspan	247 ft	211 ft
Weight	1,322 lbs	875,000 lbs
Airspeed	19-25 mph	565 mph
Cruising Altitude	100,000 ft	35,000 ft
Jet Fuel	none (solar powered)	57,285 gallons

A Boeing 747 jet is one of the largest jet airplanes in the world. How does it compare to Helios?

Solar cells across the top of the wing gather energy from the Sun. These cells change sunlight into electricity to power the 14 propellers.

Writing Journal

In your writing journal, explain whether you believe solar-powered aircraft will someday carry people and cargo. Give reasons for your views.

285

Lesson 3

What Are Waves?

Building Background

You may have made waves in a parachute in gym class. You have probably made waves in water. Waves are one way energy moves from place to place. Many familiar forms of energy, including light and sound, move in waves.

STANDARDS

1.d. *Students know* energy can be carried from one place to another by waves, such as water waves and sound waves, by electric current, and by moving objects.
5.d. Predict the outcome of a simple investigation and compare the result with the prediction.

PREPARE TO INVESTIGATE

Inquiry Skill

Observe When you observe, you gather information using your senses and using tools.

Materials

- cork
- ball
- plastic container of water
- block of wood

Science and Math Toolbox

For step 1, review **Making a Chart to Organize Data** on page H10.

Moving Energy

Procedure

1. In your *Science Notebook,* make a chart like the one shown.

2. Place a cork in a container of water, near a side. Use your hand to produce gentle waves in the water at the opposite side.

3. **Observe** Watch what happens to the waves and the cork. Record your observations in the chart.

4. Place a block of wood on the floor so the wood is standing upright. Take a few steps back. Roll a ball toward the wood.

5. **Observe** Watch what happens when the ball hits the block of wood. Record your observations in your chart.

Conclusion

1. **Communicate** Describe to someone what happened to the cork when you made waves. Explain what happened to the wood when the ball hit it.

2. **Compare** How were the results you observed in step 3 and in step 5 alike and different?

STEP 1

Observations	
Action	Result

STEP 2

STEP 4

Guided Inquiry

Experiment Predict what would happen if you placed the ball in the water instead of the cork. Repeat steps 2 and 3 using the ball and **observe** what happens.

287

Waves

READING SKILL

Draw Conclusions As you read, use the chart to record data about the crest and trough of a wave. Use the data to draw a conclusion about waves with little energy.

Data   Data

Conclusion

STANDARDS

1.d. *Students know* energy can be carried from one place to another by waves, such as water waves and sound waves, by electric current, and by moving objects.

MAIN IDEA Waves carry energy from place to place.

How Energy Travels

Suddenly the side of a mountain slides into the ocean. It's a landslide! The energy of the moving rocks and soil produces waves in the ocean. These waves reach a distant island, where they push water onto the shore. How did the energy of the landslide move through the water? It traveled as waves. A **wave** is a movement that carries energy from one place to another.

Many forms of energy can travel in waves. Mechanical energy, light energy, and sound energy can all travel in waves.

As the wave's energy passes through the water, it moves particles of water up and down. At the same time, it moves the toy boat up and down.

water particles

wave energy

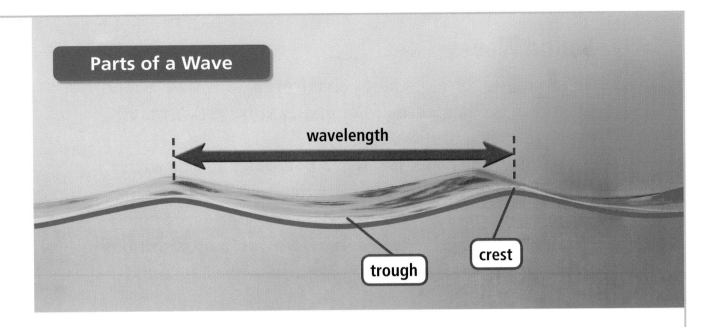

Parts of a Wave

wavelength

trough

crest

Measuring Waves

All waves have traits that can be measured. The **crest** of a wave is its highest point. The **trough** (trawf) of a wave is its lowest point. Waves with more energy have higher crests and deeper troughs.

The wavelength of a wave is the distance between one crest and the next crest or one trough and the next trough. Waves with shorter wavelengths have crests and troughs that are closer together. When crests (or troughs) are close together, each crest is followed quickly by the next. You can count how many crests pass by in a given time. This is the frequency (FREE-kwuhn see) of the wave.

DRAW CONCLUSIONS If a wave has high crests and deep troughs, what can you conclude about how much energy the wave has?

Express Lab

Activity Card 24
Model a Sound Wave

Sound Waves

Sound is a form of energy that travels in waves. Sound is produced when particles of matter **vibrate** (VY brayt), or move back and forth quickly.

A guitar string vibrates when you pluck it. The string moves back and forth so quickly that it looks like a blur. The movement of the string produces sound waves in the air around it. The sound waves move out in all directions from the vibrating string. You hear the waves as sounds.

When a guitar string is plucked, it vibrates. The energy of the vibrations travels through the air as sound waves.

A sound wave moves particles of matter back and forth. It is like a spring that is squeezed and then released. As the sound wave travels through matter, particles of matter squeeze together and then spread apart. This happens over and over again as the wave moves away from its source.

A crest is where particles of matter are bunched close together. A trough is where particles are spread far apart. This squeezing together and spreading apart happens over and over again as the wave moves away from the source.

When a sound wave travels from its source, the particles that carry the wave do not travel with the wave. The particles move back and forth, but stay in the same general location. A sound wave can travel through matter. It cannot travel through empty space.

DRAW CONCLUSIONS Can sound travel on the Moon, where there is no air? Why or why not?

A sound wave moves particles of matter back and forth. Particles of air squeeze together and then spread apart as a sound wave passes through.

▲ Dolphins use sound to communicate. Because sound waves travel a long way through water, dolphins can communicate over long distances.

Sound Moves Through Matter

Most of the time you hear sound waves that travel through the air, which is a gas. Sound waves can also travel through liquids. Dolphins use sound waves to communicate with each other under water. Sounds can also travel through solids, such as a wooden door. Sound waves travel faster through solids than liquids. They travel faster through liquids than gases.

Sound waves can reflect (rih FLEHKT), or bounce, off objects. Reflected sound waves are called echoes (EHK ohz). You can hear echoes when sound waves bounce off the face of a large building or the walls of a gym.

DRAW CONCLUSIONS Will a sound wave travel fastest through air, water, or wood?

Visual Summary

	Energy can be carried from one place to another by waves.
	Sound is the energy of vibrating matter. Sound travels in waves through matter.
	Sound waves can travel through liquids, solids, and gases. They travel fastest through solids and slowest through gases.

STANDARDS 1.d.

Technology
Visit **www.eduplace.com/cascp** to find out more about waves.

Reading Review

① MAIN IDEA How does energy travel from place to place?

② VOCABULARY What is a wave?

③ READING SKILL Imagine you visit the ocean and notice the waves are bigger in the morning than in the afternoon. What can you conclude about the amount of energy the waves had at each time of day?

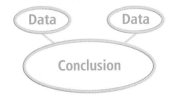

④ CRITICAL THINKING: Analyze How are sound waves and water waves alike?

⑤ INQUIRY SKILL: Observe When you swim, you make waves. What size are the waves when you move slowly? Quickly?

✔ TEST PRACTICE

What can sound waves *not* travel through?

A. water

B. air

C. empty space

D. a brick wall

Readers' Theater

Sound Safari

What happens in a sound studio? The setting is a classroom. A group of students is about to make its own sound studio. The students need to produce all kinds of sounds—growls, chirps, thunder, rattles, and echoes. How will they do it? Let's listen in!

Characters

Mr. Lee: teacher

Elaine ⎫

Rena ⎬ students

Rico ⎪

David ⎭

Sound Studio

STANDARDS

1.d. *Students know* energy can be carried from one place to another by waves, such as water waves and sound waves, by electric current, and by moving objects.

READING LINK

Elaine: I have a question. Who decided that we should put on a play called *Lost in the Jungle Cave*?

Rena: Yeah, can't we just do something simple? How about *Lost in the Library*? You don't need monkey sounds for that.

Mr. Lee: All right, everybody, let's focus on the jungle, not the library. Rena, tell about the play, *Lost in the Jungle Cave*.

Rena: Okay. In the play, MuMu the Monkey runs into a cave after a thunderstorm. Her friend LuLu the Lion looks for her in the jungle. That means we need a monkey, a thunderstorm, a lion, and other jungle noises.

Rico: This is going to be great! I can make just about any animal sound. Squeak! Chirrrrrrp! GROWWWWL!

Rena: Is that supposed to be a lion? Lions don't GROWWWWL. They ROARRRR.

David: Does anybody know what a monkey sounds like? I read someplace that monkeys are really loud. Let me give it a try. EEEK-EEEK!

Rena: The script says that MuMu the monkey calls to LuLu from inside that cave. But all she can hear is her own echo! How can we make an echo?

Mr. Lee: We can make an echo in the gym later. Now, let's take a look in this bag of tricks [*pulls out a bag*]. I've got coconut shells, copper sheets, bits of tinfoil. . . .

Rena: These are for sound effects?

Mr. Lee: Think about sounds you might hear in the jungle.

David: What about bees? BUZZZZZZZZ. How's that?

Mr. Lee: Nice try, but not all animals make sounds the way we do. Bees' wings move so fast that the air vibrates—and you hear a buzzing sound. Thunder works in a similar way.

Rena: *[confused]* But thunder doesn't buzz!

Mr. Lee: When lightning heats air, it makes the air vibrate. That creates sound waves. The sound waves carry the energy from the lightning to our ears, and we hear a loud boom.

Rico: So how can we make a thunder sound for the play?

Mr. Lee: In the 1700s, a fellow named John Dennis hung a large sheet of thin copper from the ceiling by wires. When he rattled it, it sounded like thunder.

Rena: I have an idea for the coconut shells. Listen. The lion is running to find MuMu. *[knocks coconut shell halves on table]*

David: Umm, that sounds like a horse running. There are no horses in the play.

Producing an Echo

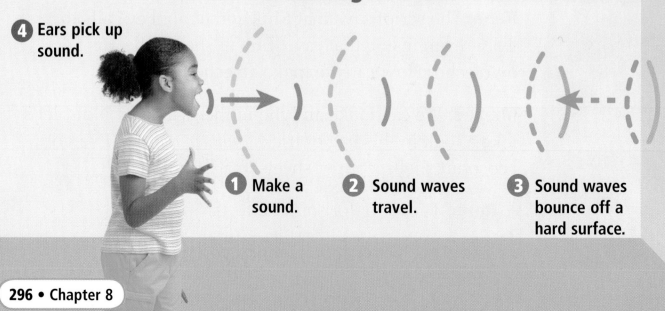

4 Ears pick up sound.

1 Make a sound.

2 Sound waves travel.

3 Sound waves bounce off a hard surface.

Elaine: Hey, if I rustle these bits of tinfoil, it sounds like animals running through leaves.

Rena: OK. MuMu is in the cave. From a distance, she hears Lulu. ROAR!

Elaine: When she is far away, the sound is soft. But she follows the sound. *[stirs the tinfoil]* As she gets closer . . .

David: The roar gets louder. ROOOOOOARRR! Finally, LuLu finds MuMu!!!!! ROOOOOOOOOAAAARRRRR! EEEK-EEEK!

Mr. Lee: Good job, team. Now all we need is the echo!

David: We need a big area with a flat wall that sound waves can bounce off, like the gymnasium.

[MR. LEE and STUDENTS walk to the gymnasium.]

David: Okay. This is the part where MuMu runs into the dark, scary cave. *[dramatically]* She cries out, but all she hears is her own echo!

David: *[shouts toward the wall]* EEEK-EEEK, EEEK-EEEK!

[They hear the echo: EEEK-EEEK, EEEK-EEEK.]

Mr. Lee: Congratulations kids, I think we're ready for the play!

Sharing Ideas

1. **READING CHECK** What makes an echo?

2. **WRITE ABOUT IT** Compare the way that a lion produces sound to the way that a bee produces sound.

3. **TALK ABOUT IT** Discuss new ways to produce sound effects using everyday objects.

What Is Electrical Energy?

Building Background

What forms of energy do you notice in this parade? If you were there, you would probably notice energy in the forms of light, motion, and sound. Although you may not notice electrical energy, it powers the parade. Electrical energy also powers the appliances and lights you use every day.

PREPARE TO INVESTIGATE

Inquiry Skill

Research When you do research, you learn more about a subject by looking in books, searching the Internet, or asking science experts.

Materials

- 2 1.3-volt batteries
- 2 battery holders
- buzzer
- insulated wires, with stripped ends

STANDARDS

1.d. *Students know* energy can be carried from one place to another by waves, such as water waves and sound waves, by electric current, and by moving objects.
5.d. Predict the outcome of a simple investigation and compare the result with the prediction.

Circuit Search

Procedure

STEP 1

1. **Research** Use the Internet, library, or other resources to find out how to make a simple electric circuit (SUR kiht). The circuit should include one or more batteries. Have your teacher check the instructions before you follow them.

2. Using the materials provided, follow the instructions to set up a circuit. Do not connect the last wire to the battery yet. **Safety:** The wires may be sharp.

STEP 2

3. **Predict** Predict what will happen when you make the last connection and complete the circuit. Record your prediction in your *Science Notebook.*

4. **Experiment** Complete the circuit by connecting the last wire to the battery holder. Observe and record what happens.

STEP 3

Conclusion

1. **Analyze Data** What form of energy does a battery contain? What form of energy does the buzzer produce?

2. **Research** Use science resources to find out what form of energy travels through the wires of the circuit.

3. **Hypothesize** Use your results to hypothesize how a doorbell works.

Guided Inquiry

Ask Questions In your *Science Notebook,* write two questions that you have about circuits. Explain how you might **use models** to find answers to your questions.

299

VOCABULARY

electric circuit   p. 301
electric current   p. 300

READING SKILL

Cause and Effect Use a graphic organizer to list some possible effects of electrical energy.

| Cause | → | Effect |

STANDARDS

1.c. *Students know* machines and living things convert stored energy to motion and heat.
1.d. *Students know* energy can be carried from one place to another by waves, such as water waves and sound waves, by electric current, and by moving objects.

Electrical Energy

MAIN IDEA Electrical energy travels along pathways called electric circuits.

Flow of Electric Charges

Most people take electricity for granted until there is a power blackout. That's when they realize that electrical energy is an important part of daily life. Electrical energy is the energy of charged particles of matter. For electricity to run lamps and TVs, some of these charged particles must move.

Charged particles of matter carry either a positive or a negative electric charge. Positively charged particles and negatively charged particles attract each other. Negatively charged particles tend to flow, or move, toward positively charged particles. This flow of charged particles is an **electric current** (KUR uhnt).

Electric current moves through a complete circuit, causing the bulb to light. ▶

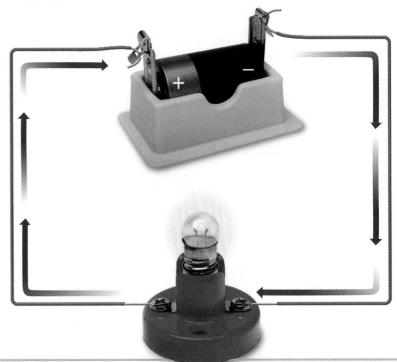

Electric current flows through a path called an **electric circuit** (SUR kiht). A circuit is made up of wires and electrical devices. It has a source of electricity, such as a battery. Electric current can flow through a circuit only if the circuit is complete. There cannot be any gap in the circuit.

 **CAUSE AND EFFECT** **What causes negative charges to flow?**

When a lamp is unplugged, there is a gap in the circuit. The lamp can be turned on only when it is plugged in and the circuit is complete. ▶

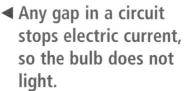

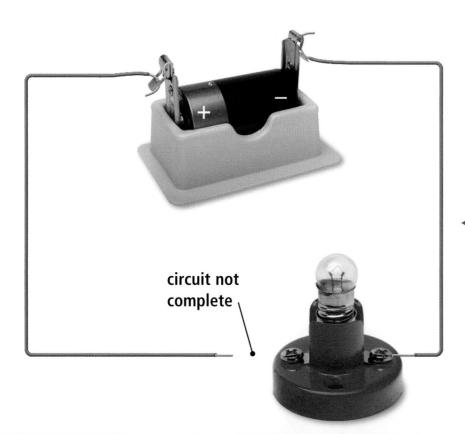

circuit not complete

◀ Any gap in a circuit stops electric current, so the bulb does not light.

Converting Electrical Energy

Electric current powers many devices. Most of these devices change electrical energy to other forms of energy. When a radio is in use, electrical energy is changed to sound energy. When a lamp is turned on, electrical energy is changed to light energy. The turning blades of a fan have mechanical energy that comes from electrical energy.

Most electrical devices have cords and plugs. Electric current flows from an outlet, through a plug to a cord. The cord is attached to the electrical device, such as a fan.

Electrical energy can be changed to sound, light, thermal, or mechanical energy.

sound energy

Express Lab

Activity Card 25
Investigate a Switch

302

The current flows from the device back through the cord. From the cord, it flows to the plug and then to the outlet. This makes a complete circuit.

A switch on a device opens or closes a gap in the circuit. When a switch is turned on, the gap in the circuit is closed. Electricity flows through the device, so it runs. When the switch is turned off, the gap in the circuit is open. The device cannot run. Even if a lamp is plugged in, it works only when its switch is turned on.

CAUSE AND EFFECT Why does an electrical device work only when its switch is turned on?

light and thermal energy

electrical energy

thermal energy

mechanical energy

▲ Warning signs can protect people from dangerous electric charges.

Electrical Energy and Your Body

Look around you. Each person in your class is using electrical energy right now. The human body uses electrical energy to function. Electrical signals in the heart keep it beating at the right pace. Electrical signals also carry messages from the brain to other parts of the body.

Where do the heart and brain get electrical energy? It comes from the chemical energy stored in food. The body changes some of the chemical energy in food to electrical energy.

Electric current from a source outside the body can be very dangerous. If a large amount of electricity passes through the body, it can stop the heart from beating. It can also change to thermal energy and cause burns.

CAUSE AND EFFECT **How does the brain use electrical energy?**

A pacemaker is an electrical device that can help a heart to beat at the right rate. ▶

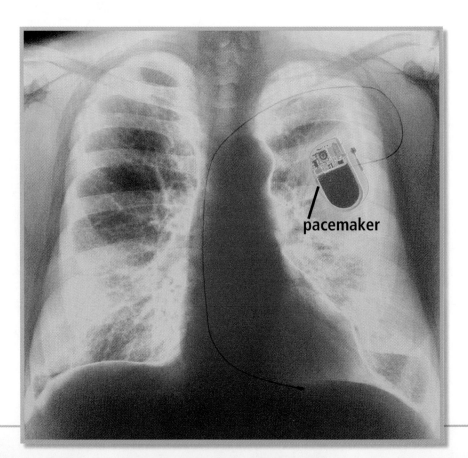

pacemaker

Visual Summary

Electrical energy is the energy of charged particles. The flow of charged particles is an electric current.

Electric current moves through a complete circuit.

Electrical devices change electrical energy to sound, light, heat, or motion.

 **STANDARDS** 1.c., 1.d.

Technology
Visit **www.eduplace.com/cascp** to find out more about electrical energy.

Reading Review

❶ **MAIN IDEA** What is electrical energy?

❷ **VOCABULARY** What is the flow of charged particles called?

❸ **READING SKILL** Energy travels from a battery through a circuit to move the hands on a wall clock. If the hands of the clock stop moving, what might be the cause?

❹ **CRITICAL THINKING: Apply** Many homes have devices called circuit breakers. If too much electric current flows through the wires, a circuit breaker can cause a gap in the circuit. How could this prevent the circuit from overheating?

❺ **INQUIRY SKILL: Research** Use the Internet or library to learn about how a battery works. Write a brief paragraph explaining what you learned.

✔ TEST PRACTICE

An electric current carries _____ from one place to another.

A. energy   **C.** sound

B. objects   **D.** waves

STANDARDS

1–2: 1.d., 3: 1.c., 4: 1.d., 5: 1.c., Test Practice: 1.d.

Math Order Whole Numbers

The volume of a sound is measured in a unit called a decibel. A soft whisper is about 30 decibels. A doorbell is about 80 decibels. The louder a sound is, the higher is the number of decibels. The table shows the decibel measurements of some sounds.

Source of Sound	Decibel Level
soft whisper	30
doorbell	80
rainfall	50
ambulance siren	120
jet taking off	150
normal conversation	60
power tools	110

1. Put the decibel measurements of the sounds in the table in order from least to greatest. What is the loudest sound shown in the chart?

2. How many decibels greater is the loudest sound than the softest sound?

3. Sounds that are louder than 85 decibels can damage your ears. Which sounds shown in the chart could hurt your ears?

Writing Narrative

Can you remember a time when the power went out in your home or school? Write a narrative story about how you and others dealt with the "blackout." Include a discussion of the types of energy you used during the blackout. If you have not lived through a blackout, use your imagination to help you describe what conditions would be like without electricity.

Automotive Mechanics

Even with regular service, most cars need repairs sooner or later. That's why automotive mechanics are always in demand. It is their job to keep cars running well. Automotive mechanics have to keep up with new technology.

What It Takes!

- A high-school diploma
- Courses in automotive repair
- On-the-job training

Mechanical Engineer

Mechanical engineers design, test, and improve all types of machines. They work on machines that produce power, such as engines and generators. They also work on machines that use power—from cake mixers to toys.

What It Takes!

- A degree in mechanical engineering
- Drafting, drawing, design, and problem-solving skills
- Knowledge of computer systems

Vocabulary

Complete each sentence with a term from the list.

1. To move back and forth quickly is to _____.
2. The energy that an object has because of its motion is called _____.
3. A movement that carries energy from place to place is a/an _____.
4. Electric current can flow only through a complete _____.
5. The lowest point of a wave is the _____.
6. The energy an object has because of its position is _____.
7. The highest point of a wave is the _____.
8. The ability to cause movement or changes in matter is _____.
9. The flow of charged particles is called _____.
10. An object rubbing against another produces a force called _____.

crest p. 289
electric circuit p. 301
electric current p. 300
energy p. 272
friction p. 282
kinetic energy p. 278
potential energy p. 278
trough p. 289
vibrate p. 290
wave 288

Test Practice

Write the letter of the best answer choice.

11. The Sun provides Earth with _____.
    A. chemical energy.
    B. light energy.
    C. mechanical energy.
    D. kinetic energy.

12. Moving charges produce a/an _____.
    A. wave.
    B. vibration.
    C. electric current.
    D. complete circuit.

13. When an object vibrates, it produces _____.
    A. chemical energy.
    B. potential energy.
    C. sound energy.
    D. light energy.

14. Chemical energy is a form of _____.
    A. sound energy.
    B. kinetic energy.
    C. light energy.
    D. stored energy.

Inquiry Skills

15. Observe At an amusement park you watch a train climb a hill on a roller coaster. Predict what will happen after the train reaches the top of the hill. Describe how the train's energy will change.

16. The energy stored in foods is measured in Calories. Look up the number of Calories in a serving of four foods that you eat in one day. (Hint: This information is often on the container the food is packaged in.) Record the food and the Calories in your *Science Notebook.* Which food had the most Calories?

Map the Concept

Label the diagram using the terms below:

trough   1. _____.
wavelength   2. _____.
crest   3. _____.

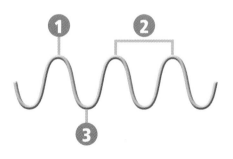

STANDARDS

1–5: 1.d., 6: 1.b., 7: 1.d., 8: 1.c., 9: 1.d., 10: 1.c., 11: 1.a., 12–13: 1.d.,
14: 1.b., 15: 1.c., 5.d., 16: 1.b., 5.c., 17: 1.b., 18: 1.c., 19: 1.b., 1.c.,
20: 1.b. Map the Concept: 1.d., Performance Assessment: 1.b.,
1.d., 5.d.

Critical Thinking

17. Synthesize Many musical instruments, such as pianos, have wires or strings that are tightly strung. What type of energy do the wires have? What type of energy do they have after you strike or pluck them to make a sound?

18. Analyze The brakes on a bicycle use friction to stop the wheels. If someone uses the brakes often, how will the temperature of the brakes change?

19. Apply Choose a battery-powered device in your home. What type of energy is stored energy converted to by that device?

20. Evaluate Support the following statement: A car that has a full tank of gasoline and is parked on a hill has energy.

Performance Assessment

Build a Circuit
Use a dry-cell battery to build an electric circuit that contains a switch and a bulb. Draw a diagram of your circuit. Predict what will happen when you work the switch. Test your prediction and record the results.

Writing Journal

Review your answers to the questions on page 267. Change your answers, as needed, based on what you have learned.

Chapter 9

Light

Light is energy you can see.

LESSON 1

Light can make the Moon shine or cast your shadow on a fence. What is light and how does it help you see?

LESSON 2

Light can make a reflection in a mirror or help magnify an image. How does light behave when it strikes an object?

LESSON 3

Flowers can have as many colors as a rainbow. When you look at a red flower, what makes it appear red?

Writing Journal

In your Writing Journal, show what you know by writing or drawing answers to each question.

Vocabulary Preview

Vocabulary

absorb p. 333
lens p. 326
light p. 316
opaque p. 318
prism p. 332
reflect p. 324
refract p. 325
shadow p. 319
translucent p. 318
transparent p. 318

Glossary
English-Spanish p. H24

Vocabulary Skill

Word Parts
translucent

The prefix *trans-* means "across" or "through." The word part *lucent* means "to give off light." Say each word part separately. Then say them together. Knowing what the parts of a word mean can help you remember the meaning of that word.

opaque
Not letting light pass through.

translucent
Letting only some light pass through.

transparent
Letting light pass through freely.

reflect

To bounce off.

Start with Your Standards

Standard Set 2. Physical Sciences (Light)

2.a. *Students know* sunlight can be blocked to create shadows.

2.b. *Students know* light is reflected from mirrors and other surfaces.

2.c. *Students know* the color of light striking an object affects the way the object is seen.

2.d. *Students know* an object is seen when light traveling from the object enters the eye.

Standard Set 5. Investigation and Experimentation covered in this chapter: 5.a., 5.d.

Lesson 1

What Is Light?

Building Background

You would probably notice colored lights on a sign at an amusement park. But you might not notice the light that surrounds you every day.

Light shines from the Sun. It also shines from colored light bulbs, like the ones below. Right now, you are using light to read this book. Without light, you could not see the world around you.

PREPARE TO INVESTIGATE

Inquiry Skill

Collaborate When you collaborate, you work with others to carry out investigations and share data and ideas.

Materials

- flashlight
- paper
- transparent tape
- sharpened pencil
- metric tape measure

STANDARDS

2.a. *Students know* sunlight can be blocked to create shadows.
5.a. Repeat observations to improve accuracy and know that the results of similar scientific investigations seldom turn out exactly the same because of differences in the things being investigated, methods being used, or uncertainty in the observation.

Shadow Shapes

Procedure

① **Collaborate** Work with a partner. Push a table or desk against a wall. Tape a sheet of white paper to the wall above the table.

STEP 2

② **Measure** Have your partner hold the end of a tape measure at the wall. Stretch the tape measure out along the table past 80 cm. Use transparent tape to mark *5 cm*, *40 cm*, and *80 cm* on the table. Label each piece of tape.

STEP 3

③ Hold a flashlight above the 80-cm mark so it points toward the paper. Have your partner hold a pencil above the 40-cm mark.

④ **Observe** Turn on the flashlight. Observe the size, shape, and edge of the pencil's shadow on the paper. Draw the shadow in your *Science Notebook*.

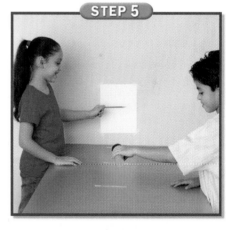
STEP 5

⑤ Turn off the flashlight. Have your partner move the pencil so it is above the 5-cm mark. Repeat step 4.

Conclusion

1. **Compare** How did the shadow look different when the pencil was held at the 40-cm and 5-cm marks?

2. **Infer** How does the distance an object is from the light affect how its shadow looks?

Guided Inquiry

Experiment Repeat these steps with paper cutouts of a square and a circle. **Compare** the shapes of the cutouts with the shapes of their shadows. Are their shadows sharp or fuzzy?

Light

MAIN IDEA Objects are seen when light traveling from them enters the eye. Shadows form when light is blocked.

VOCABULARY

light	p. 316
opaque	p. 318
shadow	p. 319
translucent	p. 318
transparent	p. 318

READING SKILL

Main Idea and Details
Use a chart to explain two things that could happen to light when it hits an object.

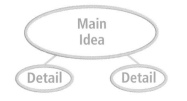

STANDARDS

2.a. *Students know* sunlight can be blocked to create shadows.
2.d. *Students know* an object is seen when light traveling from the object enters the eye.

Energy You Can See

Look around you. You can see the things around you because of light. **Light** is a form of energy that you can see. Like sound, light travels as waves. Light waves move outward, away from their source.

Unlike sound, light does not need to travel through matter. Light can travel through empty space. This is how light from the Sun reaches Earth and other planets.

Most objects do not give off their own light. You see most objects because light from another source bounces off them.

Powerful lights in this stadium make night seem like day. ▼

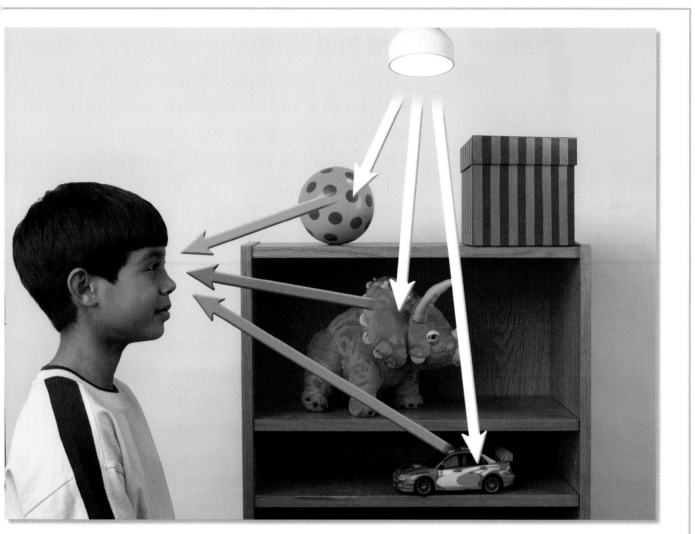

▲ The boy sees the objects when light waves bounce from their surfaces to his eyes.

How do you see an object? You see it when some of the light waves that strike its surface bounce off it and into your eyes.

Look at the picture. Light waves from an overhead bulb strike objects in the room, including a ball, stuffed animal, and toy car. Some of the light waves bounce from the objects to the boy's eye. That's why he can see these objects.

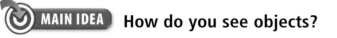 **MAIN IDEA** **How do you see objects?**

Express Lab

Activity Card 26
Create Shadows

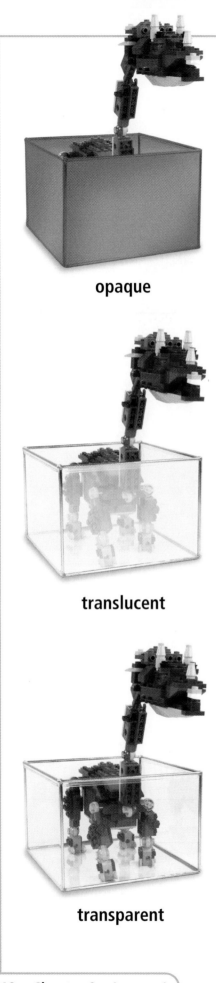

opaque

translucent

transparent

Light and Matter

You've probably noticed that you can see through some things, such as water and glass. You can't see through other things, such as a wall or your desk. Some kinds of matter—such as wood, metal, and rock—block light waves. These kinds of matter are opaque (oh PAYK). An **opaque** material does not allow light to pass through it.

Imagine you are looking at a picture on a wall. Suppose someone walks between you and that picture. Any light bouncing off the picture and traveling toward you will be blocked by the person's body. Until that person moves out of the way, you will not be able to see the picture.

Some kinds of matter, such as air and glass, are transparent (trahns PAIR uhnt). A **transparent** material allows light to pass through it. Most windows are made from transparent glass to allow sunlight to shine into buildings.

Certain materials are translucent (trahns-LOO suhnt). A **translucent** material allows some light to pass through it, but scatters the light in many directions. Frosted glass is translucent. Objects seen through translucent materials appear blurry.

MAIN IDEA How do translucent materials affect light?

◀ Light passes through transparent and translucent material, but not through opaque ones.

Shadows

Did you see your shadow today? Shadows occur when light strikes opaque objects, such as your body.

Light waves travel in straight lines from their source. If you stand in sunlight, some of the light waves strike your body. These light waves are blocked by your body. Other light waves do not strike your body. They continue past your body until they strike an opaque surface, such as the ground.

Your body causes a **shadow**, or an area where light does not strike. The shadow is shaped like you, because only the light waves that strike your body are blocked. Other light waves travel past you and shine on the ground.

An opaque object blocks all the light that strikes it. The shadow takes the shape of the outline of the object. ▼

Light waves that strike the girl's body are blocked. Other light waves go past her. ▶

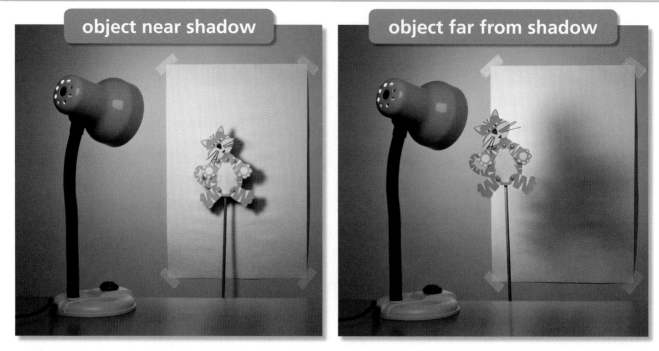

object near shadow

object far from shadow

▲ The nearer an object is to the shadow it casts, the sharper the shadow edges will be.

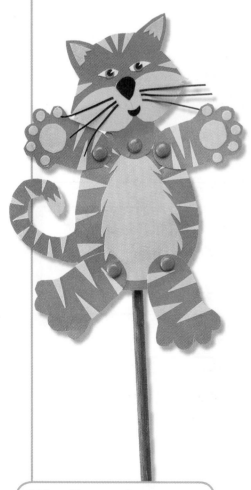

Sharp Shadows

When an object blocks light, a shadow forms in the shape of that object. Sometimes the edges of the shadow are clean and sharp. Look at the photos above. In both photos the lamp is the same distance from the wall. In the photo on the left, the puppet is only 5 cm (2 in.) from the wall. The shadow it casts has clean, sharp edges. The size of the shadow is similar to the size of the puppet.

In the photo on the right, the puppet is 15 cm (6 in.) from the wall. The shadow it casts is blurry and larger than the puppet. The farther an object is from the shadow it casts, the larger the shadow will be and the blurrier its edges.

MAIN IDEA Where should you hold your hands to produce a clear, sharp shadow on the wall?

Visual Summary

You see an object when light traveling from the object enters your eye.

Opaque objects block light. Transparent objects allow light to pass through. Translucent objects allow some light to pass through.

A shadow is an area where light does not strike. Sunlight can be blocked to produce shadows.

STANDARDS 2.a, 2.d.

Technology
Visit **www.eduplace.com/cascp** to find out more about light.

Reading Review

❶ **MAIN IDEA** How do you see objects?

❷ **VOCABULARY** Use the words *light* and *shadow* in a sentence.

❸ **READING SKILL** Provide examples of the following main idea: *When light travels, it is blocked by some materials.*

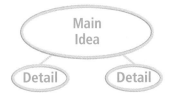

❹ **CRITICAL THINKING:**
Synthesize On a sunny day, you sit under a tree to read a book. A shadow on the book makes it hard to read. What must you do so that light shines on the book?

❺ **INQUIRY SKILL: Collaborate**
Work with a partner. A clear, empty glass vase is on a table in a well-lit room. Discuss whether or not the vase would cast a shadow.

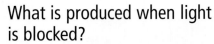 **TEST PRACTICE**
What is produced when light is blocked?

A. a shadow   **C.** a wave

B. more light   **D.** sound

STANDARDS
1: 2.d., 2–5: 2.a., Test Practice: 2.a.

How Is Light Reflected?

Building Background

When you look in a mirror you see yourself. Light strikes your body and bounces off. Some of the light bouncing off your body strikes the mirror and bounces back to your eyes. If light could not bounce off surfaces, you could not see yourself, or anything else, in a mirror.

PREPARE TO INVESTIGATE

Inquiry Skill

Ask Questions You ask questions to find out how or why something that you observe happens. Questions can lead to scientific investigations.

Materials

- flashlight   • mirror
- black construction paper
- piece of cardboard
- spray bottle with water
- safety goggles

STANDARDS

2.b. *Students know* light is reflected from mirrors and other surfaces.
5.d. Predict the outcome of a simple investigation and compare the result with the prediction.

Ways of Reflecting

Procedure

STEP 1

1. **Collaborate** Work with a group. The room should be dim. Place a mirror on the table. Hold a lighted flashlight at an angle and point it at the mirror. Record your observations. **Safety:** Do not shine the flashlight into anyone's eyes. Wear goggles.

STEP 2

2. **Predict** As you hold the lit flashlight, another student will spray a mist of water through the rays of light. Predict what the path of the light will be. Then test your prediction. In your *Science Notebook,* make a diagram to show what you observe about the path of the light.

STEP 3

3. **Observe** Have another student hold a sheet of black construction paper so the light coming from the mirror shines on the paper. In your *Science Notebook,* make another diagram to show what you observe.

Conclusion

1. Did the light travel in a curved path or in a straight line after striking the mirror?

2. **Compare** How did the light's path change when the black paper was held up in step 3?

3. **Ask Questions** With your group, brainstorm a list of questions about mirrors and the effect they have on light.

Guided Inquiry

Ask Questions Think about different materials that behave like mirrors. Make a list of some examples and ask questions about them. Try to **infer** what traits they share that would cause them to act like mirrors.

Paths of Light

VOCABULARY

lens	p. 326
reflect	p. 324
refract	p. 325

MAIN IDEA Light waves change direction depending on the surface they strike. How they change direction affects what you see.

READING SKILL

Problem and Solution
Use the chart to list some problems that might be solved by using lenses. List what kind of lenses could solve these problems.

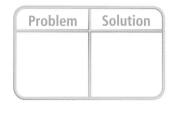

Problem	Solution

STANDARDS

2.b. *Students know* light is reflected from mirrors and other surfaces.
2.d. *Students know* an object is seen when light traveling from the object enters the eye.

Reflection

Light waves travel in straight lines. How they behave when they strike an object depends on the object's surface. Light waves **reflect** (rih-FLEHKT), or bounce, off the surfaces of most objects. When light waves reflect off a smooth, shiny mirror that you are looking at, the waves bounce directly back to your eyes. That's why you see yourself.

When light waves strike an object that does not have a smooth, shiny surface, they bounce back in many directions. You see the object, not its reflection, or reflected image.

Sometimes the surface of water is very smooth. When it is, water reflects light like a mirror. ▼

▲ Light waves bend, or refract, when they pass from one material to another.

▲ Light is refracted by this magnifying glass. How is this useful?

Refraction

Light waves can pass through some materials, but their straight path changes. Light waves refract (rih FRAKT) when they move from air to water. To **refract** is to bend. Refracted light makes objects look bent, broken, or wavy. The pencil above looks like it is broken in two pieces. That's because light is bent as it travels through the air, glass, and water.

Glass is another material that refracts light. For example, the glass in a pair of eyeglasses is curved to bend light. This helps people who wear glasses see better. A magnifying glass, which is also curved, refracts light to make objects look larger.

PROBLEM AND SOLUTION What might be the problem if you look in a mirror and your image is blurry?

Express Lab

Activity Card 27
Bend a Pencil with Light

The Human Eye

A **lens** is an object that refracts light. Often, lenses are made of glass. Eyeglasses and magnifying glasses contain lenses. Each of your eyes also has a lens. The lens in an eye is near the front part of the eyeball. It is behind the cornea and the pupil. Find these parts in the drawing below.

When you look at an object, light reflected from it enters your eye. The cornea and the lens bend the light. An image of the object appears on the retina, at the back of your eye. Nerves in your retina send the image to your brain.

PROBLEM AND SOLUTION What if the lens of an eye does not bend light correctly? What might solve this problem?

How You See

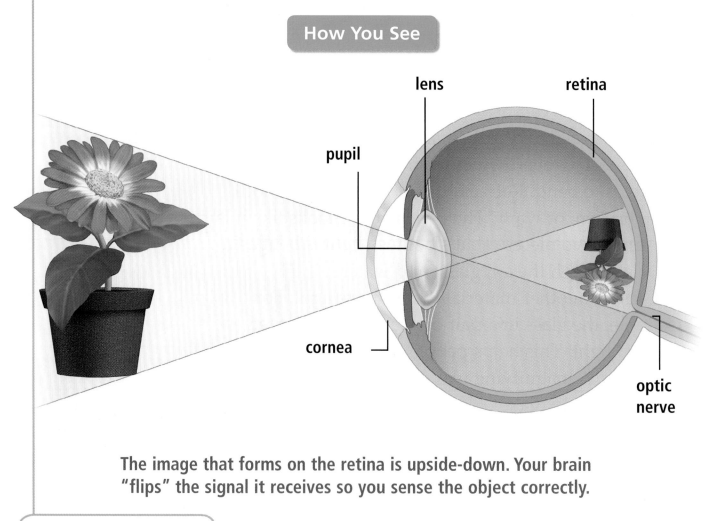

The image that forms on the retina is upside-down. Your brain "flips" the signal it receives so you sense the object correctly.

Visual Summary

Mirrors and other smooth surfaces reflect all the light that strikes them.

Light can refract, or bend, when it passes through air, water, and glass. Refracted light can make an object appear bent.

You see an object when light reflected from the object enters your eye. The lenses in your eyes refract that light to form an image on your retina. Your brain interprets that image.

 STANDARDS 2.b., 2.d.

Technology
Visit **www.eduplace.com/cascp** to find out more about reflection.

Reading Review

❶ **MAIN IDEA** How do you see your image reflected in a mirror?

❷ **VOCABULARY** What is the difference between *reflect* and *refract*?

❸ **READING SKILL** A friend cannot read very small print. What might help her read?

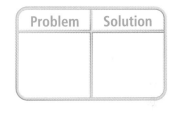

Problem	Solution

❹ **CRITICAL THINKING: Analyze** You drop a coin in a deep puddle. But each time you reach for the coin, you miss touching it. What is causing this problem?

❺ **INQUIRY SKILL: Ask Questions** Suppose you stand between two mirrors. Write two questions about what the image would be like in each mirror. Use two pocket mirrors to help you find answers to your questions.

✔ TEST PRACTICE

When light bounces off an object, the light is _____.

A. absorbed. **C.** reflected.

B. refracted. **D.** transmitted.

Mighty Mirrors

What do all these mirrors do? They collect sunlight over a huge area. Then they direct all that energy into a very small area. The place where all this sunlight comes together gets extremely hot. How hot? Would you believe 4,000°C, or 7,200°F? That's so hot you could actually melt a diamond, the hardest substance on Earth!

This huge sunlight collection and concentration system is called a solar furnace. Scientists can use the extreme thermal energy of a solar furnace to test the effects of high temperatures on various materials.

People can use thermal energy collected in small solar ovens like this to cook food.

The Odeillo solar furnace in the Pyrenees Mountains of France is the world's biggest. The curved face of the collector is over 36 meters high and has 1,830 individual mirrors.

Writing Journal

In your journal, write about the advantages and disadvantages of relying on solar power to do cooking or supplying energy to a home or business.

What Is Color?

Building Background

You see objects of different colors all around you. Sometimes you can see a rainbow of colors when you look at an object, such as this cut glass ball.

When light strikes an object, it affects how the object looks. Different colors of light striking an object can affect the color you see when you look at that object.

PREPARE TO INVESTIGATE

Inquiry Skill

Predict When you predict, you state what you think will happen based on observations and experiences.

Materials

- flashlight
- blue cellophane
- red cellophane
- piece of white paper

STANDARDS

2.c. *Students know* the color of light striking an object affects the way the object is seen.
5.d. Predict the outcome of a simple investigation and compare the result with the prediction.

Colored Lights

Procedure

1. Place a sheet of white paper on a table. The room should be dim.

2. **Observe** Shine a flashlight on the paper. Record in your *Science Notebook* the color that the paper appears to be.

3. **Experiment** Hold a piece of blue cellophane in front of the flashlight lens. Shine the light on the paper. Record the color that the paper appears to be.

4. **Predict** Hold a piece of red cellophane in front of the flashlight lens. Predict the color that the paper will appear to be. Test your prediction. Compare your prediction with what you observe.

Conclusion

1. **Infer** How does the color of the cellophane affect the color of the light that you see coming from the flashlight?

2. In steps 3 and 4, how does the color of the light affect the color that the white paper appears to be?

3. **Predict** In step 3, suppose you shined the flashlight on a sheet of green paper. What color do you think the paper would appear to be? If possible, test your prediction.

STEP 2

STEP 3

STEP 4

Guided Inquiry

Experiment Plan to test other combinations of colored cellophane and colored paper. **Predict** the outcome of each test before you carry it out. Compare your results with your predictions.

Color

MAIN IDEA When light strikes an object, the color of the light affects the way the object is seen.

The Colors of Sunlight

Look at the bands of color that appear as light shines through the piece of glass in the photo. This shows that white light is made up of all the colors of the rainbow. A **prism** is a piece of glass or other transparent object, shaped like a triangle, that separates white light into these colors.

Sunlight also contains all the colors of the rainbow. When it is raining, you might see a rainbow if there is also some sunlight. That is because raindrops act like prisms. When sunlight passes through raindrops, the white light separates into colors. This forms a rainbow.

Raindrops act like tiny prisms to create a rainbow. ▼

A prism separates white light into colors. ▼

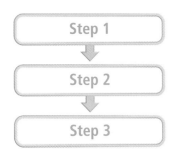

▲ An orange absorbs most of the light from sunlight. It reflects orange light. This is the color we see.

Seeing Colors

When white light shines on a colored object, the surface of the object will **absorb** (uhb SAWRB), or take in, some of the light waves that strike it. So the object absorbs some colors. The object reflects other colors. You see the reflected colors but not the absorbed colors. Bananas look yellow because they reflect yellow light. They absorb other colors. A lime looks green because it reflects green light and absorbs the other colors of light.

SEQUENCE What happens to sunlight after it strikes a banana?

Express Lab

Activity Card 28
Make Colored Light

333

Colored Light

The color of an object depends on the color of light it reflects. It also depends on the color of the light shining on it.

White light is made up of all the colors of the rainbow. White objects reflect all of these colors. If you shine white light on a white sneaker, it will reflect all of the colors in the light. It will look white. If you shine red light on the sneaker, it will reflect the red light and look red. If you shine a blue light on the sneaker, it will look blue.

SEQUENCE **How could you cause a white golf ball to appear blue, then red, then yellow?**

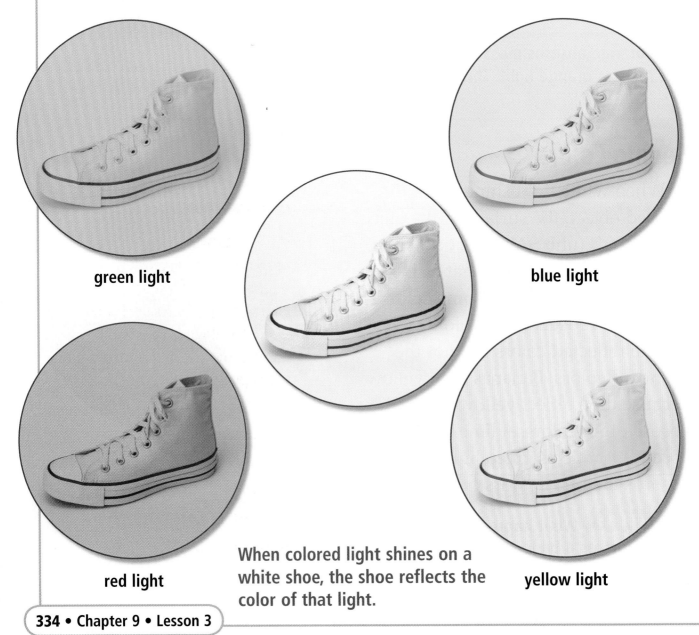

green light

blue light

red light

yellow light

When colored light shines on a white shoe, the shoe reflects the color of that light.

Visual Summary

Sunlight includes all the colors of the rainbow. A rainbow forms when sunlight separates into colors as it passes through raindrops.

When white light strikes an object, you see only the reflected colors. The other colors are absorbed.

Light affects how an object looks. White objects appear to change color under colored light.

STANDARDS 2.c.

Technology
Visit www.eduplace.com/cascp to find out more about color.

Reading Review

① MAIN IDEA Give an example of how the color of light can affect how an object appears.

② VOCABULARY Use the terms *absorb* and *reflect* in a sentence.

③ READING SKILL List the steps that produce a rainbow.

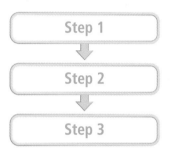

Step 1
Step 2
Step 3

④ CRITICAL THINKING: Evaluate Your friend tells you that red apples would look blue in red light. How would you evaluate this statement?

⑤ INQUIRY SKILL: Predict Imagine you have a prism, a flashlight, and a sheet of white paper. What would you see if you shined the flashlight through the prism, toward the paper?

✓ **TEST PRACTICE**
If red light shines on a white car, what color will the car appear to be?

A. white　**C.** yellow
B. black　**D.** red

STANDARDS
1–5: 2.c., Test Practice: 2.c.

335

COMPUTER HELP FOR ANIMATED CARTOONS

Many of the studios that produced the first animated cartoons were in California. The term *animated* means "full of movement."

How are animated cartoons made? In the past, an artist drew a series of pictures. Each picture was traced onto a clear plastic sheet, called a cel (SEHL). The artist then colored the picture using paints.

Paints had to be carefully mixed so that the colors of characters and objects would be the same in every picture. Finally, the finished pictures were photographed and transferred to film. Artists had to draw and paint up to 24 pictures for every second of an animated cartoon. It could take 9 months to produce a 30-minute color cartoon.

In the past, each cel in an animated cartoon had to be painted by hand.

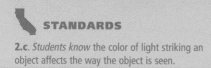
STANDARDS

2.c. *Students know* the color of light striking an object affects the way the object is seen.

READING

Today, computers help artists save time in producing animated cartoons. First, the artist makes a drawing. The use of a computer can then help the artist color the drawing. The artist needs to color a character only once. Then the computer colors that character in the same way in every drawing in the cartoon. This saves many hours of work.

At a California studio, an artist made this sketch. ▼

▲ **Another artist colors the character once. Then the computer fills in the colors on every other drawing of that character.**

Sharing Ideas

1. **READING CHECK** How do artists use computers to color the characters in animated cartoons?

2. **WRITE ABOUT IT** Would you color the pictures of an animated cartoon using paints or a computer? Explain.

3. **TALK ABOUT IT** Discuss why it is important that the color of a character look the same throughout an animated cartoon.

Math Conduct a Survey

Ask each student in your class to choose his or her favorite color from the colors listed in the chart. Record each answer in your *Science Notebook.* Then organize your results in a tally chart.

1. In your *Science Notebook,* write the number of students who choose each color as their favorite.

2. Which color was the favorite of the greatest number of students? Which color was the least favorite?

3. Display the results of your survey on a bar graph. Write the name of each color on the x-axis and the number of students on the y-axis.

Favorite Color	
Color	**Tally**
blue	
green	
orange	
purple	
red	

Writing Letter

Think of a question you have about light or color. Now think of an expert who might be able to answer your question.

Write a letter to that person to tell him or her what you know. Then ask your question. If you have an idea what the answer might be, include your idea. Explain the reason you think this might be the answer.

Dr. Patricia Bath

People can sometimes develop problems with their eyes as they grow older. The lens of the eye can become cloudy, making it hard to see.

How can cloudy lenses be fixed? In 1981, Dr. Patricia Bath of Los Angeles invented a new and better way to deal with this problem. She used laser light to remove cloudy lenses. Then she put in new lenses. Unlike older treatments, the laser method was quick and painless.

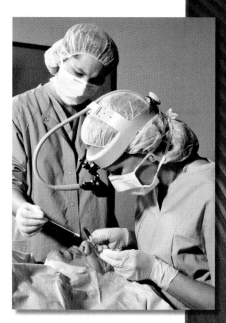

▲ Laser eye surgery

Dr. Bath continues to research and to invent new ways to help her eye patients. Her work has saved the sight of thousands of people.

Vocabulary

Complete each sentence with a term from the list.

1. Material that allows light to pass through is _____.

2. When light waves bounce off an object, they _____.

3. A material that blocks light is _____.

4. When an object blocks light, it creates a/an _____.

5. To take in light is to _____ it.

6. An object that lets some light through but scatters it in all directions is _____.

7. To bend light is to _____ it.

8. A form of energy that you can see is called _____.

9. A piece of glass that bends light and is used in eyeglasses is a/an _____.

10. A piece of glass that separates white light into colors is a/an _____.

absorb p. 333
lens p. 326
light p. 316
opaque p. 318
prism p. 332
reflect p. 324
refract p. 325
shadow p. 319
translucent p. 318
transparent p. 318

Test Practice

Write the letter of the best answer choice.

11. A sweater looks blue if it _____.

   A. refracts blue light.
   B. reflects blue light.
   C. absorbs blue light.
   D. reflects all light.

12. When light from an object bounces off a mirror, you see a/an _____.

   A. reflection.
   B. absorption.
   C. refraction.
   D. subtraction.

13. A red apple is behind an opaque object. The apple can be _____.

   A. seen, but not clearly.
   B. seen clearly.
   C. not seen at all.
   D. seen, but it appears green.

14. If a red light shines on a white flower, the flower will appear _____.

   A. yellow.
   B. black.
   C. white.
   D. red.

Inquiry Skills

15. Predict What would happen if you shined a red light on a sheet of black paper? What color do you think the paper would appear? How would you find out?

16. While playing outside in the afternoon, you notice that a long shadow seems to follow you everywhere. What causes the shadow?

Map the Concept

Use the terms below to fill in the blanks.

Earth	the Sun
mirror	rainbow
opaque	reflection
prism	shadow

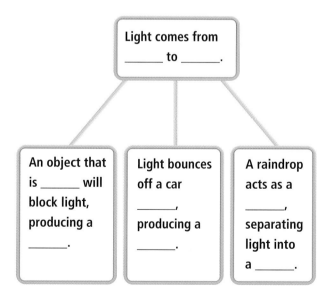

Light comes from _____ to _____.

An object that is _____ will block light, producing a _____.

Light bounces off a car _____, producing a _____.

A raindrop acts as a _____, separating light into a _____.

STANDARDS

1: 2.d., 2: 2.b., 3–4: 2.a., 5: 2.c., 6: 2.a., 2.b., 7–10: 2.d., 11: 2.b., 2.c., 12: 2.b., 13: 2.a., 2.d., 14: 2.c., 15: 2.c., 5.d., 16: 2.a., 17–19: 2.b., 20: 2.d., Map the Concept: 1.a., 2.a., 2.b., Performance Assessment: 1.a., 5.a.

Critical Thinking

17. Apply You are going outside at night and want to be visible to drivers. Should you wear a shirt that absorbs light or reflects light? Explain.

18. Analyze A toy bear is on a dresser in front of a mirror. Why does the mirror produce a reflection, but the bear does not?

19. Synthesize You want to see into a dark closet. A light above you is aimed in the wrong direction and too high to reach. How could you make this light shine into the closet?

20. Evaluate A flower is in a glass vase filled with water. Its stem looks bent. Your friend says the water made the stem so soft that it bent. Do you think this is the reason? Explain.

Performance Assessment

Design a Solar Collector

Solar panels collect sunlight to be converted into other forms of energy. Think about what you have learned in this chapter. What features would help a solar panel to collect the most light? List the features and explain how you could test them.

Writing Journal

Review your answers to the questions on page 311. Change your answers, as needed, based on what you have learned.

Write the letter of the best answer choice.

1. Which type of energy does Earth receive from the Sun?

   A. mechanical energy
   B. light energy
   C. sound energy
   D. chemical energy

2. Which picture shows an example of reflection?

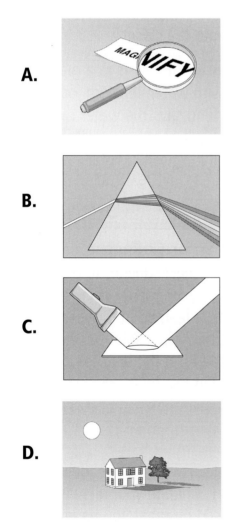

   A.

   B.

   C.

   D.

3. If you throw a ball straight up into the air, what kind of energy does it have at its highest point?

   A. potential energy
   B. chemical energy
   C. sound energy
   D. kinetic energy

4. When you turn on a lamp you change _____.

   A. light energy to electrical energy.
   B. kinetic energy to potential energy.
   C. electrical energy to light energy.
   D. light energy to chemical energy.

5. What is the source of stored energy in the circuit shown below?

   A. a light bulb
   B. wires
   C. a battery
   D. gasoline

6. You can see an object because light from that object is _____.

   A. refracted

   B. reflected

   C. blocked

   D. absorbed

7. You see a shadow because _____.

   A. some objects reflect light.

   B. some objects refract light.

   C. some objects block light.

   D. some objects let light pass through them.

8. What part of a wave is the arrow pointing to in the picture below?

   A. crest

   B. trough

   C. energy

   D. wavelength

Answer the following in complete sentences.

9. How does a plucked guitar string produce sound? Explain your answer.

10. What happens when a white sneaker is held under a blue light? Explain why this happens.

◤ **STANDARDS**

1: 1.a., 2: 2.b., 3: 1.b., 4: 1.c., 5: 1.b.,
6: 2.d., 7: 2.a., 8–9: 1.d., 10: 2.c.

Wrap-Up

You Can...

Discover More

The cars of a roller coaster are pulled up the first, and highest, hill by an electric motor. An invisible change occurs as the cars climb the hill. The cars store energy. That energy changes form as the cars go over the top of the hill.

When the cars of a roller coaster are pulled up a hill, they gain energy called **potential energy**.

When the cars reach the top of the hill, the force of gravity pulls them down the hill.

As the cars speed down the hill, the potential energy of the cars changes to **kinetic energy**, the energy of motion.

PE Potential Energy
KE Kinetic Energy

This pattern of changing energy continues through the ride. The energy the cars have at the top of the first hill moves the cars along the entire ride. That is why the cars do not need any electrical energy after the first hill.

Simulations Go to www.eduplace.com/cascp to see how potential and kinetic energy affect your coaster.

Science and Math Toolbox

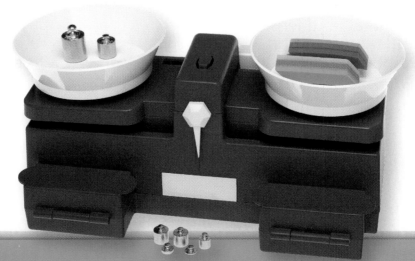

Using a Hand Lens

A hand lens is a tool that magnifies objects, or makes objects appear larger. This makes it possible for you to see details of an object that would be hard to see without the hand lens.

Look at a Coin or a Stamp

1 Place an object such as a coin or a stamp on a table or other flat surface.

STEP 1

2 Hold the hand lens just above the object. As you look through the lens, slowly move the lens away from the object. Notice that the object appears to get larger and a little blurry.

STEP 2

3 Move the hand lens a little closer to the object until the object is once again in sharp focus.

STEP 3

Making a Bar Graph

A bar graph helps you organize and compare data.

Make a Bar Graph of Animal Heights

Animals come in all different shapes and sizes. You can use the information in this table to make a bar graph of animal heights.

① Draw the side and the bottom of the graph. Label the side of the graph as shown. The numbers will show the height of the animals in centimeters.

② Label the bottom of the graph. Write the names of the animals at the bottom so that there is room to draw the bars.

③ Choose a title for your graph. Your title should describe the subject of the graph.

④ Draw bars to show the height of each animal. Some heights are between two numbers.

Heights of Animals

Animal	Height (cm)
Bear	240
Elephant	315
Cow	150
Giraffe	570
Camel	210
Horse	165

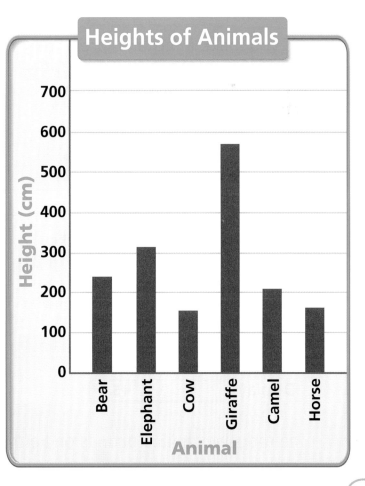

Heights of Animals

H3

Using a Calculator

After you've made measurements, a calculator can help you analyze your data.

Add and Multiply Decimals

Suppose you're an astronaut. You may take 8 pounds of Moon rocks back to Earth. Can you take all the rocks in the table? Use a calculator to find out.

Weight of Moon Rocks	
Moon Rock	**Weight of Rock on Moon (lb)**
Rock 1	1.7
Rock 2	1.8
Rock 3	2.6
Rock 4	1.5

 To add, press:

1 . 7 + 1 . 8 +
2 . 6 + 1 . 5 =

Display: (7.6)

2 If you make a mistake, press the left arrow key and then the Clear key. Enter the number again. Then continue adding.

3 Your total is 7.6 pounds. You can take the four Moon rocks back to Earth.

4 How much do the Moon rocks weigh on Earth? Objects weigh six times as much on Earth as they do on the Moon. You can use a calculator to multiply.

Press: 7 . 6 × 6 =

Display: (45.6)

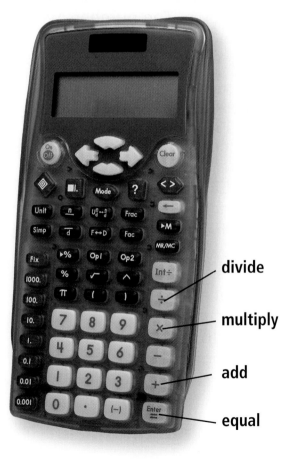

divide

multiply

add

equal

The rocks weigh 45.6 pounds on Earth.

Making a Tally Chart

A tally chart can help you keep track of items you are counting. Sometimes you need to count many different items. It may be hard to count all of the items of the same type as a group. That's when a tally chart can be helpful.

Make a Tally Chart of Birds Seen

A group of bird watchers made a tally chart to record how many birds of each type they saw. Here are the tallies they have made so far.

- Every time you count one item, make one tally.

- When you reach five, draw the fifth tally as a line through the other four.

- To find the total number of robins, count by fives and then ones.

- You can use the tally chart to make a chart with numbers.

What kind of bird was seen most often?

- Now use a tally chart to record how many cars of different colors pass your school.

Birds Seen

Type of Bird	Tally
Cardinal	||
Blue jay	卌 卌 卌
Mockingbird	||||
Hummingbird	卌 ||
House sparrow	卌 卌 卌 卌 |
Robin	卌 卌 ||

Birds Seen

Type of Bird	Number
Cardinal	2
Blue jay	15
Mockingbird	4
Hummingbird	7
House sparrow	21
Robin	12

Using a Tape Measure or Ruler

Tape measures and rulers are tools for measuring the length of objects and distances. Scientists most often use units such as meters, centimeters, and millimeters when making length measurements.

Use a Tape Measure

1. Measure the distance around a jar. Wrap the tape around the jar.

2. Find the line where the tape begins to wrap over itself.

3. Record the distance around the jar to the nearest centimeter.

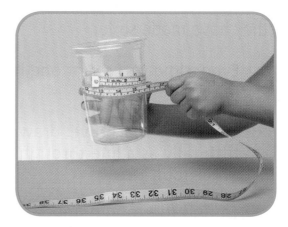

Use a Metric Ruler

1. Measure the length of your shoe. Place the ruler or the meterstick on the floor. Line up the end of the ruler with the heel of your shoe.

2. Notice where the other end of your shoe lines up with the ruler.

3. Look at the scale on the ruler. Record the length of your shoe to the nearest centimeter and to the nearest millimeter.

Measuring Volume

A beaker, a measuring cup, and a graduated cylinder are used to measure volume. Volume is the amount of space something takes up. Most of the containers that scientists use to measure volume have a scale marked in milliliters (mL).

Beaker
50 mL

Measuring cup
50 mL

Graduated cylinder
50 mL

Measure the Volume of a Liquid

1. Measure the volume of juice. Pour some juice into a measuring container.

2. Move your head so that your eyes are level with the top of the juice. Read the scale line that is closest to the surface of the juice. If the surface of the juice is curved up on the sides, look at the lowest point of the curve.

3. Read the measurement on the scale. You can estimate the value between two lines on the scale.

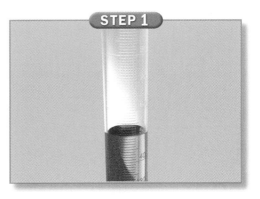

STEP 1

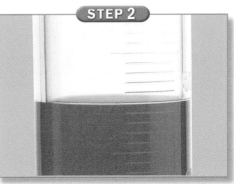

STEP 2

Using a Thermometer

A thermometer is used to measure temperature. When the liquid in the tube of a thermometer gets warmer, it expands and moves farther up the tube. Different scales can be used to measure temperature, but scientists usually use the Celsius scale.

Measure the Temperature of a Liquid

1 Half fill a cup with warm tap water.

2 Hold the thermometer so that the bulb is in the center of the liquid. Be sure that there are no bright lights or direct sunlight shining on the bulb.

3 Wait a few minutes until you see the liquid in the tube of the thermometer stop moving. Read the scale line that is closest to the top of the liquid in the tube. The thermometer shown reads 22°C (72°F).

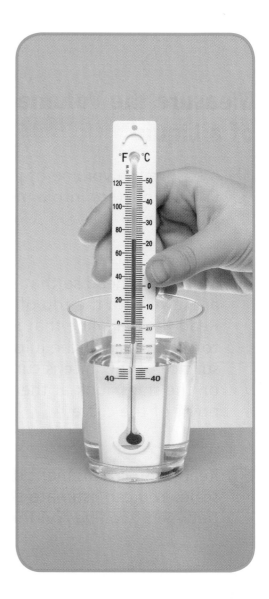

Using a Balance

A balance is used to measure mass. Mass is the amount of matter in an object. To find the mass of an object, place it in the left pan of the balance. Place standard masses in the right pan.

Measure the Mass of a Ball

1. Check that the empty pans are balanced, or level with each other. When balanced, the pointer on the base should be at the middle mark. If it needs to be adjusted, move the slider on the back of the balance a little to the left or right.

2. Place a ball on the left pan. Then add standard masses, one at a time, to the right pan. When the pointer is at the middle mark again, each pan holds the same amount of matter and has the same mass.

3. Add the numbers marked on the masses in the pan. The total is the mass of the ball in grams.

Making a Chart to Organize Data

A chart can help you keep track of information. When you organize information, or data, it is easier to read, compare, or classify it.

Classifying Animals

Suppose you want to organize this data about animal characteristics. You could base the chart on the two characteristics listed—the number of wings and the number of legs.

1 Give the chart a title that describes the data in it.

2 Name categories, or groups, that describe the data you have collected.

3 Make sure the information is recorded correctly in each column.

Next, you could make another chart to show animal classification based on number of legs only.

My Data

Fleas have no wings. Fleas have six legs.

Snakes have no wings or legs.

A bee has four wings. It has six legs.

Spiders never have wings. They have eight legs.

A dog has no wings. It has four legs.

Birds have two wings and two legs.

A cow has no wings. It has four legs.

A butterfly has four wings. It has six legs.

Animals–Number of Wings and Legs

Animal	Number of Wings	Number of Legs
Flea	0	6
Snake	0	0
Bee	4	6
Spider	0	8
Dog	0	4
Bird	2	2
Butterfly	4	6

Reading a Circle Graph

A circle graph shows a whole divided into parts. You can use a circle graph to compare the parts to each other. You can also use it to compare the parts to the whole.

A Circle Graph of Fuel Use

This circle graph shows fuel use in the United States. The graph has 10 equal parts, or sections. Each section equals $\frac{1}{10}$ of the whole. One whole equals $\frac{10}{10}$.

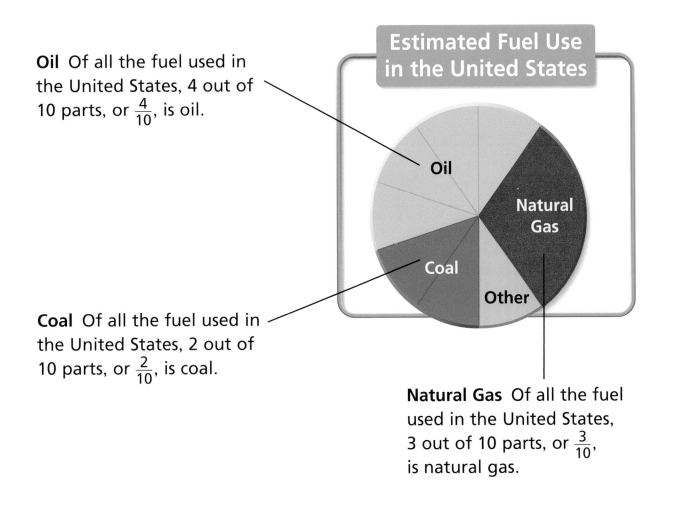

Estimated Fuel Use in the United States

Oil Of all the fuel used in the United States, 4 out of 10 parts, or $\frac{4}{10}$, is oil.

Coal Of all the fuel used in the United States, 2 out of 10 parts, or $\frac{2}{10}$, is coal.

Natural Gas Of all the fuel used in the United States, 3 out of 10 parts, or $\frac{3}{10}$, is natural gas.

Measuring Elapsed Time

A calendar can help you find out how much time has passed, or elapsed, in days or weeks. A clock can help you see how much time has elapsed in hours and minutes. A clock with a second hand or a stopwatch can help you find out how many seconds have elapsed.

Using a Calendar to Find Elapsed Days

This is a calendar for the month of October. October has 31 days. Suppose it is October 22 and you begin an experiment. You need to check the experiment two days from the start date and one week from the start date. That means you would check it on Wednesday, October 24, and again on Monday, October 29. October 29 is 7 days after October 22.

Days of the Week
Monday, Tuesday, Wednesday, Thursday, and Friday are weekdays. Saturday and Sunday are weekends.

Last Month
Last month ended on Sunday, September 30.

October

Sunday	Monday	Tuesday	Wednesday	Thursday	Friday	Saturday
	1	2	3	4	5	6
7	8	9	10	11	12	13
14	15	16	17	18	19	20
21	22	23	24	25	26	27
28	29	30	31			

Next Month
Next month begins on Thursday, November 1.

Using a Clock or a Stopwatch to Find Elapsed Time

You need to time an experiment for 20 minutes.

It is 1:30 P.M.   **Stop at 1:50 P.M.**

You need to time an experiment for 15 seconds. You can use the second hand of a clock or watch.

Start the experiment when the second hand is on number 6.

Stop when 15 seconds have passed and the second hand is on the 9.

You can use a stopwatch to time 15 seconds.

Press the reset button on a stopwatch so that you see 0:00₀₀.

Press the start button. When you see 0:15₀₀, press the stop button.

Measurements

Volume

1 L of sports drink is a
little more than 1 qt.

Area

A basketball court covers about 4,700 ft².
It covers about 435 m².

Metric Measures

Temperature

- Ice melts at 0 degrees Celsius (°C)
- Water freezes at 0°C
- Water boils at 100°C

Length and Distance

- 1,000 meters (m) = 1 kilometer (km)
- 100 centimeters (cm) = 1 m
- 10 millimeters (mm) = 1 cm

Force

- 1 newton (N) =
  1 kilogram × 1(meter/second)
  per second

Volume

- 1 cubic meter (m³) = 1 m × 1 m × 1 m
- 1 cubic centimeter (cm³) =
  1 cm × 1 cm × 1 cm
- 1 liter (L) = 1,000 milliliters (mL)
- 1 cm³ = 1 mL

Area

- 1 square kilometer (km²) =
  1 km × 1 km
- 1 hectare = 10,000 m²

Mass

- 1,000 grams (g) = 1 kilogram (kg)
- 1,000 milligrams (mg) = 1 g

Temperature

The temperature at an indoor basketball game might be 27°C, which is 80°F.

Length and Distance

A basketball rim is about 10 ft high, or a little more than 3 m from the floor.

Customary Measures

Temperature

- Ice melts at 32 degrees Fahrenheit (°F)
- Water freezes at 32°F
- Water boils at 212°F

Length and Distance

- 12 inches (in.) = 1 foot (ft)
- 3 ft = 1 yard (yd)
- 5,280 ft = 1 mile (mi)

Weight

- 16 ounces (oz) = 1 pound (lb)
- 2,000 pounds = 1 ton (T)

Volume of Fluids

- 8 fluid ounces (fl oz) = 1 cup (c)
- 2 c = 1 pint (pt)
- 2 pt = 1 quart (qt)
- 4 qt = 1 gallon (gal)

Metric and Customary Rates

km/h = kilometers per hour

m/s = meters per second

mph = miles per hour

Health and Fitness Handbook

Health means more than just not being ill. There are many parts to health. Here are some questions you will be able to answer after reading this handbook.

- How do my body systems work?
- What nutrients does my body need?
- How does being active help my body?
- How can I be safe at home?
- How can I prevent food from making me ill?

The Digestive System

Your digestive system breaks down food into materials your body can use. These materials are called nutrients.

1 Digestion starts in your mouth.
- Your teeth break food into small pieces. Saliva mixes with the food. Saliva has chemicals that break down food more.
- Your tongue pushes the chewed food into your esophagus when you swallow.

2 Food travels through the esophagus to the stomach.
- Acid and other chemicals in the stomach break down the food even more.
- The food moves to the small intestine.

3 More chemicals flow into the small intestine. They come from the liver, pancreas, and other organs.
- These chemicals finish breaking down the food into nutrients.
- The nutrients are absorbed into the blood.
- The blood carries the nutrients to all parts of the body.

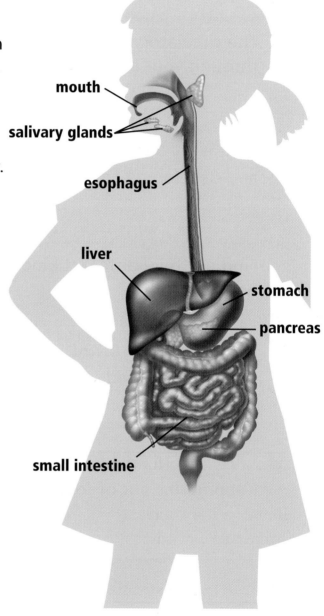

mouth

salivary glands

esophagus

liver

stomach

pancreas

small intestine

The Circulatory System

Your circulatory system moves blood through your body. There are three major parts to the circulatory system: the heart, blood vessels, and blood.

Heart Your heart has four chambers, or sections.

- The right two chambers take blood from the body and pump it to the lungs.
- There, the blood picks up oxygen and gets rid of waste.
- The left two chambers take blood from the lungs and pump it to the rest of the body.

Blood Vessels Two kinds of vessels carry blood through your body.

- **Arteries** carry blood from the heart to the body.
- **Veins** carry blood from the body to the heart.

Blood Your blood carries oxygen from your lungs to your body cells.

- Blood carries nutrients from your digestive system.
- Blood carries wastes away from the cells to organs that remove the wastes from the body.

heart

arteries (red)

veins (blue)

Some Nutrients You Need

Nutrients are materials your body needs for energy and to grow. Three important nutrients are proteins, carbohydrates, and fats. Eating these nutrients in the right amount can help you stay at a healthful weight.

Proteins

Uses Your body uses proteins to build new cells and for cell activities. You need proteins to grow and develop.

Sources meat, chicken, fish, milk, cheese, nuts, beans, eggs

Fats

Uses Your body uses fat to store energy. You need to eat only a small amount of fat, because your body makes some on its own.

Sources oils and butter

Carbohydrates

Uses Carbohydrates are your body's main source of energy. Simple carbohydrates give quick energy. Complex carbohydrates give long-lasting energy. Complex carbohydrates should make up the largest part of your diet.

Sources simple carbohydrates: fruits and milk products

complex carbohydrates: whole-grain bread, cereal, pasta, potatoes

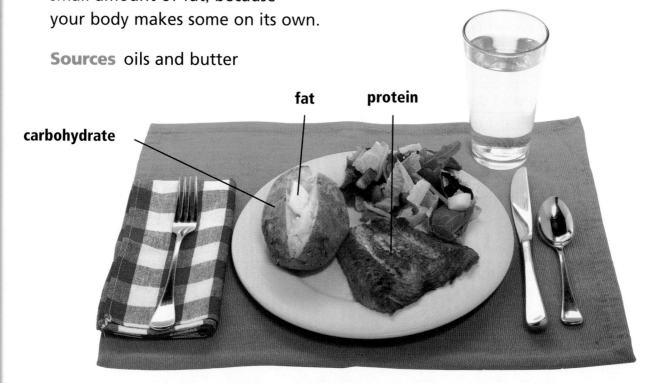

carbohydrate

fat

protein

Kinds of Physical Activity

Do you run, jump, and play every day? There are different kinds of physical activity. Each helps your body in a different way.

Endurance

Some activities help your body work hard for longer periods of time.

Activities That Build Endurance

- swimming
- jumping rope
- soccer
- in-line skating
- riding a bike
- walking fast
- basketball
- hockey

Do one of these activities for 20 to 60 minutes three to five times a week.

Flexibility

Stretching helps your muscles move smoothly.

Activities That Build Flexibility

- touching your toes
- stretching your arms
- sit and reach
- stretching your side

Do flexibility exercises two to three times a week.

Strength

These exercises make your muscles stronger. Ask an adult to show you how to do them safely.

Activities That Build Strength

- sit-ups
- push-ups
- pull-ups

Do strength training two to three days each week.

Home Safety Checklists

Most accidents happen at home. Here are some tips for staying safe.

Fire Safety

✔ Have smoke detectors. Check the batteries twice each year.

✔ Don't play with matches or candles.

✔ Only use the stove or oven if an adult is there.

✔ Have a family fire plan. Practice your plan.

Poison Safety

✔ Some chemicals and cleaners are poisons. So are some medicines. Keep them in high places away from small children.

✔ Post the phone number for Poison Control by the phone.

Kitchen Safety

✔ Never leave the kitchen while cooking.

✔ Store knives out of the reach of children.

✔ Wipe up spills immediately. Keep the floor clear of clutter.

Electrical Safety

✔ Keep electrical cords out of areas where someone could trip on them.

✔ Don't use electrical appliances near water.

✔ Unplug small appliances when you are not using them.

✔ Make sure electric cords are not damaged. They could start a fire.

Food Safety

Foods and drinks can carry germs. These germs can cause disease. Remember these four steps to keep food safe.

Clean

✔ Wash your hands before and after you cook. Wash them again if you handle raw meat, poultry, or fish.

✔ Wash all the dishes and utensils you use.

✔ Wash your hands before you eat.

Separate

✔ Keep raw meat, poultry, and fish away from other foods.

✔ Keep cooked food away from raw food.

Chill

✔ Some foods need to be kept cold. Put leftovers in the refrigerator as soon as possible. This slows down the growth of germs.

✔ If you are having a picnic, keep foods in an icechest until you are ready to cook or serve them

Cook

✔ Cook food thoroughly. Cooking kills many germs.

✔ Use a thermometer to make sure foods are hot enough.

Glossary

English-Spanish Glossary

A

absorb (uhb SAWRB) To take in. (333)

　absorber Tomar.

adaptation (ad dap TAY shun) A way of acting or a body part that helps a living thing survive. (8)

　adaptación Forma de actuar de un ser vivo; parte del cuerpo que le ayuda a sobrevivir.

ancestor (an SEHS tur) A species or form of a species that lived long ago and to which modern species can be traced back. (90)

　antepasado Especie o forma de especie que vivió hace mucho tiempo y con la cual se puede averiguar sobre los orígenes de una especie actual.

aquatic habitat (uh KWAT ihk HAB ih tat) A place where organisms live in or on water. (26)

　hábitat acuático Lugar donde los organismos viven dentro o cerca del agua.

atom (AT uhm) The smallest particle of some kinds of matter that has the properties of that kind of matter. (202)

　átomo La partícula más pequeña de ciertos tipos de materia que tiene las mismas propiedades que ese tipo de materia.

axis (AK sihs) An imaginary line through the center of an object. (155)

　eje Línea imaginaria que pasa por el centro de un objeto.

B

behavior (bee HAYV yur) The way that an organism usually acts in a certain situation. (12)

　comportamiento Forma en la que usualmente actúa un organismo en una situación determinada.

biome (BY ohm) A large area that has similar living things and about the same temperature and rainfall throughout. (8)

　bioma Zona extensa que tiene similares seres vivos, temperaturas y lluvias.

C

chemical change (KEHM ih kuhl chaynj) A change in matter in which one or more new kinds of matter form. (251)

　cambio químico Cambio en la materia mediante el cual se forman uno o más tipos nuevos de materia.

chemical property (KEHM ih kuhl PRAHP-uhr tee) A property that describes how matter can react with other kinds of matter. (250)

　propiedad química Propiedad que describe la reacción de un tipo de materia con otros tipos de materia.

community (kuh MYOO nih tee) A group of organisms that live in the same area and interact with each other. (44)

comunidad Grupo de organismos que viven en la misma zona e interactúan unos con otros.

competition (kom PIH tish uhn) The struggle of one organism against another to gain resources. (45)

competencia Lucha de un organismo contra otro para obtener recursos.

compound (KAHM pound) A substance made of two or more elements that are joined together. (242)

compuesto Sustancia formada por dos o más elementos que se unen.

condense (kuhn DEHNS) To change form from a gas to a liquid. (224)

condensar Cambiar de forma gaseosa a líquida.

constellation (kahn stuh LAY shuhn) A group of stars that forms a pattern shaped like an animal, person, or object. (180)

constelación Grupo de estrellas que forman una figura parecida a un animal, persona u objeto.

crescent moon (KREHS uhnt moon) The phase of the Moon when a thin part of the Moon's near side is sunlit. (168)

luna creciente o menguante La fase de la Luna en la cual una parte delgada de la luna recibe luz del Sol.

crest (krest) The highest point of a wave. (289)

cresta Punto más alto de una onda.

desert (deh ZURT) An area that receives less than about 25 cm (10 in.) of precipitation in a year. (18)

desierto Zona que recibe menos de unos 25 cm (10 pulg.) de precipitación al año.

drought (drowt) A long time with little to no rainfall. (55)

sequía Período largo de tiempo durante el cual no llueve nada o llueve poco.

dwarf planet (DWORF PLAN iht) A round orbiting body much like a planet, but smaller.

planeta enano Cuerpo celeste redondo similar a un planeta, pero de menor tamaño que orbita alrededor del Sol.

ecosystem (EE koh SIHS tehm) All the living and nonliving things that exist and interact in one place. (45)

ecosistema Todos los seres vivos y las cosas sin vida que existen e interactúan en un lugar.

electric circuit (EE lek trik SUR kiht) A path through which electric current can flow. (301)

circuito eléctrico Recorrido a través del cual puede circular la corriente eléctrica.

electric current (EE lek trik KUR uhnt) The flow of charged particles. (300)

corriente eléctrica Flujo de partículas con carga.

element (EHL ih mehnt) A pure form of matter in which all of the atoms are the same kind. (238)

elemento Forma pura de materia cuyos átomos son todos del mismo tipo.

endangered species (ehn DAYN jurd SPEE-sheez) A species that has so few members that the entire species is at risk of dying out. (76)

especies en peligro Especie con tan pocos miembros que está en peligro de desaparición.

energy (EHN ur jee) The ability to cause matter to change or move. (272)

energía Capacidad que tiene la materia de cambiar o moverse.

environment (ehn VY ruhn muhnt) All the living and nonliving things that surround and affect an organism. (16)

medio ambiente Todos los seres vivos y las cosas sin vida que rodean y afectan a un organismo.

equator (ee KWAY tur) An imaginary line that circles Earth halfway between the North and South Poles. (161)

ecuador Línea imaginaria que rodea a la Tierra y está a la misma distancia del Polo Norte que del Polo Sur.

era (IHR uh) A major division of time. (82)

era División grande del tiempo.

evaporate (ih VAP uh rayt) To change form from a liquid to a gas. (222)

evaporar Cambiar de forma líquida a gaseosa.

extinct species (ihk STIHNGKT SPEE sheez) A species that has died off. (72)

especie extinta Especie que ha desaparecido.

F

forest (FAWR ihst) A large area in which there are many trees growing close together. (8)

bosque Zona grande donde muchos árboles crecen juntos.

fossil (FAHS uhl) The preserved remains of an organism that lived long ago. (80)

fósil Restos que se conservan de un organismo que vivió hace mucho tiempo.

freeze (freez) To change form from a liquid to a solid. (224)

congelar Cambiar de forma líquida a sólida.

friction (FRIHK shuhn) A force that occurs when one object rubs against another object. (282)

fricción Fuerza que tiene lugar cuando un objeto roza con otro.

full moon (ful moon) The phase of the Moon when all of the Moon's near side is sunlit. (169)

luna llena Fase de la Luna en la cual todo su lado más cercano recibe luz del Sol.

G

gas (gas) Matter that has no definite shape and no definite volume. (214)

gas Materia que no tiene forma o volumen definidos.

gas giant (gas JY ent) A very large planet made up mostly of gases. (136)

gigante gaseoso Planeta muy grande compuesto en su mayor parte por gases.

grassland (GRAS land) An area made up of large, flat land that is covered with grasses. (10)

pastizal Zona formada por terrenos grandes y llanos, cubiertos de hierbas.

H

habitat (HAB ih tat) The place where a plant or animal lives. (12)

hábitat Lugar donde vive una planta o animal.

I

inner planets (IHN ur PLAN ihts) The four planets closest to the Sun—Mercury, Venus, Earth, and Mars. (122)

planetas interiores Son los cuatro planetas más cercanos al Sol: Mercurio, Venus, la Tierra y Marte.

K

kinetic energy (kuh NEHT ihk EHN ur jee) The energy of motion. (278)

energía cinética Energía del movimiento.

L

lens (lehnz) An object that refracts light. (326)

lente Objeto que refracta la luz.

light (lyt) A form of energy that you can see. (316)

luz Forma de energía que se puede ver.

liquid (LIHK wihd) Matter that takes the shape of its container and has a definite volume. (213)

líquido Materia que toma la forma de su recipiente y que tiene volumen definido.

M

magnify (MAG nuh fy) To make an object appear larger. (112)

aumentar Hacer que un objeto parezca más grande.

matter (MAT uhr) Anything that has mass and takes up space. (200)

materia Cualquier cosa que tiene masa y ocupa espacio.

melt (mehlt) To change form from a solid to a liquid. (221)

derretir Cambiar de forma sólida a líquida.

mixture (MIHKS chur) Matter made up of two or more substances that are physically combined, or mixed. (244)

mezcla Materia en la que se combinan o mezclan físicamente dos o más sustancias.

moon (moon) A small, rounded body in orbit around a planet. (121)

luna Cuerpo pequeño y redondo que orbita alrededor de un planeta.

N

new moon (noo moon) The phase of the Moon when the Moon's near side receives no sunlight. (168)

luna nueva Fase de la Luna durante la cual su lado más cercano no recibe luz del Sol.

O

opaque (OH payk) Not allowing light to pass through. (317)

opaco Que no permite que pase la luz.

orbit (OHR biht) To move in a path around an object. (121)

orbitar Hacer un recorrido alrededor de un objeto.

outer planets (OW tur PLAN ihts) The four planets farthest from the Sun—Jupiter, Saturn, Uranus, and Neptune. (123)

planetas exteriores Son los planetas más alejados del Sol: Júpiter, Saturno, Urano, y Neptuno.

P

paleontologist (pay lee ehn TAHL uh jihst) A scientist who studies fossils and forms of life that no longer exist. (81)

paleontólogo Científico que estudia fósiles y formas de vida que ya no existen.

periodic table (PEER ee ahd ik TAY buhl) An arrangement of all the elements that gives information about their atoms and properties. (240)

tabla periódica Disposición de todos los elementos, con información sobre sus átomos y propiedades.

phases of the Moon (FAYZ ihz uhf thuh moon) The different ways the Moon looks throughout the month. (170)

fases de la luna Distintos aspectos que toma la Luna durante el mes.

physical change (FIHZ ih kuhl chaynj) A change in size, shape, or form of matter. (204)

cambio físico Cambio de tamaño, apariencia o forma de la materia.

physical property (FIHZ ih kuhl PRAHP uhr-tee) A trait of matter that can be measured or observed with the senses. (200)

propiedad física Rasgo de la materia que se puede medir u observar mediante los sentidos.

planet (PLAN iht) A large body in space that moves around a star. (120)

planeta Cuerpo sideral de gran tamaño que se mueve alrededor de una estrella.

pollution (puh LOO shuhn) The addition of any harmful materials to the environment. (58)

contaminación Liberación de sustancias perjudiciales para el medio ambiente.

population (pahp yuh LAY shuhn) All the living organisms of the same kind that live in an area. (44)

población Todos los organismos vivos del mismo tipo que viven en una zona.

potential energy (puh TEHN shuhl EHN ur-jee) The energy of position. (278)

energía potencial Energía de posición.

prism (prihzm) A transparent object that separates white light into all the colors of the rainbow. (332)

prisma Objeto transparente que separa la luz blanca en todos los colores del arco iris.

Q

quarter moon (KWAHR tur moon) The phase of the Moon when half of the Moon's near side is sunlit. (169)

media luna Fase de la Luna en la que la mitad más cercana recibe luz del Sol.

R

reflect (rih FLEHKT) To bounce off. (324)

reflejar Rebotar.

refract (rih FRAKT) To bend. (325)

refractar Cambiar de dirección.

relative (reh LUH tihv) A species that shares a common ancestor with another species. (91)

pariente Especie que comparte un antepasado común con otra especie.

reproduce (ree proh DOOS) To make new living things of the same kind. (46)

reproducir Crear nuevos seres vivos del mismo tipo.

resource (REE sawrs) A thing found in nature that is useful to organisms. (45)

recurso Objeto que se encuentra en la naturaleza y es útil para los organismos.

revolve (rih VAHLV) To move in a path around another object. (160)

girar Moverse siguiendo un recorrido alrededor de otro objeto.

rotate (ROH tayt) To turn on an axis. (155)

rotar Girar alrededor de un eje.

S

season (SEE zuhn) One of the four parts of the year—spring, summer, fall, and winter. (161)

estación Cada una de las cuatro partes del año: primavera, verano, otoño e invierno.

shadow (sha DOH) An area where light does not strike the ground. (319)

sombra Zona donde la luz no llega al suelo.

solar system (SOH lur SIHS tuhm) The Sun, planets, moons, and other objects that orbit the Sun. (121)

sistema solar Está formado por el Sol, los planetas, las lunas y otros objetos que orbitan alrededor del Sol.

solid (SAHL ihd) Matter that has a definite shape and a definite volume. (211)

sólido Materia que tiene forma y volumen definidos.

space probe (spays prohb) A craft that helps scientists explore outer space. (132)

sonda espacial Máquina que ayuda a los científicos a explorar el espacio exterior.

species (SPEE sheez) A group of the same type of living thing that can mate and produce other living things of the same kind. (72)

especie Grupo de seres vivos que pueden reproducirse y crear seres vivos del mismo tipo.

star (stahr) A ball of hot gases that gives off light and other forms of energy. (178)

estrella Bola de gases calientes que produce luz y otras formas de energía.

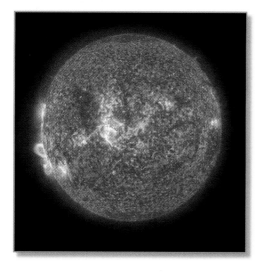

Sun (suhn) The nearest star to Earth. (120)

Sol La estrella más cercana a la Tierra.

telescope (TEHL ih skohp) A tool that makes distant objects appear larger, brighter, and sharper. (112)

telescopio Instrumento que hace parecer más grandes, brillantes y claros los objetos distantes.

thermal energy (THUHR muhl EHN uhr jee) The energy of moving particles in all matter. (218)

energía térmica Energía de las partículas en movimiento que existen en la materia.

trait (trayt) A feature such as a body part or a behavior. (91)

rasgo Característica propia de una parte del cuerpo o de un comportamiento.

translucent (trans LU sehnt) Allows only some light to pass through. (318)

traslúcido Que permite pasar sólo parte de la luz.

transparent (trans PAYR uhnt) Lets light pass through. (318)

transparente Que deja pasar la luz.

trough (trawf) The lowest point of a wave. (289)

valle Punto más bajo de una onda.

tundra (TUHN drah) A cold, treeless area that has short, cool summers and long, cold winters. (16)

tundra Zona fría sin árboles donde los veranos son cortos y frescos y los inviernos largos y fríos.

vibrate (VY brayt) To move back and forth quickly. (290)

vibrar Moverse hacia un lado y otro rápidamente.

waning moon (WAY nihng moon) The phases of the Moon when a decreasing amount of the Moon's near side is sunlit. (169)

luna menguante Fase de la Luna en la cual disminuye la cantidad de luz del Sol que recibe su lado más cercano.

wave (wayv) A movement that carries energy from one place to another. (288)

onda Movimiento que lleva energía de un lugar a otro.

waxing moon (WAHK zihng moon) The phases of the Moon when an increasing amount of the Moon's near side is sunlit. (169)

luna creciente Fase de la Luna en la cual aumenta la cantidad de luz del Sol que recibe su lado más cercano.

Index

Index

Index

Museum, London. (bl) Ken Lucas/Taxi/ GettyImages. **88** Jonathan Blair/Corbis. **90** Dave King/DK Images. **91** Superstock. **92** (cr) Fritz Prenzel/Animals Animals. (bl) ZSSD/Minden Pictures. **93** (t) Colin Keates /DK Images. (b) Art Wolfe/Photo Researchers, Inc. **94** (l) © Sally A, Morgan; Ecoscene/Corbis. (r) George J. Sanker/DRK Photo. **95** © Sally A, Morgan; Ecoscene/Corbis. **98** Super- stock. **99** Courtesy of the Museum of Paleontology, University of California, Berkeley, Photographed by David K. Smith. **104** Fritz Poelking/Elvele Images/ Alamay. Unit B Opener: Stockli, Nelson, Hasler/NASA. CA Field Trip: Courtesy of Palomar Observatory and California Institute of Technology. **105** Planetary Visions/Eumetsat Meteosat-6/Planetary Visions. **106–107** GoodShoot/Super- Stock. **107** (t) Tony Freeman/Photo Edit Inc. (cl) SPL/Photo Researchers, Inc. (cr) JPL/Nasa. (b) AP Wide World Photo. **108** (c) US Geological Survey/Photo Researchers, Inc. (b) Burke/Triolo Productions/Brand X Pictures/Alamy. **108–109** (bkgrd) Nasa/Getty Images. **110–111** Taxi/Getty Images. **112** Steve Vidler/Superstock. **113** (t) Dr. Seth Shostak/Photo Researchers, Inc. (b) Denis Scott/Corbis. **114** (t) Photri. (br) © Phil Degginger/NASA/Color-Pic, Inc. **115** (t) Burke/Triolo Productions/Brand X Pictures/Alamy. (c) Steve Vidler/ Superstock. (b) Denis Scott/Corbis. **116** (c) NASA/JPL-Caltech/UMD. **116–117** (bkgrd) Dennis Di Cocco/Peter Arnold, Inc. **117** (c) Detlev Van Ravensway/Photo Researchers, Inc. **118–119** © Phil Degginger/NASA/SOHO-EIT/Color-Pic Inc. **122** (l) Digital Vision Ltd./Super- stock. (tr) USGS/Photo Researchers, Inc. (cr) Digital Vision Ltd./Superstock. (br) ©Phil Degginger/Nasa/JPL/Color-Pic, Inc. **122–123** (bkgrd) © Bryan Allen/Color- Pic, Inc. **123** (tr) Goodshoot/Superstock. (cr) © Phil Degginger/Nasa/JPL/Color-Pic, Inc. (cl) Pixtal/Superstock. (bl) NASA/ Photo Researchers, Inc. (br) Nasa Jet Propulsion Labrotory /Nasa-JPL. **125** (tl) USGS/Photo Researchers, Inc. (tcl), (bcl) Digital Vision Ltd./Superstock. (tcr) NASA/Photo Researchers, Inc. (tr) Pixtal/ Superstock. (cr) Goodshoot/Superstock. (bl), (bcr) © Phil Degginger/NASA/JPL/ Color-Pic, Inc. (br) NASA Jet Propulsion Labrotory/Nasa-JPL. **126** (bl) US Geological Survey/Photo Researchers, Inc. **126–127** (bkgrd) © Bill Frymire/ Masterfile. **128** (c) USGS/Photo Researchers Inc. (b) © Phil Degginger/ Nasa/JPL/Color-Pic, Inc. **129** (c) Digital Vision Ltd./Superstock. (b) Photri- Microstock. **130** (c) Digital Vision Ltd./ Superstock. (b) © Thomas Ligon/ARC Science Simulations/Photo Researchers, Inc. **131** © Phil Degginger/Nasa/JPL/ Color-Pic, Inc. **132** (tl) NASA/Photri. (tr) Nasa. (b) © Phil Degginger/Nasa/Color- Pic, Inc. **133** (t) USGS/Photo Researchers Inc. (tc) Digital Vision Ltd./Superstock. (bc) Digital Vision Ltd./Superstock. (b) © Phil Degginger/NASA/JPL/Color-Pic, Inc. **134–135** (bkgrd) © Phil Degginger/Nasa/ JPL/Color-Pic, Inc. **136** (l), (cr) © Phil Degginger/Nasa/JPL/Color-Pic, Inc. **137** (c) Jpl/Nasa. (t) Digital Vision Ltd./

Superstock. **138** © Phil Degginger/Nasa/ Color-Pic, Inc. **139** (c) © Phil Degginger/ Nasa/JPL/Color Pic, Inc. (t) Nasa/JPL. **140** Nasa/JPL. **141** (t), (bc), (b) © Phil Degginger/NASA/JPL/Color-Pic, Inc. (tc), (tr) Jpl/Nasa. **145** Gary Hochman, NET Television, Lincoln, Nebraska, for the Wonderwise Project. **148–149** (bkgrd) P. Parvianinen/Photo Researchers, Inc. **149** (tr) Frank Cezus/ Photogrpaher's Choice/Getty Images. (cl) Royalty-Free/ Corbis. (cr) W.H. Mueller/Masterfile. (bl) Frank Zullo/Photo Researchers, Inc. **150** (t) John Sanford/Photo Researchers, Inc. (b) Mpia-hd, Birkle, Slawik/Photo Researchers, Inc. **150–151** (bkgrd) Chris Cook/Photo Researchers, Inc. **152–153** (bl) M.P. Kahl/DRK Photo. **154** (l) Joe Sohm/The Image Works. (r) ML Sinibaldi/Corbis. **158–159** (bkgrd) © Comstock. **162** George Wuerthner. **163** Gibson Stock Photography. **164–165** David Young-Wolff/Photo Edit. Inc. **166** (bl) PhotoLink/Photodisc Blue/Getty Images. (bl-inset) John Sanford/Photo Researchers, Inc. **166–167** (bkgrd) Lawrance Brennon/Masterfile. **171** John Sanford/Photo Researchers, Inc. **172** (c) Kevin Kelley/The Image Bank/Getty Images. (b) ©Phil Degginger/Nasa/JPL/ Color Pic, Inc. **173** (t) Kevin Kelley/The Image Bank/Getty Images. (b) John Sanford/Photo Researchers, Inc. **174** Reproduced by permission of Rt. Hon. Lord Egremont, from Petworth House Archives HMC 241/9. **175** (tl) The Granger Collection, New York. (br) Hulton Archive/Getty Images. **176–177** (bkgrd) Bill Frymire/Masterfile. **178** Jerry Schad/Photo Researchers, Inc. **179** Photri. **183** Jerry Schad/Photo Research- ers, Inc. **186** John Sanford/Photo Researchers, Inc. **187** (tr) Mike Dowd/ AP/Wide World Photos. Unit C Opener: Roberto Soncin Gerometta/ Lonely Planet Images. CA Field Trip: (bkgrd) Dennis Flaherty. (tr) Larry Ulrich Stock Photography. (br) © Tom Bean/DRK Photo. **193** Henryk T. Kaiser/Index Stock Imagery. **194–195** (bkgrd) R. Todd King. **195** (c) PhotoPix/Photonica/Getty Images. (b) © Adam Wollfitt/Corbis. **196** (t) © Royalty Free/Corbis. (b) Tony Arruza/ARRUZ/Bruce Coleman Inc. **196–197** (bkgrd) © P. Freytag/zefa/ Corbis. **198–199** Art Resource. **203** (l) Courtesy: IBM Research, Almaden Research Center/©The Nobel Founda- tion. (r) © Douglas Whyte/Corbis. **205** Courtesy: IBM Research, Almaden Research Center/© The Nobel Founda- tion. **208** (bl) Dennis Flaherty/Photo Researchers, Inc. **208–209** © Marc Muench/Corbis. **210–211** HMCo. **212–213** Tony Arruza/ARRUZ/Bruce Coleman, Inc. **214** Rick Berkowitz/Index Stock Imagery. **215** (t) HMCo. (b) Rick Berkowitz/Index Stock Imagery. **216–217** Rolf Hicker/Panoramic Images. **219** (tl) © Bob Daemrich/The Image Works. (tr) Thinkstock/Picturequest. **220** (l) Lester Lefkowitz/The Image Bank/Getty images. (br) Greg Pease/ Stone/Getty Images. **221** (t), (bc) Charles D. Winters /Photo Researchers, Inc. (tc) Russel Lappa/Photo Researchers, Inc. (b)

John Cancalosi/ Peter Arnold Inc. **224** Frank Siteman/Mira. **226–227** Bettmann/Corbis. **229** (tl) William Whitehurst/Corbis. (cr), (br) Ainaco/ Corbis. (bkgrd) MacDuff Everton/Corbis. **232–233** (bkgrd) Ed Pritchard/Stone/ Getty Images. **233** (tr) Dave King/DK Images. (cl) © Royalty Free/Corbis. **234** (t) Image Source/Superstock. **236–237** (bkgrd) Todd Phillips/Index Stock Imagery. **238** (bl) DK Images. (br) Courtesy of the Oakland Museum of California. **246** ©Corbis. **247** (tr) AGE Fototstock/Superstock. (cr) © European Communities,1991. **248** Stephen Kline/ Bruce Coleman Inc. **248–249** (bkgrd) Digital Vison/Getty Images. **251** (t) © E. R. Degginger/Color Pic, Inc. (br) Oote Boe/Alamy Images. **252** (bl)Tony Freeman/Photo Edit, Inc. (br) Tom Pantages/Tom Pantages Stock Photos. **253** © Phil Degginger/ Color-Pic, Inc. **255** (c) Oote boe/Alamy Images. (bc) Tom Pantages Stock Photos. (b) Tony Freeman/Photo Edit, Inc. **258** © Ariel Skelly/Corbis. **259** Courtesy of Dr. Wilson Ho. Unit D Opener: Lester Lefkowitz/ Corbis. CA Field Trip: (bkgrd) John Elk III. (tr) John Poimiroo/Roaring Camp Railroad. (br) John Elk III. **265** Robert Landau/Corbis. **266–267** David Pu'u/ Corbis. **267** (t) Craig Tuttle/Corbis. (tc) Lawrence Migdale. (bc) © Jason Hosking/zefa/Corbis. (b) Miles Ertman/ Masterfile. **268** (t) HMCo. (c) Hmco/ Lawrence Migdale. (b) © Phil Deggin- ger/Color-Pic, Inc. **268–269** Tony Freeman/Photo Edit, Inc. **270** (bl) Francisco Cruz/Superstock. **270–271** (bkgrd) © Imagestopshop/Alamy. **273** (tc) © Phil Degginger/ Color-Pic, Inc. (bc) F. Damm/Masterfile. (bbc) Dave Rudkin/ DK Images. (b) David Young-Wolff/ Photo Edit, Inc. **274** Photolibrary.com PTV.LTD./Index Stock Imagery. **275** © Phil Degginger Photography/ Color-Pic, Inc. **276–277** Jean-Michel Foujols/ Stock Image/PictureQuest. **278** Jeff Schultz/ Alaska Stock. **279** Tony Freeman/Photo Edit, Inc. **280** (bl) Larry Gilberson/AP/ Wide World. (c) Myrleen Ferguson Cate/Photo Edit, Inc. **281** Pat Morris/ Ardea London. **283** (t) Tony Freeman/ Photo Edit, Inc. (c) Myrleen Ferguson Cate/Photo Edit, Inc. **286–287** Tom Pantages Stock Photos. **288–289** DK Images. **290** (l) Tony Freeman/Photo Edit, Inc. (c) © Phil Degginger/Color-Pic, Inc. **292** Doug Perrine/DRK Photo. **293** (t) DK Images. (c) © Phil Degginger/ Color-Pic, Inc. (b) Doug Perrine/DRK Photo. **298** (bl) Gail Mooney/Masterfile. **298–299** (bkgrd) Frank Wiese/Associated Press/AP Wide World Photos. **300–301** ©HMCo. **304** (tl) Rob Casey/Fogstock/ Alamy Images. (c) Science Photo Library/Photo Researchers, Inc. **305** ©HMCo. **306** David Woods/Corbis. **307** (tl) Steve Craft/Masterfile. (bkgrd) Image DJ/Alamy Images. **310–311** Mehau Kulyk/Victor de Schwanberg/ Science Photo Library/Photo Research- ers, Inc. **311** (t) Grant Faint/The Image Bank/Getty Images. (c) © David Young- Wolff/Photo Edit, Inc. (b) Anthony Marcieca/Science Photo Library/Photo Researchers, Inc. **312–313** (bkgrd) Dorr/

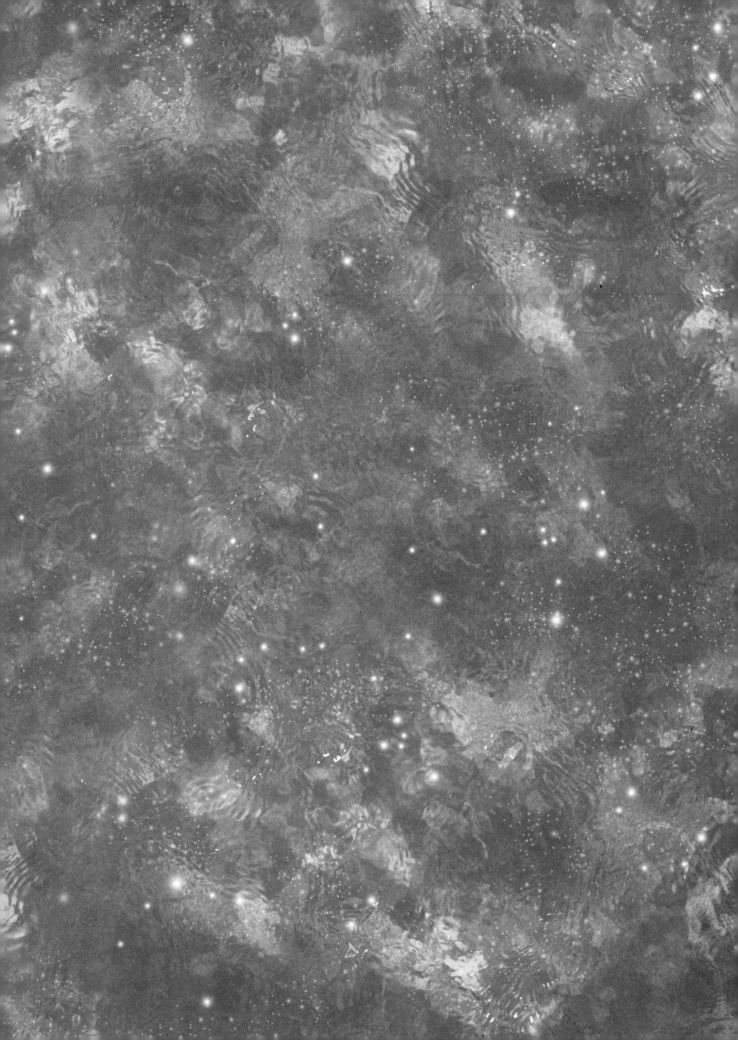

CUCINARE

Healthy and Authentic Italian Cooking
for the Whole Family

Published in 2020 by
Harper Design
An Imprint of HarperCollins *Publishers*
195 Broadway
New York, NY 10007
Tel: (212) 207-7000
Fax: (855) 746-6023
harperdesign@harpercollins.com
www.hc.com

Distributed throughout the world by
HarperCollins *Publishers*
195 Broadway
New York, NY 10007

ISBN 978-0-06-295883-9

Printed in Singapore

First printing, 2020

Photographs on pp. 13 (bottom left), 23 (right and bottom left), 24, 28 (except bottom right), 32, 39, 44, 47 (except bottom right), 54, 57 (top), 62 (bottom), 66 (right), 72 (except top left), 75 , 79, 80, 90, 93 (top), 100, 103, 106, 109 (right), 117, 120 (left), 124 (except top left), 128, 132, 135, 141 (right), 151, 152 (top left), 156 (left), 162, 165, 176 (left)
© Marco Bianchi

Photographs on pp. 4, 10, 13 (top and bottom right), 16, 18, 20, 23 (top left and bottom right), 27, 28 (bottom right), 31, 35, 36, 40, 42, 47 (bottom right), 50, 52, 57 (bottom), 58, 61, 62 (top), 65, 66 (left), 68, 71, 72 (top left), 76, 83, 84, 89 , 93 (bottom), 94, 96, 99, 105, 109 (left), 111, 112, 114, 118, 120 (right), 123, 124 (top left), 126, 131, 136, 138, 141 (left), 142, 144, 146, 152 (top right and bottom), 155, 156 (right), 158, 161, 166, 171, 172, 175, 176 (right), 179, 183, 184 © Alex Alberton and Silvia Pellegrinato

MARCO BIANCHI

{ CUCINARE }

**Healthy and Authentic Italian Cooking
for the Whole Family**

HARPER
DESIGN

An Imprint of HarperCollins Publishers

{ CONTENTS }

WELCOME!

To me, cooking is an act of love—love of ourselves, the people we love, and all we hold dear. Even talking about food and health is, in my opinion, a way of expressing that love. The book that you are holding in your hands is dedicated to all of you—those who have followed me for years and demonstrate their affection for me every day, and those who have just decided to purchase it out of curiosity. You will find a lot of recipes in these pages, of course, but you'll find more, too: tips for wellness, health advice, some tricks to use in the kitchen, and lots of snapshots of moments in my own daily life.

I aimed to use this book to illustrate a new phase in my life and my career, and I want all of you to be a part of it! My goal remains the same: to promote the rules of good nutrition in my own way, with simple, direct language that begins with a foundation built on science and ends with your tables filled with natural, healthy food—with a lot of fun along the way.

Before I begin, I'd like to put a few things out there. Recently, as I've chatted with people in real life or on social media, I am frequently asked what reasons underlie my diet choices. They're enthusiastic and curious.

My first answer is that I have one rule: There is no single food that can be considered "poison" in and of itself. It all depends on the quantity and quality and on our subjective attitudes. We all take in nutrients from food in the same way.

That's why it's important to talk about science and research and data— even though, I will admit, data isn't always easy to interpret. Data may be murky and inaccessible, and that's why I always try to answer questions as clearly and pleasantly as possible, giving practical advice that can be applied in everyday life. We need to learn to eat not just with our stomachs, but also with our heads. That may sound difficult and boring, monotonous, and even trivial, but I promise you it is not. Eating with your head means learning to respect food, ingredients, and the planet where we live.

On that subject, I naturally cannot help but mention Professor Umberto Veronesi, whom I remember with affection and esteem. It's his "fault" that I am so determined to spread the word about science. I still remember when he told me, "Science is the most powerful tool humanity has to improve people's quality of life and perspective." Nothing truer nor more useful was ever spoken.

It all began with an email. I suggested a crazy project to him, and fewer than forty-eight hours later he called me to talk about it. This was in 2009. At the time I was a biochemistry research technician who simply wanted to go beyond the laboratory . . . He and I would go on to create a relationship of mutual respect, meetings, brainstorming, plans, and goals. Even though he was a very busy man, he was also accessible, funny, energetic, and very knowledgeable about everything—a true philosopher.

When a film director contacted him about a project related to vegetarians, he got me involved. Then, he invited me to contribute a piece to a book he was writing on nutrition. I asked him to be in the opening segment for my TV series and to write the foreword to one of my books, but I also invited him to be a guest at my wedding, because he was a man who I knew would have the right words at one of the most important moments in my life. After that, he asked me to stop addressing him as professor and use his first name, because we were family. I was never able to do it, however!

Each time we met, I was infused with positive energy and with a great desire to learn more, deepen my knowledge, and most of all to share that knowledge. "A researcher has to be curious and be hungry for knowledge," he often told me. "Keep going, because the world needs science and reason."

My friends, the fact that I am here today telling you about science as I do every day is something I owe solely to him. He was a man who taught me about life—a wonderful person who believed in my abilities and kept pushing me forward.

I hope that I have painted you a clear picture of my love for science, and that you will be tempted by the recipes in this book, but by including photos of my daily life, I also hope to impress upon you that to me living a free and conscious life is a choice: no labels, no obligation or requirement that you cook in one particular style.

I love nourishing myself this way, and I love cooking with my head for my family, my friends, and the other people I love, because cooking is the best way I know to express love.

COOKING IS . . .

Cooking is truly an act of love for ourselves and those around us. Even offering a recipe to a friend is a gesture of affection. It's a little like the way we interact on social media. That's why I wanted to include some of your thoughts in this book. (Though I have to say, it was really, really hard to choose the people to include!)

VALENTINA Cooking is an act of love . . . like caressing someone's heart. It's taking care of yourself and the people you love; that's why we cook with our hearts. It's consoling someone we love and lifting up someone when they're down. It's filling the kitchen with delicious smells that bring us back to our childhoods. It also can be a way to capture a person's heart. It means filling a plate with thousands of colors and still tasting simple flavors. Nursing a baby is the first act of love. Cooking brings us back to that time of warmth and joy.

BRUNA To me, cooking is a way to spend a half hour with my daughter, sweet and fragile Hikikomori, because she has to come out of her room—the comfort zone where she's been hiding out for the last four years—to eat.

MARCO Time in the kitchen is often spent waiting. In the kitchen we walk a sensory path toward beauty and we nourish our love. As the saying goes, "To wait is the infinitive of the verb 'to love.'"

GIULIA Cooking is letting go of all the tension, worry, and sadness, and, like magic, putting only joy, love, and happiness on the plate!

LAURA Cooking is a moment of healthy solitude, wonderful sharing, and deep understanding of others.

MATTEO Cooking is getting back in touch with nature and its smells and tastes. The taste of a dish is easily accessed and manipulated by big business, but there's always the flavor of the human hand, an experience that is infinitely more complex and permits food to bear the individual signature of those who cooked it, tended to it, thought about it, and its own special qualities. Taste cannot be falsified and requires time and effort. That taste is, basically, the taste of love.

SABRINA Cooking is mixing, cooking, and serving emotions.

MICHELA Cooking is care and love. My mother always cooked when she couldn't tell me how she felt in words; today I do the same with my family. In my kitchen sometimes there is fatigue and stress; other times there is joy and a love of life. What I mean is, look at what I'm cooking and you'll know how I feel today.

TINA Either you like cooking or you don't, because it's passion, love, ecstasy for the mind, the eyes, and the palate. I love creating things in the kitchen, especially for my family.

SILVANA Cooking is the thought of love, and I love.

SHARON As a child I played with my sister at guessing the ingredients in the dishes that our Iranian mother was making. And when something was particularly good, she told us, "There's a special ingredient that makes everything taste better—love." ♥

CINZIA If you "take care" of anyone in any way, you experience life day by day, moment by moment, and that care never feels wasted. One of the ways I take care of my loved ones is to cook, because cooking is a choice, a ritual, a gesture that makes me feel good. Cooking nourishes not only the body, but the soul.

Veru   Marco   Vivienne

OPERATING INSTRUCTIONS

This isn't your usual cookbook.

It doesn't contain any miracle diets.

It's not a memoir.

It's not a scientific encyclopedia.

This is a book about unbridled passion for good, healthy, practical cooking in the spot where the Mediterranean diet and preventive health meet and provide ideas about what to put on the table every day.

Ideas good for grown-ups and kids, for the whole family.

Let's imagine we're going grocery shopping. We purchase five or six items and then head home to cook something tasty. That's how to read this book: the ingredients chosen and photographed for each basket represent a base for a handful of recipes that don't waste one bit of what you've bought.

Obviously, in order to help you cook well and to use the ingredients in the baskets as best as possible, I'm starting with the presumption that you always—and I mean always—have certain ingredients in your pantry and

your freezer, such as extra-virgin olive oil, cold-pressed organic corn and sunflower oil, whole-grain and partially whole-grain flours, various types of whole (or pearled) grains (including barley, farro, corn, quinoa, rice), onions, lemons, garlic, aromatic herbs (frozen are fine), tomato sauce, fat-free milk, various types of nondairy milk, and Greek yogurt.

Only when you have a fully equipped pantry will you be able to cook without making mistakes and also guarantee that you are healthy and that your palate is treated to great-tasting food with preventive power.

Every once in a while in this book you'll come across a page I have hashtagged #tasteandhealth. There you'll find factoids from the world of science (remember that my background is as a biochemistry research technician) and my years of lab work—especially my current position as scientific educator for the Fondazione Umberto Veronesi.

10 THINGS I DO FOR BETTER HEALTH

Here are the reasons behind some of the choices I make in the kitchen. Don't make the mistake of thinking that good taste and pleasure are not compatible with healthy eating.

Why do I choose whole-grain items? Why do I eat very little sugar? Why do I love extra-virgin olive oil so much?

The answers to these—and other—questions can be found in the following pages. I hope these answers will clear up any questions you have and provide clear explanations of scientific data in order to help you understand how easy it is to eat with your head in a healthy way.

Recommended
daily allowance
of salt

1

{ **Why do I limit salt and replace some of it with herbs and spices and always say to cook in "lightly salted water"?** }

It's simple! The average Italian man consumes more than 4,100 milligrams of sodium (about 1¾ teaspoons or 10.6 grams salt) per day, and the average Italian woman consumes nearly 3,200 milligrams sodium (about 1⅓ teaspoons or 8.2 grams salt). Both are nearly double the 2,000 milligrams sodium (about 1 teaspoon or 5 grams salt) suggested by the World Health Organization (WHO). It's important to find alternatives for flavoring your food. Too much salt causes hypertension, cardiovascular disease, obesity, osteoporosis, and cancer.

{ Why do I always specify "whole-grain" whenever possible? }

Fiber is synonymous with good health, and getting a good daily dose of fiber in your diet protects you. Not only does fiber keep you regular, but it's also associated with lowering total cholesterol and LDL (that's "bad" cholesterol) and improving postprandial glycemia. Fiber is also a prebiotic: That means it selectively nurtures the growth and activity of intestinal micro-biota, lactobacillus and bifidobacteria, the "good" bacteria in our intestines. An active intestine is synonymous with a strong and capable immune system!

The recommended "dose" of fiber is 25 to 30 grams per day, according to WHO guidelines.

Why are my desserts less sweet than traditional treats?

The WHO updated its guidelines for sugar consumption and strongly recommends cutting back so that sugar (meaning glucose, fructose, and table sugar) represents less than 10 percent of total daily intake. However, the WHO goes further and recommends that sugar actually represent less than 5 percent of daily intake (about 25 grams or 6 teaspoons). Indeed, sugar raises your blood sugar quickly and encourages inflammation and cell growth.

Since cells use sugar as their primary source of fuel, there is a theory that excess consumption of sugar may cause inflammation and growth of tumors, which means it can both increase the risk of getting sick and aggravate any existing disease.

{ Why do I choose some fats over others? }

Extra-virgin olive oil (EVOO) helps keep your cardiovascular system young, strong, and healthy, because it contains good fats. It also fights tumors with polyphenols. And that's not all. This oil contains oleocanthal, a compound with anti-inflammatory properties that acts like a typical nonsteroidal anti-inflammatory. (That's what can make your throat burn slightly after you swallow extra-virgin olive oil.) EVOO is rich in polyphenols, so consuming it at every meal improves postprandial glycemia and the lipid profiles of those with prediabetes. All of these benefits are also found in nut and seed oils.

{ Why do I include so many vegetables in every recipe? }

Because we eat too few vegetables. We should be eating five servings of fruits and vegetables every day: two servings of vegetables and three of fruit, for a total of about 2 pounds (900 grams). Try to make your plate as colorful as possible by using a variety of ingredients. That way you'll take in plenty of minerals (potassium, magnesium, copper, zinc, calcium, iron, and so on), antioxidants (anthocyanins, lutein, flavonoids, and so on), and vitamins (A, C, E, folate, and more).

{ Why do I sometimes call for dairy milk and sometimes call for plant-based milks? }

Should you choose dairy milk (*vaccino*) or plant-based milks like soy (*soia*) and almond (*mandoria*)? Only you can answer that question. Are you lactose intolerant, allergic to milk, or diabetic, or are you subject to blood sugar swings or high cholesterol? Then you've probably already selected a type of milk that works for you. Always keep an eye on added sugar and the type of beverage. Rice milk is very starchy, for instance, and added sugar raises its glycemic index further; by comparison, fat-free milk as well as lactose-free fat-free milk have less impact on your body if consumed in line with the recommended daily allowance. Each recipe has a type of milk that works best, just as with individual palates and bodies. We don't all digest food the same way, so let's vary our diets. Your body will thank you!

VACCINO

SOIA

MANDORLA

CUISINE

SOIA

GRECO

VACCINO

Do you prefer soy, Greek, or dairy milk?

{ Why do I say you need to move a little each day? }

Moving consumes calories, but more important, it reduces the level of "bad" cholesterol (LDL) and raises the level of "good" cholesterol (HDL, or high-density lipoprotein, which carries excess cholesterol from tissues to the liver, which then works to remove it).

Walking lowers blood pressure and helps to control the risk of type 2 diabetes and of certain tumors that are influenced by hormonal activity, which can be stabilized through exercise.

I do CrossFit and functional fitness training, which combines aerobic and anaerobic exercise in a total workout that lasts less than a half hour.

Exercise makes us happy. Try it and you'll see!

{ Why don't I use 00 flour? }

The answer is simple: Italian "tipo 00" flour is the type of flour that offers the fewest benefits, because it's the most refined type. (The American equivalent is unbleached all-purpose flour.) As wheat is processed to make white flour, the most nutritious parts are removed. These include the germ, which is rich in vitamins, minerals, and amino acids, and the bran, which provides fiber. In the end, you're left with just starch, which is pure sugar. White flour doesn't do anything for your body; in fact, it raises the level of blood sugars.

Instead, use whole wheat flour, as it still contains all the nutrients, such as vitamins, minerals, and fiber.

In Italy, there are also a number of flours that fall in between refined white and whole wheat flours:

Tipo 0 flour: This is slightly less refined than "tipo 00" and contains a few parts of the bran and therefore has more fiber.

Tipo 1 flour: This falls in the middle of the range and has even more bran and fiber than tipo 0.

Tipo 2 flour: This is semi whole wheat flour and is a compromise between white flour and whole wheat flour.

Vary the
colors and flavors
you enjoy every day!

{ Why don't I cook (or eat) fresh meat or processed meat (cold cuts and preserved meat)? }

If you go over the weekly recommendation of a little over 1 pound (500 grams) of red meat (pork, beef, lamb, horse) or less than 2 ounces (50 grams) of processed meat, you increase your risk of cardiovascular disease and cancer—especially cancer of the gastrointestinal tract and especially rectal cancer, which is affected by the consumption and overeating of meat. This has been reported by the World Cancer Research Fund, which provides solid, reliable data.

What should you be eating instead? Legumes and grains, which provide a nutritionally complete meal. Legumes and grains are rich in vitamins (B1, B2, B3, B6, folate, and biotin) and protein and are the perfect replacement for animal protein sources.

{ Why am I always photographed barefoot and often with a cup of coffee in my hand? }

The answer to this is simple, too. Very simple. Ever since I was a kid I've walked barefoot at home and anywhere else that I could. (We don't grow out of all of our childhood habits.) I love to feel the ground beneath my feet without anything coming between us.

As for coffee, up to five or six espressos a day offer protection. Coffee is a friend to your arteries, because it's full of powerful antioxidants. Of course, this amount of caffeine might not be a good idea for people with certain health issues.

Coffee is also good for your liver, because it can prevent diseases such as cirrhosis, and it stops the formation of gallstones, which can be painful. And contrary to popular belief, caffeine has an analgesic effect: It's a vasoconstrictor. That means it narrows the blood vessels so that less blood flows through them—that makes it excellent for preventing headaches.

{ BASKET № 1 }

Finely Ground Cornmeal,
Fresh Anchovies,
Soy Milk,
Parsley,
Ground Turmeric,
Chickpeas

RECIPES

Herbed

Pink

Classic

Tuna

Eggless Mayonnaise

✓ **MAKES 1⅓ CUPS (300 GRAMS)**

¾ cup plus 2 tablespoons (220 ml) organic sunflower oil

¼ cup plus 3 tablespoons (100 ml) unsweetened soy milk

2 tablespoons apple cider vinegar or lemon juice

1 teaspoon mustard

½ teaspoon ground turmeric

Pinch of salt

In a container with high sides, combine all the ingredients. Mix with an immersion blender on high speed until dense and creamy.

This mayonnaise will keep in the refrigerator in a tightly sealed container for about 10 days.

Variations

1 Tuna

Drain 2 (4.5 oz/125 g) cans water-packed tuna. Flake into the mayonnaise after it is blended. Mix with a fork until combined.

2 Zing

Do you like a flavor punch? Add zest to your mayonnaise with cornichons and capers. Chop 5 cornichons and 1 tablespoon capers and fold them into the blended mayonnaise.

3 Spicy

Grate a ½-inch (1-cm) piece fresh ginger and add to the ingredients before blending into a mayonnaise.

4 Herbed

Mince 10 chives and the leaves of 2 sprigs of dill and add them to the mayonnaise after it is blended.

5 Pink

Add a chunk of cooked beet to the ingredients before blending the mayonnaise.

#tasteandhealth

Some nutrients are recommended to help combat inflammation. Among the most effective of these substances is a fatty acid called eicosapentaenoic acid (**EPA**), which yields the greatest anti-inflammatory effect when there is little arachidonic acid in the body. **FATTY FISH** have especially high levels of EPA.

Crispy Anchovies with Lemon

Ileana, the mother of my friend Andrea, first introduced me to this dish! You're going to love it. From sea to table, anchovies are a humble food, but really delicious. This dish is habit-forming: You've been warned!

SERVES 4

10½ ounces (300 g) cleaned fresh anchovies, boned and butterflied
2 to 3 tablespoons finely ground cornmeal
⅓ cup (50 g) pine nuts
Pinch of salt
Grated zest and juice of 2 to 3 organic lemons
Extra-virgin olive oil spray

Preheat the oven to 350°F to 400°F (180°C to 200°C). Line a baking sheet or pan with parchment paper.

Arrange the anchovies on the pan skin side down in a single layer. Sprinkle the cornmeal over the anchovies and press down gently to adhere. Sprinkle on the pine nuts, salt, lemon zest, and lemon juice.

Spray with olive oil and bake until browned on top, about 20 minutes.

You'll be astounded by the incredible smell of lemon that fills your kitchen!

Pan de Mej

This recipe makes 6 large corn buns, but you can make them any size or shape that you like. I've even used this dough to make little tiny cookies.

MAKES 6 LARGE BUNS (ABOUT 4½ INCHES/11 CM IN DIAMETER)

1¼ cups (200 g) finely ground cornmeal
¾ cup (100 g) rice flour or whole-grain durum flour
⅔ cup (80 g) organic powdered sugar
1½ teaspoons baking powder
Grated zest of 1 organic lemon
¼ cup (60 ml) organic corn oil
⅓ cup (75 ml) milk

Preheat the oven to 340°F (170°C). Line a baking sheet with parchment paper.

In a large bowl, combine the cornmeal, rice flour, sugar, baking powder, and lemon zest.

Stir the oil and milk into the dry ingredients and mix with a fork until combined. Divide the dough into 6 portions and form into buns, or use an ice cream scoop to make spheres.

Place the buns on the prepared pan and flatten them gently with your fingertips. Bake until the tops crack, about 20 minutes.

Variations

1 Add 1 teaspoon matcha green tea powder to the dough to give the buns a pleasant color and make them even better for you!

2 For a chocolate chip version, knead ⅔ cup (100 grams) chocolate chips into the dough and replace the dairy milk with almond milk.

#tasteandhealth

How I love **GREEN TEA**! Its benefits for your cardio-vascular system (due to its high content of polyphenols, especially catechins) are well known, and its cancer-fighting abilities are still being studied. You should definitely always have green tea in your cupboard. (Obviously, I'm talking about tea leaves—not sweetened green tea-flavored beverages.) I especially love matcha, which is aromatic, herbaceous, and a beautiful green color. It's especially good for those with allergies, as it contains a catechin called epigallocatechin. Articles published in various international scientific journals suggest that this antioxidant blocks the histamine and immuno-globulin E involved in immune responses and typical allergy symptoms.

Green Toasts

You need an immersion blender and a mini food processor to prepare many of my recipes. Always have them at the ready.

SERVES 4

Salt

1⅔ cups (250 g) shelled fresh or frozen peas

2½ ounces (70 g) goat cheese

5 fresh mint leaves

3 tablespoons plus 1 teaspoon (50 ml) extra-virgin olive oil

Pink peppercorns, to taste

Multigrain bread, sliced and toasted

In a saucepan of lightly salted water, cook the peas until just bright green, then drain and allow to cool.

Transfer the peas to a mini food processor. Add the goat cheese, mint leaves, oil, and pink peppercorns. With the machine running, add enough water (about 3 tablespoons/50 ml) in a thin stream to make a creamy spread.

Spread the pea mixture on the toasts.

Don't use canned peas. They won't give you the bright green color you want!

Falafel

I love falafel hot or cold. They even win over people who claim not to like beans dressed with olive oil and lemon juice!

✓ SERVES 4

Salt
⅔ cup (100 g) frozen shelled
 edamame
Leaves of 1 sprig parsley
1 yellow onion, peeled and
 cut into chunks
2 cups (500 g) canned chickpeas,
 drained and rinsed
5 tablespoons extra-virgin
 olive oil
Juice of 1 lemon
1 tablespoon ground cumin
½ teaspoon ground turmeric
3 tablespoons (30 g) finely
 ground cornmeal

Preheat the oven to 400°F (200°C). Line a baking pan with parchment paper.

In a saucepan of lightly salted water, blanch the edamame. Drain and let cool slightly.

In a food processor, combine the parsley and onion and process. Add the edamame, chickpeas, oil, lemon juice, cumin, and turmeric and process until the mixture forms a dense paste with a few chunkier chickpeas in it. Season to taste with salt.

Use a small ice cream scoop (or your hands) to form small balls of the mixture. Roll the balls in the cornmeal and set them on the prepared pan as you make them.

Bake until golden, at least 15 minutes.

P.S. You can also cook the falafel on the stovetop in a lightly but thoroughly oiled nonstick pan.

BASKET Nº 2

Walnuts, Almonds, Hazelnuts, "Tipo 2" or White Whole Wheat Flour, Apples, Extra-Virgin Olive Oil, Lentils, Raspberries

RECIPES

#tasteandhealth

There is a great deal of scientific evidence showing that **WALNUTS** protect against chronic illnesses, including **METABOLIC SYNDROME** and **TYPE 2 DIABETES**. Eating walnuts also seems to improve body mass index (BMI) and body adiposity without causing weight gain: Participants in the PREDIMED study and in NHS and HPFS studies who ate large amounts of walnuts had lower body mass and smaller waist measurements. Like all nuts, walnuts do not contain cholesterol. Indeed, they can lower cholesterol if you make them a regular part of your diet!

Lentil and Walnut Salad

The trick to using herbs and spices is to keep them in a visible spot in your kitchen. We do the opposite with salt and keep very little at hand.

SERVES 4

1½ cups (300 g) cooked lentils, well drained

1⅓ cups (150 g) walnuts, finely chopped

¾ cup (80 g) drained oil-packed sun-dried tomatoes, finely chopped

1 leek, white and light-green parts, minced

Leaves of 1 bunch parsley, minced

Finely grated zest and juice of 1 organic lemon

Extra-virgin olive oil

Piece of fresh ginger

In a large bowl, combine the cooked lentils, walnuts, sun-dried tomatoes, leek, and parsley and toss to combine well. Drizzle on the lemon juice, toss, and taste. Dress with a little olive oil if needed.

Sprinkle the lemon zest on top and grate a little ginger over the salad just before serving.

P.S. Sun-dried tomatoes are a source of concentrated iron, phosphorous, and, most of all, carotenoids. If you prefer not to use the type in oil, use dry-pack or salt-preserved dried tomatoes. You'll have to soak them in water for at least 30 minutes to soften. If they were salt-packed, rinse them very well to eliminate excess salt.

Granola

This is one of my most requested recipes and one that I love because it contains so many ingredients that are good for your health (especially thyroid health, thanks to all the iodine and sele-nium) in the proper amounts, and also because I see it as a way of being good to yourself starting with breakfast. I never go without breakfast: a cup of coffee, nice and bitter, yogurt, and granola!

MAKES 5 TO 6 CUPS (600 TO 700 G)

5½ cups (500 g) rolled oats
½ cup (50 g) almonds, coarsely chopped
⅓ cup (50 g) hazelnuts, coarsely chopped
¼ cup (40 g) raisins, coarsely chopped
¾ cup (80 g) unsweetened shredded coconut
Pinch of salt
¼ cup (60 ml) organic corn oil
2 tablespoons plus 2 teaspoons (40 ml) organic sunflower oil
½ cup (130 ml) maple syrup
¼ cup plus 2 tablespoons (130 g) honey

Preheat the oven to 320°F (160°C). Line a baking sheet with parchment paper.

In a large bowl, combine the dry ingredients. Add the oils, maple syrup, and honey. Sprinkle on a couple of tablespoons of water and toss with your hands or a spatula until thoroughly combined. Spread on the prepared pan and bake for 20 minutes.

Remove the pan from the oven and mix the granola without breaking up any clumps. Bake until crunchy, an additional 10 to 20 minutes.

Remove from the oven and allow to cool. Use your hands to break up into irregular pieces.

Granola will keep for a couple of months in a tightly sealed glass container.

I never skip breakfast!

Kisses

As a kid I was curious about everything. I alternated between spending time with my mother, Cristina, in the kitchen—where she was often preparing these cookies—and spending time in my room, where I "studied" insects under a microscope.

MAKES 15 SANDWICH COOKIES

⅔ cup (100 g) blanched hazelnuts

1⅔ cups (200 g) white whole wheat flour or Italian "tipo 2" flour

⅔ cup (80 g) organic powdered sugar

¼ cup (60 ml) organic corn oil

⅔ cup (100 g) dark chocolate (72% cacao)

Preheat the oven to 350°F (180°C). Line a baking sheet with parchment paper and set aside.

In a mini food processor, grind the hazelnuts to a paste. The paste should feel oily.

In a bowl, combine the hazelnut paste, flour, sugar, and corn oil. Pull off a piece of the dough and with your hands shape it into a small ball. Place the ball on the prepared pan. Continue with remaining dough to make an even number of cookies. Flatten the balls slightly and bake until set and light golden, about 20 minutes.

Meanwhile, melt the chocolate in the top of a double boiler and cool until it has a thick consistency.

When the cookies have cooled, sandwich them in pairs with melted chocolate in between.

Variation

For friends with celiac disease: Replace the wheat flour with rice flour. Your cookies will be delicious!

Apple-Walnut Salad with Balsamic-Honey Dressing

Apples are packed with polyphenols, phytosterols, vitamin C, and pectin. Always keep a good supply on hand, and be sure to eat the peel (as long as it's organic, of course!).

SERVES 4

SALAD

2 heads Belgian endive, slivered
1 head radicchio, slivered
2 Granny Smith apples, peeled
  (if not organic) and diced
1¾ cups (200 g) walnuts, roughly
  chopped
⅓ cup (50 g) raisins

DRESSING

¼ cup (60 ml) extra-virgin
  olive oil
¼ cup plus 2 tablespoons
  (90 ml) balsamic vinegar
1 teaspoon honey
Pinch of salt

FOR THE SALAD: In a salad bowl, combine the Belgian endive, radicchio, apples, walnuts, and raisins.

FOR THE DRESSING: In a small bowl, whisk together the olive oil, balsamic, honey, and salt.
   Drizzle the dressing over the salad and toss until well combined.

#tasteandhealth

A study published in the *Journal of the International Society of Sports Nutrition* demonstrated that young runners in the twenty to thirty age group have their best performances when they eat energy bars or raisins as supplements. **RAISINS** are energy in its purest form.

They are a good source of sugars and also contain fiber, calcium, and oleanolic acid (a powerful anti-inflammatory), in addition to potassium, calcium, and phosphorous. Thanks to their high content of phytonutrients, they are effective anti-inflammatories and antioxidants.

Ricotta Berry Tartlets

SERVES 6 TO 8

CRUST

2 cups (250 g) white whole wheat
flour or Italian "tipo 2" flour
⅔ cup (80 g) organic powdered
sugar
Finely grated zest of 1 organic
lemon
¼ cup (60 ml) organic
sunflower oil

FILLING

Generous 1 cup (250 g)
Italian-style ricotta cheese or
well-drained regular ricotta
½ cup (70 g) organic powdered
sugar
⅓ cup (60 g) quartered
strawberries
½ cup (60 g) raspberries

FOR THE CRUST: In a bowl, combine the flour, sugar, and lemon zest. Add the oil and ¼ cup (60 ml) water and knead together to form a smooth and compact dough. Shape the dough into a ball, wrap in plastic wrap, and refrigerate for 1 hour.

MEANWHILE, FOR THE FILLING: In a bowl, vigorously whisk the ricotta with the sugar until a cream-like density is reached.

Preheat the oven to 350°F (180°C).

Roll out the dough and cut out rounds to line disposable aluminum mini tartlet pans or silicone mini tartlet pans. (You can also roll the dough into a single large round and use it to line a 9-inch/23-cm tart pan.)

Put a few tablespoons of the ricotta filling in each tartlet shell and bake until light brown on top, 30 to 40 minutes. (The large tart will take about 10 minutes longer.) Cool the tart completely and top with the strawberries and raspberries.

Variations

These are so delicious! You can also vary them by folding about ¼ cup (50 g) diced candied fruit or about ½ cup (70 g) chocolate chips into the ricotta. Or fill the tartlets with ⅔ cup (200 g) of a healthy hazelnut spread and skip the ricotta completely. Top hazelnut tartlets with ¾ cup (70 grams) chopped hazelnuts.

Pancakes with Bananas, Raspberries, and Honey

Every night I set my alarm for 6:00 or 7:00 a.m. All night long I dream of recipes, and in the morning I jot them down as I'm making breakfast.

MAKES 12 PANCAKES

1¾ cups plus 1 tablespoon (220 g) white whole wheat flour or Italian "tipo 2" flour
1½ cups (350 ml) milk
¼ cup (30 g) organic powdered sugar
½ teaspoon baking powder
1 tablespoon organic corn oil (for the pan)
2 bananas, sliced
1 pint (250 g) raspberries
2 tablespoons honey

In a large bowl, beat together the flour and milk, then beat in the sugar and baking powder. Be sure there are no lumps. (You can use an immersion blender if you like.)

Heat a nonstick pan over medium heat and add just a drop of oil. Pour about ¼ cup (60 ml) of the batter into the pan. When bubbles appear on the surface, flip the pancake and cook the other side. Repeat with the remaining batter and more oil.

Stack the pancakes, placing the banana slices, raspberries, and honey in between and on top of them.

Serve them with lots of fruit and honey.

#tasteandhealth

No doubt about it: Hazelnuts are good for our DNA. Indeed, a recent study showed that regularly consuming **HAZELNUTS** can stabilize levels of LDL cholesterol—the "bad" kind—and triglycerides. And that's not all: They stop cellular aging and have anti-inflammatory and antiviral properties thanks to their selenium, vitamin E (the star antioxidant), and flavonoids.

Crumble

I started cooking with my daughter, Vivienne, when she was only fifteen months old. The first thing we made together was crumble—the best I've ever tasted!

Crumble is delicious with yogurt in the morning. You can also combine it with fresh fruit for a fantastic fruit crumble dessert: Cut fruits such as pears and apples into very small dice, spread in a pan, sprinkle the crumble on top, and bake. Or, if you prefer larger pieces of fruit, sauté them briefly before putting them in the pan.

MAKES APPROXIMATELY 2½ CUPS (300 G) CRUMBLE

¾ cup (120 g) blanched hazelnuts
1⅔ cups (200 g) white whole wheat flour or Italian "tipo 2" flour
¼ teaspoon baking powder
¼ cup plus 1 tablespoon (60 g) muscovado sugar
¼ cup (60 ml) organic sunflower oil
2 teaspoons honey

Preheat the oven to 340°F (170°C). Line a baking sheet with parchment paper.

Soak the hazelnuts in warm water for 50 minutes. Drain, but absolutely do not dry them! In a mini food processor, grind the nuts to coarse.

Transfer the hazelnuts to a bowl and stir in the flour, baking powder, sugar, oil, and honey.

Spread the mixture on the prepared pan. It should be in large, irregular pieces and not densely packed. Don't worry if it looks sandy.

Bake until crisp, about 20 minutes.

Variations

MAKES 2½ CUPS (300 G) CRUMBLE

Omit the wheat flour and use ¾ cup (100 g) brown rice flour and ½ cup plus 1 tablespoon (100 g) finely ground cornmeal.

1 **Do you have friends with celiac disease or are you interested in eating less gluten?**
Here's a gluten-free version!

2 **Interested in trying a cocoa crumble?**
Add a heaping tablespoon of sifted unsweetened cocoa powder.

BASKET Nº 3

Chickpea Flour,
"Tipo 2" or White
Whole Wheat Flour,
Leeks, Pumpkin,
Extra-Virgin Olive Oil,
Frozen Peas

RECIPES

Savory Leek Tart

This is the perfect appetizer. Slice it into wedges and serve it right on a cutting board as the first course for a dinner with friends. It can be made in advance, too. In fact, it tastes even better if it has a chance to sit!

✓ **SERVES 6**

CRUST

2⅔ cups (300 g) white whole wheat flour or Italian "tipo 2" flour
Pinch of salt
Pinch of baking soda
⅓ cup (80 ml) extra-virgin olive oil
2 tablespoons apple cider vinegar

FILLING

Extra-virgin olive oil, for sautéing
4 leeks, thinly sliced
Salt and pepper
Generous 1 cup (250 g) Italian-style ricotta cheese or well-drained regular ricotta

FOR THE CRUST: In a bowl, combine the flour, salt, baking soda, oil, and vinegar and knead by hand, adding water a tablespoon or so at a time, until you have a smooth and compact dough. (You will need about ½ cup/120 ml water.) Shape into a ball, wrap in plastic wrap, and refrigerate for 1 hour.

MEANWHILE, FOR THE FILLING: In a nonstick skillet, heat a few tablespoons olive oil over medium-high heat. Add the leeks, season with a pinch of salt and pepper, and cook until softened. When the leeks are soft, add the ricotta. Stir until well combined, then remove from the heat.

Preheat the oven to 350°F (180°C). Line the bottom of a 6-inch (15-cm) pie pan or earthenware dish with a round of parchment paper.

Roll out the crust and use it to line the prepared pan. Fill the crust with the ricotta filling and bake until the crust is well done, 45 to 50 minutes.

Variation

Replace the leeks and ricotta with 2 cups (400 g) diced peeled pumpkin or winter squash, 5 ounces (150 g) soft goat cheese, and fresh thyme leaves.

Cook the pumpkin in a nonstick pan with a drizzle of oil, a spoonful or two of water, and a little salt and pepper. When the squash is soft, blend with the goat cheese and thyme. Make and fill the tart shell as above and bake at 350°F (180°C) until the crust is well done, 45 to 50 minutes.

With leeks

With pumpkin

Eggless Leek Frittata

My daughter, Vivienne, goes crazy for this dish. Her personal preference is the addition of a little fresh rosemary (picked by her) at the end and some grated aged sheep's cheese in place of the salt. She's a real gourmet! Obviously, you can customize it any way you like.

✓ SERVES 4 TO 6

2 cups plus 3 tablespoons (200 g) chickpea flour
1⅔ cups (400 ml) lukewarm water
¼ teaspoon salt
Pinch of pepper
Extra-virgin olive oil
2 leeks, thinly sliced

In a large bowl, whisk together the chickpea flour and water by hand or using an immersion blender until thoroughly blended. There should not be any lumps.

Stir in the salt and pepper and a couple of tablespoons of extra-virgin olive oil. Stir again and let the batter rest in the refrigerator for 20 minutes.

Stir the leeks into the batter.

Lightly oil a nonstick skillet with olive oil and place over medium-high heat until the pan is very hot. Pour enough batter into the pan to fill the whole pan but be no deeper than ¼ inch (0.5 cm). Cook for about 10 minutes, then flip the frittata out onto a plate. Return it to the pan browned side up and cook the second side for another 10 minutes. Continue with more batter and oil (how many frittatas you can make will depend on the size of your pan).

P.S. You can also bake the frittata. Preheat the oven to 425°F (220°C). Line an 8-inch (20-cm) baking pan with parchment paper. Pour in the batter and bake until set and nicely browned, about 20 minutes. Brush the surface of the pan lightly with oil. There's no need to flip the frittata if you bake it. Once it is cooked, cut into squares and serve warm!

Pumpkin Soup with Ginger

Pumpkin has been used for its calming effects since ancient times. It also assists in the production of serotonin and is rich in beta-carotene, which protects us from free radicals and is a good anti-inflammatory.

✓ SERVES 4

3 tablespoons extra-virgin olive oil

1 winter squash (2½ lbs/1.2 kg), such as pumpkin, kabocha, or kuri, peeled, seeded, and diced

1 shallot, minced

1¼ cups (300 ml) milk

Salt and pepper

1 piece ginger, peeled, grated to taste

¾ cup (200 g) canned cannellini, drained and rinsed

In a Dutch oven or soup pot, heat the oil over medium heat. Add the squash, shallot, and a few tablespoons of water and cook the squash to soften. When the squash is about halfway cooked, add the milk and season with salt and pepper. Grate in the ginger, stir to combine, and continue cooking until the squash is soft.

Add the beans and ½ cup (120 ml) water, then use an immersion blender to puree until smooth. Your soup is ready.

Variation

To make this into a one-pot meal, add 3 potatoes (sweet potatoes work well) or 1⅔ cups (320 g) black rice, brown basmati rice, or barley, along with 2¼ cups (500 ml) milk, or simply serve with a few slices of toasted whole-grain bread.

#tasteandhealth

GINGER is a plant in the same family as cardamom and hails from the Far East. It contains various healthful substances—zingiberene and gingerols—that are strong anti-inflammatories and anti-oxidants that fight cancer. It also aids digestion and has a positive effect on the gastro-intestinal system. It is often used to calm the nausea of motion sickness and morning sickness, as well as alleviate indigestion and flatulence. Fresh ginger may be grated, or you can crush it using a garlic press (though do set one aside just for this purpose). Dried ginger (the kind without sugar) is excellent! When I begin to lose my voice, I find it the best remedy. I eat a little cube every 2 hours during the day, and by evening I'm back to normal!

Pumpkin and Chickpea Spread

Use every part of the pumpkin! Save the seeds and eat them raw or roast them. Not only do they make a tasty snack, but they're rich in cucurbitin, which is a big help with many urinary issues in both men and women. Serve with crackers or crudites.

✓ SERVES 4

2¾ cups (14 oz/400 g) diced, peeled, and seeded winter squash, such as pumpkin, kabocha, or kuri
Extra-virgin olive oil
⅔ cup (150 g) canned chickpeas, drained and rinsed
⅔ cup (100 g) feta cheese
Fresh thyme leaves

In a nonstick skillet, braise the squash in a small amount of olive oil with a few tablespoons of water over medium heat until softened.

Transfer the squash to a blender and add the chickpeas and feta. Puree to spreading consistency.

Transfer the mixture to a bowl, brush the surface of the spread with olive oil and sprinkle with the fresh thyme. Cover and refrigerate for 1 hour to firm up.

Pea, Zucchini, and Goat Cheese Pesto

This is the perfect condiment to elevate any dish and make it unique! Use this pesto on pasta or barley, or spread it on toasted whole wheat bread! If you prepare the pesto in advance, oil the surface so it won't turn brown and will maintain its great taste!

✓ MAKES ABOUT 2 CUPS (500 G)

3 zucchini, sliced into rounds
1 cup (150 g) frozen peas
1 shallot, diced
¼ cup (60 ml) extra-virgin olive oil
3 ounces (80 g) goat cheese
Salt and pepper

In a large skillet, cook the zucchini slices, peas, and shallot in a small amount of water until tender. When they are about halfway done, add the olive oil and continue cooking.

Transfer the mixture to a blender, add the goat cheese and a pinch of salt and pepper, and puree.

Variation

✓ MAKES ABOUT 2 CUPS (500 G)

1⅓ cups (200 g) frozen peas
2⅔ cups (400 g) frozen shelled edamame
1 yellow onion, thinly sliced
Salt and pepper
3 tablespoons extra-virgin olive oil
Scant ½ cup (100 g) Italian-style ricotta cheese or well-drained regular ricotta

Edamame, Pea, and Ricotta Pesto
In a skillet, cook the peas, edamame, and onion in a few tablespoons of water with a pinch of salt and pepper. When they are about halfway done, add the olive oil and continue cooking.

Transfer half of the cooked pea mixture to a blender. Add the ricotta and puree. Your pesto is ready! Use this pesto on pasta, ravioli, barley, farro—anything you like, really. Serve the dish garnished with the remaining whole peas and edamame and a generous grinding of black pepper.

Buon appetito Vivienne!

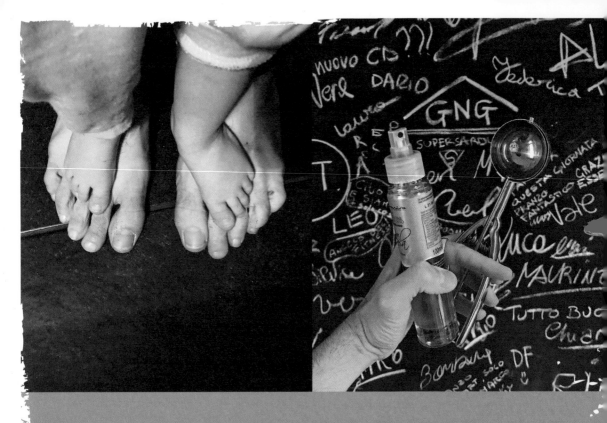

#tasteandhealth

LEGUMES contain as much protein as meat and twice as much as grains. They also contain four essential amino acids (lysine, threonine, valine, and tryptophan) and, when combined with grains, meet our daily requirements for those substances.

According to a study published in the *American Journal of Clinical Nutrition,* eating a serving of about ¾ cup (130 g) of beans per day can help with weight loss. Participants in the study lost ¾ pound (0.34 kg) over six weeks without changing their diets, simply by adding a serving of legumes each day. That change also led to a 31 percent increase in feeling full and satisfied.

Greek Chickpea and Zucchini "Meatballs"

A spray bottle of oil and at least two ice cream scoops of varying sizes are musts for the kitchen. Use them to make excellent vegetarian "meatballs" that can be baked or cooked on the stovetop until crisp but not greasy!

✓ SERVES 4

2 zucchini
5 tablespoons extra-virgin olive oil
10 fresh mint leaves, minced
Salt and pepper
¼ cup (40 g) chickpea flour

Preheat the oven to 350°F (180°C). Line a baking sheet with parchment paper.

Grate the zucchini on the largest holes of a box grater into a bowl.

Add the oil and mint to the zucchini and season with salt and pepper. Add the chickpea flour and mix until well combined.

Using a standard ice cream scoop (or your hands), form the mixture into balls and place them on the prepared pan.

Spray the balls with a small amount of olive oil and bake until firm and lightly browned, about 20 minutes.

Variations

1 Replace the zucchini with two standard-size sweet potatoes. So good!

2 You can also use an equal amount by weight of two standard-size finely grated carrots in place of the grated zucchini. Bake for same amount of time as above.

Mediterranean Sushi

I call this Mediterranean sushi, though it's really a whole wheat flat bread wrapped around an eggless frittata. If there's anything in the ingredient list you don't like, feel free to leave it out—except for the chickpea flour, of course! But if you don't make this you're really missing out!

✓ **SERVES 4**

2 cups plus 3 tablespoons (200 g) chickpea flour

1⅔ cups (400 ml) lukewarm water

¼ teaspoon salt

8 oil-packed sun-dried tomatoes (50 g), minced

½ teaspoon curry powder

Extra-virgin olive oil

Three 8-inch (20-cm) round whole wheat flatbreads (such as piedina, naan, or flour tortillas), preferably made with extra-virgin olive oil

About 1 cup (200 g) spreadable cheese

In a large bowl, beat the chickpea flour and water with a whisk or immersion blender until smooth. There should be no lumps.

Stir in the salt, sun-dried tomatoes, curry powder, and a couple of tablespoons of olive oil. Stir again to combine, then refrigerate for about 30 minutes.

Lightly oil an 8-inch (20-cm) nonstick skillet and heat over medium-high heat until very hot. Add enough batter to cover the bottom of the pan and come a scant ⅛ inch (a few millimeters) up the sides of the pan. Cook for 10 minutes, flip and return to the pan, then cook on the second side for 10 minutes. Repeat to make 3 of these eggless frittatas and allow them to cool.

Gently reheat the flatbreads on the stovetop (the same pan you used is fine) and spread a spoonful of cheese on each. Arrange an eggless frittata on top of the cheese. Roll up and cut into spirals.

P.S. These Mediterranean sushi rolls are good cold, but you can also reheat them on the stovetop before serving if you prefer.

Fill with
seasonal
herbs!

{ BASKET № 4 }

**Beets,
Chickpeas, Avocado,
Celery, Feta Cheese,
Apple, Ginger**

RECIPES

Beet Chips

Beets are an excellent source of iron. Beet chips are sweet—kids love them. Try them and you'll see!

✓ **SERVES 4**

3 beets
Extra-virgin olive oil spray
Salt and pepper

Preheat the oven to 425°F (220°C). Line a baking sheet with parchment paper.

Use a mandoline to very thinly slice the beets. Arrange them on the prepared pan. Spray with olive oil and season with salt and pepper

Bake until crispy and purple, about 40 minutes.

P.S. Beets stain everything, and I mean everything—cutting boards, hands, and even urine, so don't panic if your children pee red after chowing down on these chips!

Beet Cake

This cake is excellent for athletes in training. It combines betaine from beets with the polyphenol and antioxidant activity of cocoa powder and helps to increase muscle strength.

MAKES ONE 9-INCH (23-CM)
CAKE/8 TO 10 SERVINGS

4 ounces (120 g) cooked beets, store-bought or homemade
¾ cup (180 ml) unsweetened almond milk
1 cup (150 g) almonds, roughly chopped
1 cup (130 g) all-purpose flour
⅔ cup (70 g) whole wheat flour
¼ cup plus 2 tablespoons (80 g) muscovado sugar
1 teaspoon unsweetened cocoa powder
1 tablespoon baking powder
Scant ⅓ cup (70 ml) organic corn oil
3½ ounces (100 g) dark chocolate (72% cacao), cut up

Preheat the oven to 350°F (180°C). Line the bottom of a 9-inch (23-cm) cake pan with a round of parchment paper.

In a mini food processor, puree the cooked beets with about half of the almond milk.

In a bowl, mix together the almonds, flours, sugar, cocoa powder, and baking powder. Add the pureed beet mixture to the dry ingredients along with the corn oil and stir to combine.

Place the chocolate and the remaining almond milk in the top of a double boiler and melt, whisking together. Stir into the batter.

Pour the batter into the prepared pan. Bake until a toothpick inserted in the center comes out clean, about 50 minutes. If the toothpick comes out with some batter clinging to it, the cake still needs to bake a little longer.

Hummus

I make hummus at least twice a week to spread on bread or toasts, or as a dip for seasonal vegetables.

√ **MAKES ABOUT 2 CUPS (500 G)**

2 cups (500 g) canned chickpeas, drained and rinsed
2 tablespoons tahini
½ clove garlic
Pinch of ground cumin
Pinch of sweet paprika
¼ cup (60 ml) extra-virgin olive oil
Juice of 1 lemon

In a food processor, puree all the ingredients until smooth. (Omit the garlic if raw garlic is hard for you to digest.) The resulting creamy spread can be served with raw vegetables, toasted bread, focaccia—anything you like. You can even eat it with a spoon!

Variation

To make beet hummus, use ½ Tropea red onion (Italian torpedo onion) in place of the garlic and add 7 ounces (200 g) cooked beets (about two small beets). Puree all the ingredients together, adding a tablespoon or two of water, if necessary, to make a creamy mixture.

Beet Hummus   Classic Hummus

HUMMUS

#tasteandhealth

CHICKPEAS are one of my favorite legumes. I love them in everything. They're rich in magnesium and folate and reduce homocysteine—high levels of this amino acid in the blood increase the risk of heart attack and stroke.

That's not the only heart-health benefit of eating chickpeas: They also lower LDL ("bad") cholesterol and contain lots of omega-3s, which means they prevent depression and lower triglycerides, which in turn fosters a regular heartbeat and decreases the chance of arrhythmia.

Chickpea, Celery, and Feta Salad

Celery is the cook's best friend. You can use every part of it, and it's a good low-calorie snack that has lots of potassium.

✓ **SERVES 4**

2 cups (500 g) canned chickpeas, drained and rinsed
1 cup (150 g) diced feta cheese
1 stalk celery, finely diced
Extra-virgin olive oil
Juice of 1 lemon

In a bowl, combine the chickpeas, feta, and celery. Dress with a drizzle of olive oil and the lemon juice.

P.S. Don't strip the leaves from your celery and toss them! Chop the leaves and serve them like lettuce in a salad: they contain vitamin C, chlorophyll, and lots of key minerals.

Variations

1 In place of the feta use a soft, spreadable cow's milk cheese, such as Quartirolo Lombardo cheese, or an aged sheep's milk cheese.

2 For a vegan salad, use smoked tofu in place of the cheese.

Avocado Tartare with Lime and Red Onion

Avocado is a source of good fats that protect the cardiovascular system. The Italian avocados from Sicily are excellent—give them a try!

SERVES 4

2 avocados, finely diced
1 small red onion, minced
Juice of 1 lime
Salt and pepper
Extra-virgin olive oil

In a bowl, combine the avocados and onion. Drizzle the lime juice over the avocado and onion. Season with salt and pepper and drizzle on a little olive oil.

Use a ring mold to arrange the tartare on plates.

If you don't have a ring mold, you can serve the tartare in a bowl or use it to top toasted bread for a special bruschetta.

You can serve it on bruschetta!

Beet, apple, and ginger

Celery, apple, and ginger

Celery, Apple, and Ginger Juice

This juice and the alternative below are anti-inflammatory and help you digest. They are also very rich in minerals. One thing I would like to note: pineapple does not "melt fat," as is often said, but instead aids in the digestion of protein.

✓ SERVES 4

½ piece (3 g) fresh ginger, peeled
2 Granny Smith apples, cut into chunks
2 stalks celery, cut into chunks
¼ pineapple, peeled and cut into chunks

Scrub the apples and celery. Combine all the ingredients in a juicer. Taste the results!

P.S. Celery leaves are full of chlorophyll, so don't throw them away! Don't throw away the pineapple core either, because that is the most concentrated source of its nutrients and is perfect for using in juices!

Alternative

✓ SERVES 4

1 raw beet, peeled and cut into chunks
2 Granny Smith apples, cut into chunks
¼ piece (2 g) fresh ginger, peeled
1 grapefruit, peeled, pulled into sections

Beet, Apple, and Ginger Juice

Combine all the ingredients in a juicer. Taste the results!

You can use a lemon or a lime in place of the grapefruit if you prefer.

{ BASKET № 5 }

Coconut, Carrots, Chocolate, Eggplant, Fresh Mint

RECIPES

Carrot-Yogurt Shots

Gathering together is an important part of cooking. Cooking with friends and eating all together is one of the best parts of life! It's the foundation of the food pyramid.

✓ **SERVES 6 TO 8**

11 ounces (300 g) carrots
  (4 to 6 medium), sliced
½ cup (80 g) blanched almonds
½ cup (120 g) nonfat Greek yogurt
Extra-virgin olive oil
Salt
Fresh thyme leaves

In a saucepan, combine the carrots with water to cover and bring to a boil. Cook the carrots until soft, then drain.

Transfer the carrots to a food processor and add the almonds. Process, adding as much water as necessary to make a creamy smooth puree.

In a bowl, whisk the yogurt with a little oil and a pinch of salt.

Put a spoonful of the yogurt mixture into the bottom of each of 6 to 8 liqueur glasses or small jars. Top with the carrot puree. Garnish with a few thyme leaves.

P.S. Add a few crumbled saffron threads to the yogurt for an even more colorful treat.

Variation

For a vegan version, omit the yogurt. Puree 4 ounces (120 g) soft tofu with some oil, salt, and thyme. Layer with the carrot-almond mixture as directed.

Carrots
and almonds

Yogurt

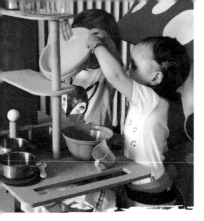

Chocolate Roll

This dessert is great year-round. I always have it in my favorite storage area—my freezer. You can customize it any way you like. Make it and cut it into cubes. You'll find you keep reaching for another piece, and another, and another . . .

SERVES 8 TO 10

- 1 pound 5 ounces (600 g) dark chocolate (72% cacao)
- 1 espresso cup (3 to 4 tablespoons) brewed espresso
- 1¼ cups (300 ml) soy milk or almond milk
- 2 tablespoons organic corn oil
- 1 pound (500 g) whole wheat digestive biscuits or graham crackers
- ⅓ cup (50 g) blanched hazelnuts

Place the chocolate, espresso, and milk in the top of a double boiler. Melt the chocolate and whisk to combine. Stir in the oil. Crumble the cookies and stir them in as well. Fold in the hazelnuts (left whole).

Transfer the mixture to a silicone loaf pan and freeze for 5 hours until very firm.

Once the roll is firm, it is ready to serve.

Unmold. (It will come out of the silicone mold easily.) Cut into slices and then into cubes!

You can use other nuts in place of the hazelnuts, or fold in chopped dried apricots, prunes, dried figs, or any other dried fruit.

Individual Chocolate Lava Cakes

Making individual cakes means each diner gets to cut into one and see the chocolate flow. But they are also good cold: The centers will thicken up a little and won't be as runny, but they'll still be soft.

✓ **MAKES 6 TO 8 CAKES**

7 ounces (200 g) dark chocolate (72% cacao), cut into chunks

½ cup plus 3 tablespoons (200 ml) soy milk or almond milk

2 tablespoons organic corn oil

⅓ cup (30 g) unsweetened cocoa powder

¼ cup plus 1 tablespoon (60 g) muscovado sugar

⅔ cup (80 g) white whole wheat flour or Italian "tipo 2" flour

2 teaspoons baking powder

Pinch of salt

Preheat the oven to 350°F (180°C).

Melt the chocolate with the milk in a double boiler. Whisk together, then add the oil, cocoa powder, sugar, flour, baking powder, and salt and whisk vigorously to combine, whisking in as much air as possible.

Divide the batter among six to eight 2.5-inch (7-cm) ramekins. Transfer the ramekins to a baking sheet and bake 12 to 13 minutes.

Variations

✓ **INGREDIENTS FOR COFFEE-FLAVORED CAKES**

7 ounces (200 g) dark chocolate (72% cacao), cut into chunks

½ cup plus 3 tablespoons (200 ml) soy milk or almond milk

1 espresso cup (3 to 4 tablespoons) brewed coffee

⅓ cup (30 g) unsweetened cocoa powder

2 tablespoons very finely ground coffee

¼ cup plus 1 tablespoon (60 g) muscovado sugar

3 tablespoons (40 ml) organic corn oil

⅓ cup (80 g) white whole wheat or Italian "tipo 2" flour

2 teaspoons baking powder

Pinch of salt

1 **Coffee-Flavored Lava Cakes**
Preheat the oven to 350°F (180°C). Melt the chocolate with the milk in a double boiler and whisk together. Add the remaining ingredients and whisk vigorously to combine, whisking in as much air as possible. Divide the batter among the ramekins and bake as directed above.

2 **Coconut-Flavored Lava Cakes**
For a coconut version, incorporate 1 scant cup (100 g) coconut flour in place of the wheat flour.

#tasteandhealth

Everyone who follows me knows that I could eat chocolate all day long, as long as it's **DARK CHOCOLATE** (at least 72 percent cacao!). There is a great deal of scientific literature on chocolate's benefits. Indeed, according to many studies, the **FLAVONOIDS** in cacao have beneficial effects on blood pressure and cholesterol and also decrease headaches and fight stress. A recent study at Brown University (in Providence, Rhode Island) associated consumption of cacao with prevention of diabetes and heart disease.

Clearly dark chocolate is **A HEALTHY ADDITION TO YOUR DIET**. It's a mood enhancer and stimulates the creation of serotonin, which means it makes you feel relaxed and happy. It also contains a lot of nutrients, such as copper, iron, zinc, and a good dose of magnesium (520 mg in 100 g of chocolate). If you pair it with unsweetened coffee, its anti-inflammatory powers increase considerably!!!

Coconut Treats

These are quick and easy. When I make them with Vivienne, the batter mysteriously tends to disappear before I can get them in the oven. That's why I work quickly using an ice cream scoop!

✓ **MAKES 20 COOKIES**

2 cups (200 g) unsweetened shredded coconut

1¼ cups plus 3 tablespoons (170 g) white whole wheat flour or Italian "tipo 2" flour

½ cup (70 g) organic powdered sugar

1½ teaspoons baking powder

1 cup plus 1 tablespoon (250 ml) milk

3 tablespoons light-flavored extra-virgin olive oil or organic sunflower oil

Preheat the oven to 325°F (160°C). Line a baking sheet with parchment paper.

In a bowl, stir together the coconut, flour, sugar, baking powder, milk, and oil. Use a standard ice cream scoop to make small balls of dough and place them on the prepared baking sheet.

Bake until lightly browned, 17 to 20 minutes.

Coconut, Carrot, and Chocolate Treats never last long!

Variations

1 Add 1 cup (50 g) grated carrots and ¼ teaspoon ground turmeric to the dough.

2 Add a generous ½ cup (80 g) chocolate chips and replace the dairy milk with soy milk.

Carrot Muffins

Desserts made with carrots are tricky because carrots contain a lot of water that is released as they bake. These muffins are exceptional tasting and they come out beautifully every time, as long as you follow the recipe exactly!

✓ MAKES 12 MUFFINS

MUFFINS

¾ cup plus 1 tablespoon (100 g) whole wheat flour
1 cup (130 g) semolina flour
¼ cup (50 g) muscovado sugar
2 teaspoons baking powder
Generous pinch of ground cinnamon
Generous 1 cup (250 g) nonfat dairy yogurt or nondairy yogurt, or generous ¾ cup (250 g) 0% Greek yogurt
5 tablespoons mild-flavored extra-virgin olive oil or organic sunflower oil
3 tablespoons maple syrup or honey
5 cups (250 g) grated carrots (about 10 medium)
½ cup (100 g) chopped hazelnuts

GLAZE (OPTIONAL)

6 tablespoons organic powdered sugar
Pinch of pepper

Preheat the oven to 350°F (180°C). Line the cups of a 12-cup muffin tin with paper liners.

FOR THE MUFFINS: In a large bowl, stir together the flour, semolina, sugar, baking powder, cinnamon, yogurt, oil, and maple syrup. Fold in the carrots and hazelnuts.

Divide the batter among the muffin cups and bake until lightly browned, about 25 minutes. Let the muffins cool.

IF DESIRED, FOR THE GLAZE: In a small bowl, combine the powdered sugar and 2 tablespoons water.

Dip each muffin upside down in the glaze, then turn right side up and allow the glaze to dry. Sprinkle with a pinch of pepper just before serving!

Variation

For gluten-free muffins, simply replace the whole wheat flour and the semolina flour with ¾ cup (100 g) rice flour and ¼ cup (50 g) potato starch.

Pasta with Eggplant, Taggiasca Olives, Capers, and Mint

This dish takes me back to a vacation in Greece and a fantastic pastitsio I enjoyed there that used these ingredients—a delicious memory.

SERVES 4

Salt

12 ounces (320 g) short-cut whole wheat pasta

¼ cup (60 ml) extra-virgin olive oil, plus additional for drizzling

1 pound (450 g) eggplant (about 1 medium)

⅔ cup (80 g) pitted Taggiasca or Niçoise olives

¼ cup plus 2 tablespoons (50 g) capers, rinsed and drained

5 tablespoons tomato paste

10 fresh mint leaves, minced

Try it warm!

In a large pot of lightly salted boiling water, cook the pasta, stirring frequently, until al dente. Drain, rinse under running water, and transfer to a large bowl. Drizzle with a little olive oil and set aside.

Dice the eggplant and place it in a dry nonstick skillet. Cook over medium heat, stirring constantly, until it releases its natural liquids. When the eggplant is soft, add the ¼ cup olive oil, olives, capers, and tomato paste. Cook for about 10 minutes.

Toss together the pasta, eggplant mixture, and mint.

P.S. This dish is meant to be served at room temperature, but I can attest that it is also delicious served slightly warm with aged ricotta cheese grated over the top just before serving.

#tasteandhealth

TOMATOES get their red hue from lycopene, a carotenoid that is an antioxidant and fights cancer and aging. Our bodies don't synthesize lycopene, so it has to be introduced through diet.

Tomato paste and cooked ripe tomatoes have higher lycopene content than raw tomatoes. That's because heat releases lycopene from inside the cells of the tomato and makes it easier for the digestive system to absorb.

Matcha Crêpes

Matcha is a highly prized green tea packed with polyphenols. To make matcha, green tea leaves are dried and then ground into a powder.

✓ MAKES ABOUT 6 CRÊPES

⅔ cup (70 g) whole-grain farro flour

¼ cup (30 g) organic powdered sugar

1 teaspoon matcha powder

¾ cup (170 ml) soy milk

2 tablespoons organic corn oil

4 ounces (120 g) dark chocolate (85% cacao), shaved

In a bowl, combine the flour, sugar, and matcha powder. Beat in the soy milk and corn oil.

Heat an 8-inch (20-cm) nonstick pan over medium heat. Add just enough batter to cover the bottom of the pan (about 3 tablespoons), tilting the pan so it goes to all the edges. Cook on the first side for a few minutes until set and lightly browned on the bottom, then carefully flip and cook the second side.

Transfer the crepe to a plate and scatter the chocolate over the crêpe while it's still hot so it will melt. Fold and serve.

Continue to make more crêpes in the same manner.

P.S. You can find matcha powder in organic food stores, herbal shops, and grocery stores specializing in ethnic and Asian foods.

Chocolate shavings melt instantly!

{ BASKET Nº 6 }

"Tipo 2" or White Whole Wheat Flour, Spices, Cannellini, Cabbage, Ginger

RECIPES

Cannellini and Tuna "Meatballs"

Frying strictly forbidden? Absolutely not, as long as it's done properly in a generous amount of peanut or extra-virgin olive oil, though you should still only indulge in peanut oil once or twice a month. If we want to eat something crispy more often, I use the oven and a good oil sprayed from a bottle!

SERVES 4

2 cups (500 g) canned cannellini, drained and rinsed

1 can (3 oz/100 g) water-packed tuna, drained

1 shallot, peeled and cut into chunks

Leaves of 1 bunch parsley

1¾ cups (200 g) dried whole wheat breadcrumbs

Salt

Extra-virgin olive oil, plus olive oil spray

Preheat the oven to 400°F (200°C). Line a baking sheet with parchment paper.

In a food processor, pulse together the beans, tuna, shallot, and parsley. Don't puree the mixture too smooth. You want a fairly chunky mixture. If it seems too wet to hold together, add ½ to ⅔ cup (50 to 80 g) bread-crumbs.

Season with salt and drizzle with olive oil.

Spread the remaining breadcrumbs on a large dinner plate or sheet pan. Use a standard ice cream scoop to form "meatballs" of the bean mixture, dredge them in the breadcrumbs, and transfer to the prepared pan.

Spray the surface of the "meatballs" with olive oil and bake until lightly browned, about 20 minutes.

Variations

Prefer not to use tuna? Replace it with ⅔ cup (60 g) grated cheese or 3 ounces (80 g) tofu.

Gingerbread Men

Christmas wouldn't be Christmas without gingerbread men. Serve them with hot chocolate, give them to friends as gifts, and use them to decorate your tree!

✓ MAKES 6 TO 8 COOKIES

2 cups (250 g) white whole wheat flour or Italian "tipo 2" flour
¼ cup plus 1 tablespoon (60 g) muscovado sugar
1 teaspoon baking soda (or alternately 3 teaspoons baking powder)
1 teaspoon ground ginger
1 teaspoon ground cinnamon
1 teaspoon grated nutmeg
Pinch of salt
1 tablespoon honey
¼ cup (60 ml) organic corn oil
Scant ⅓ cup (70 ml) soy milk

Preheat the oven to 325° to 350°F (160° to 170°C). Line a baking sheet with parchment paper.

In a large bowl, combine the flour, sugar, baking soda, spices, and salt. Add the honey, corn oil, and soy milk (a little at a time) and stir to combine. The mixture should form a dough that can be kneaded by hand.

On a lightly floured surface, roll out the dough to about 1 inch (a few millimeters) thick and cut out cookies using the classic gingerbread man cutter. Gather the scraps and re-roll to cut out more cookies.

Transfer to the prepared pan and bake until lightly browned, about 10 minutes.

The perfect Christmas gift!

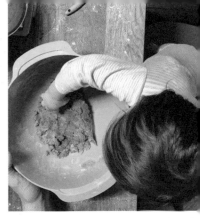

Fresh thyme leaves make this dish smell incredible!

Barley Risotto-Style with Pepper and Goat Cheese Cream

I love barley, oats, and farro cooked risotto-style, in soups, and in cold and warm salads. This is one of my favorite recipes! It combines peppers with barley for a delicious, healthful dish that will also keep your cholesterol in check!

✓ SERVES 4

Salt

1⅔ cups (320 g) pearled barley

2 medium red bell peppers (about 5 oz/150 g each), cut into thin strips

1 spring onion, sliced

Fresh thyme leaves

Extra-virgin olive oil

7 ounces (200 g) goat cheese

2 tablespoons (20 g) capers, drained

¼ cup (40 g) pine nuts, toasted

In a saucepan, bring 3⅓ cups (790 ml) lightly salted water to a boil. Add the barley and cook until the grains have completely absorbed the liquid.

Meanwhile, in a skillet, cook the peppers, spring onion, and thyme to taste with a little water and a little oil. When the vegetables are soft, transfer them to a blender and puree with the goat cheese. With the machine running, drizzle in a little olive oil.

Transfer a couple of spoonfuls of the cooked barley to a mini food processor and puree with a couple of spoonfuls of warm water. Return the barley puree to the pan of whole cooked barley and stir in the pepper and goat cheese cream. Cook over medium heat for 5 minutes to combine the ingredients.

Serve garnished with more thyme, capers, and pine nuts dotted here and there.

Variation

For a delicious twist, replace the goat cheese with the same amount of Greek yogurt. Garnish with a few sun-dried tomatoes.

#tasteandhealth

PEPPERS are one of summer's culinary superstars. They're used fresh in all kinds of sauces, and we also like to put them up in jars so we can eat them in the fall and winter as well. Peppers are full of phosphorous and potassium, as well as vitamins: they contain more **VITAMIN C** than any other vegetable! In 4 ounces (100 g) of peppers there are 153 mg. (The same amount of oranges contains only 50 mg.) Peppers are also rich in flavonoids, which strengthen the cardiovascular system by making blood vessels more elastic and protect against prostate disease.

Mini Focaccia Breads with Seeds and Olives

These make a healthy appetizer and a delicious savory snack. Homemade focaccia is good for you and tastes great!

MAKES 8 TO 10 MINI FOCACCIA

1 envelope (2¼ teaspoons) active dry yeast or ⅓ cake (about 8 g) compressed fresh yeast

½ cup plus 1 tablespoon (135 ml) milk, warm

1½ cups (190 g) all-purpose flour

½ cup (60 g) whole wheat flour

Pinch of salt

2 tablespoons extra-virgin olive oil

½ cup (60 g) pitted whole Taggiasca or Niçoise olives

½ cup (70 g) sunflower, poppy, fennel, or other seeds

In a small bowl, dissolve the yeast in the milk. Place the flours and salt in a large bowl and make a well in the center. Add the milk mixture and mix to form a dough, kneading until well combined. Knead in the oil. If the dough feels very dry, add water, about a tablespoon at a time, until you have a soft, smooth dough. Knead the dough briskly, then shape into a ball, place in a bowl, cover, and let rise at room temperature for 1 hour.

Knead in the olives and the seeds and divide the dough into 8 to 10 equal portions. Shape each portion into a disk and place on parchment-lined baking sheets. Allow to rise at room temperature for 2 hours.

Preheat the oven to 425°F (220°C).

Bake the focaccia for 5 minutes, then reduce the oven temperature to 350°F (180°C) and bake until golden, an additional 5 to 7 minutes.

Stuffed Cabbage with Cannellini Puree

Many of you ask me for dishes that are quick and easy and can be made in advance and use seasonal produce. Here's one! These little bundles are delicious.

✓ SERVES 4

½ head (400 g) cabbage
1 cup (250 g) canned cannellini, drained and rinsed
¼ cup plus 2 tablespoons (50 g) capers, rinsed and drained
Pepper
Extra-virgin olive oil

Make miniature stuffed cabbage!

Separate the cabbage into leaves. Bring a large pot of water to a boil and blanch the leaves until tender, 7 to 8 minutes, taking care not to tear them. Drain and cool. If you want to make bite-sized stuffed cabbage, cut the leaves in half.

In a blender, puree the beans, capers, a pinch of pepper, and a drizzle of olive oil.

Spread a little of the bean filling in the center of one of the cooled cabbage leaves and fold the leaf around the filling. Repeat with remaining leaves and filling.

Serve at room temperature. You can also tie each packet with a chive for a pretty effect.

P.S. Cabbage is economical and you can use every part of it. It stays good for a long time. Mince the less attractive outer leaves and cook them with minced onion as the base for risotto. The prettiest leaves are great for stuffed cabbage, and the rest can go into a soup made with barley, cannellini, carrots, and leeks.

Pan dei Morti Cookies

Pan dei morti are chocolate cookies traditionally made in Italy for All Soul's Day (aka Day of the Dead) on November 2. This is my version.

MAKES 8 TO 10 COOKIES

3 tablespoons (40 g) muscovado sugar

¾ cup (100 g) almonds

¾ cup plus 1 tablespoon (100 g) white whole wheat flour or Italian "tipo 2" flour

1 tablespoon unsweetened cocoa powder

½ teaspoon baking powder

1 teaspoon mixed ground spices including one or more of the following: cardamom, cinnamon, cloves, coriander

3½ ounces (100 g) large dates (about 4), pitted

2 tablespoons organic corn oil

About ¼ cup plus 3 tablespoons (100 ml) soy milk

1 tablespoon organic powdered sugar

Preheat the oven to 350°F (180°C). Line a baking sheet with parchment paper.

In a food processor, grind the muscovado sugar and almonds to a powder. Add the flour, cocoa powder, baking powder, mixed spices, and dates and grind to a paste.

Transfer the mixture to a large bowl. Beat in the oil and then gradually add the soy milk until you have a soft dough. You may not need all of the soy milk.

Use a tablespoon to place portions of the dough on the prepared pan and shape them into ovals. Bake until lightly browned, 15 to 20 minutes.

Remove the cookies from pan and allow them to cool. Sprinkle with the powdered sugar once they are cool.

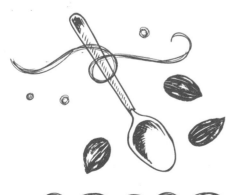

{ BASKET № 7 }

Sun-Dried Tomatoes, Frozen Baby Peas, Salmon, Fresh Tomatoes, Whole-Grain Durum Flour

RECIPES

Home-Style Cake

This is the sort of humble plain cake that goes well with a bit of fruit preserves or yogurt or a glass of milk. This is a cake I made on the spur of the moment with what I had on hand, and you should feel free to approach it in the same spirit.

✓ **MAKES ONE 9-INCH (23-CM) CAKE/8 SERVINGS**

¾ cup (120 g) finely ground cornmeal

¾ cup (150 g) finely ground whole-grain durum flour

¼ cup (30 g) buckwheat flour

1 tablespoon baking powder

¼ cup plus 2 tablespoons (70 g) muscovado sugar

Firmly packed ⅓ cup (60 g) raisins

½ cup (60 g) chopped walnuts

3 tablespoons (40 ml) organic corn oil

¾ cup (180 ml) milk

Preheat the oven to 350°F (180°C). Line the bottom of a 9-inch (23-cm) cake pan with a round of parchment paper.

In a large bowl, combine the cornmeal, flours, baking powder, and sugar. Add the raisins and walnuts and toss with the dry ingredients. Add the corn oil and milk and stir to combine.

Pour the batter into the prepared pan and bake until a tester comes out clean, about 30 minutes.

Variation

Because it's not overly rich, it's perfect for breakfast. Try slicing it in half horizontally to make two layers and filling it with about ½ cup (150 g) of your favorite fruit preserves or 1 cup (250 g) ricotta whipped with a couple of table-spoons of honey.

Pea and Mint Mousse on Toast

If you use a good, satisfying whole wheat bread, a couple of slices of this and lunch is done!

✓ **MAKES 6 TOASTS**

1⅔ cups (250 g) frozen baby peas
15 fresh mint leaves
2 ounces (50 g) goat cheese
1 tablespoon plus 2 teaspoons (25 ml) mild-flavored extra-virgin olive oil
Salt and pepper
6 slices whole wheat bread, toasted

In a saucepan of boiling water, blanch the peas. Drain and transfer to a food processor.

Set aside 6 mint leaves for garnish and add the remaining 9 leaves to the peas in the food processor along with the goat cheese, oil, and a pinch each of salt and pepper. Puree the pea mixture until creamy. If necessary, add water in very small amounts to thin to a spreadable consistency. You won't need more than 2 tablespoons.

Spread the mixture on the toast and garnish each toast with a mint leaf.

Variations

Use the same amount of fava beans or edamame in place of the peas.

#tasteandhealth

Use **COFFEE** as an anti-inflammatory? Why not! Caffeine begins to circulate within thirty minutes of being ingested and is 99 percent absorbed within one hour. It peaks two hours after you drink it and has a half-life of two and a half to four and a half hours.

Coffee protects your heart and stops some kinds of tumors from forming, and it has anti-inflammatory powers that seem to be connected to its polyphenol content—and in particular the chlorogenic acid it contains. Caffeine influences the gastrointestinal system by increasing the secretion of hydrochloric acid and pepsin in the stomach, so it's not for those who suffer from gastritis or ulcers. However, caffeine does not cause reflux, gastritis, or ulcers in healthy people.

Tube Cake with Yogurt Sauce

✓ MAKES ONE TUBE CAKE/
ABOUT 8 SERVINGS

CAKE

Corn oil and flour, for the pan
1 cup (120 g) all-purpose flour
⅔ cup (80 g) whole wheat flour
½ cup (80 g) potato starch
¼ cup plus 2 tablespoons (80 g)
    muscovado sugar
¾ cup (100 g) almonds, chopped
1 tablespoon baking powder
⅓ cup (80 ml) organic corn oil
1 cup (250 ml) milk
Finely grated zest of 2 organic lemons

TOPPING

1 cup (300 g) Greek yogurt
2 tablespoons organic powdered sugar
½ pint (150 g) raspberries

Preheat the oven to 350°F (170°C). Lightly oil and flour an 8-inch (20-cm) tube pan.

FOR THE CAKE: In a bowl, combine the flours, potato starch, sugar, almonds, and baking powder. Stir in the oil, milk, and lemon zest. Mix briskly to incorporate as much air as possible.

Pour the batter into the prepared pan and bake until lightly browned, about 40 minutes. Cool the cake in the pan.

MEANWHILE, FOR THE TOPPING: In a small bowl, whisk together the yogurt and powdered sugar.

Serve wedges of the cake with the yogurt sauce on top and garnished with raspberries.

Variation

✓ MAKES ONE TUBE CAKE/
ABOUT 8 SERVINGS

Corn oil and flour, for the pan
1 cup (120 g) all-purpose flour
⅔ cup (80 g) whole wheat flour
½ cup (80 g) potato starch
1 tablespoon unsweetened cocoa powder
¼ cup plus 2 tablespoons (80 g)
    muscovado sugar
½ cup (80 g) hazelnuts, chopped
1 tablespoon baking powder
⅓ cup (80 ml) organic corn oil
1 cup (250 ml) almond milk or soy milk
Generous ½ cup (80 g) chocolate chips

Chocolate-Hazelnut Tube Cake

Preheat the oven to 350°F (170°C). Lightly oil and flour an 8-inch (20-cm) tube pan. In a bowl, combine the flours, potato starch, cocoa powder, sugar, hazelnuts, and baking powder. Stir in the oil, almond milk, and chocolate chips. Mix briskly to incorporate as much air as possible.

Pour the batter into the prepared pan and bake until lightly browned, about 40 minutes. Cool the cake in the pan.

Roasted Cherry Tomatoes with Onions

Red onions are a great ally in the fight against inflammation because they contain a significant amount of quercetin, an anti-oxidant that helps to rid the body of unwanted substances. These tomatoes are wonderful on toasted bread or used as a sauce for whole-wheat pasta.

✓ **SERVES 4**

1 pound (500 g) cherry tomatoes
2 red Tropea onions (Italian torpedo onions), or 1 medium red onion, cut into wedges
Oregano and/or rosemary sprigs
Extra-virgin olive oil
Salt and pepper

Preheat the oven to 425°F (220°C).

Halve the tomatoes and arrange in a baking pan. Add the onion wedges and scatter on the herbs. Drizzle with oil and season with salt and pepper.

Roast until the tomatoes and onions are lightly browned, about 20 minutes.

Variation

If you like, you can also toss the tomatoes with a few anchovy fillets or a few small balls of buffalo mozzarella just before serving.

Before

After

Pasta with Arugula Pesto and Crispy Salmon

I "stole" this first course from friends who made it for me at their house. It won me over from the first bite.

✓ SERVES 4

Salt

12 ounces (340 g) whole wheat farfalle pasta

6 cups (150 g) arugula

¼ cup (60 ml) extra-virgin olive oil

⅔ cup (100 g) feta cheese

14 ounces (400 g) salmon fillet

¼ cup plus 3 tablespoons (100 ml) orange juice

¼ cup (30 g) oil-packed sun-dried tomatoes, drained and minced

¼ cup (30 g) hemp hearts

¼ cup (30 g) chopped pistachios

In a large pot of lightly salted boiling water, cook the pasta to al dente. Drain and cool under running water. Return to the cooking pot.

In a food processor or blender, combine the arugula, oil, and feta and puree. Add a tablespoon or two of water to make a creamy pesto.

In a dry nonstick skillet over high heat, add the salmon, sprinkle lightly with salt and cook for 2 minutes per side. Add the orange juice and cook until the juice has evaporated and the surface of the fish is crispy and caramelized.

Add the arugula pesto to the pasta and toss to coat. Add a couple of tablespoons of water and reheat briefly.

Transfer the pasta to individual plates and top each portion with slices of the salmon. Garnish with the minced sun-dried tomatoes, hemp hearts, and pistachios.

Variation

If desired, replace the arugula with baby spinach.

#tasteandhealth

Watch out for animal fats and some vegetable fats, such as peanut oil, that are high in **ARACHIDONIC ACID**, which causes **INFLAMMATION**. That's why the magic word when it comes to eating meat (especially red meat), cold cuts, and eggs is "moderation." Fatty fish and plant foods can be eaten in abundance, though, because they help fight inflammation.

Even dairy products contain arachidonic acid, but they supply important nutrients such as calcium and vitamin D. Your best bet is to eat low-fat and nonfat dairy products (1.5 percent fat at most) and cheeses that are 45 percent fat at most. The lower the fat content, the less arachidonic acid they contain.

#tasteandhealth

FODMAP is an acronym that stands for "Fermentable Oligosaccharides, Disaccharides, Monosaccharides, and Polyols." That's a mouthful that simply means **SUGARS WITH A TENDENCY TO FERMENT** (fructose, lactose, fructans, xylitol).

A diet high in these sugars can exacerbate the most common symptoms of **IRRITABLE BOWEL SYNDROME**, or IBS (bloating, gas, abdominal pain, irregularity). A University of Michigan study published in *Gastroenterology* showed that a low-FODMAP diet reduces those symptoms.

When IBS is in the acute phase, it's a good idea to follow a low-FODMAP diet for a while.

What are the foods to avoid or limit, and which should be eaten in large quantities? When it comes to **FRUIT**, choose bananas, oranges, grapes, and cantaloupe; avoid watermelon, peaches, apples, and pears, which are easily fermented. For **VEGETABLES**, look for zucchini, lettuce, tomatoes, and green beans, and avoid asparagus, onions, garlic, beets, and cabbage. Fish and gluten-free items such as rice, quinoa, and amaranth are also recommended as part of a low-FODMAP diet. Only lactose-free **DAIRY PRODUCTS** are permitted.

Keep in mind, however, that a low-FODMAP diet should not be followed for an extended period and any eliminated foods should gradually be reintroduced.

Pizza

Not a week goes by that I don't serve pizza for lunch or dinner. The common denominator all my pizzas share? Lots of vegetables, a small amount of cheese, and plenty of sauce!

✓ SERVES 4 TO 6

½ teaspoon active dry yeast or ⅙ cake (3 g) compressed fresh yeast

1 cup plus 2 tablespoons (267 ml) warm water

3 cups (380 g) all-purpose flour

1 cup (120 g) whole wheat flour

Scant 2 tablespoons (25 g) extra-virgin olive oil, plus more for drizzling

½ teaspoon (10 g) salt

¼ cup (about 50 g) tomato sauce

Grilled peppers, or other cooked vegetables, to taste

Dissolve the yeast in ¼ cup (60 ml) of the warm water. In a large bowl, combine the flours and olive oil. Stir in the yeast mixture, then gradually knead in enough warm water to make a smooth dough. Knead in the salt. Shape the dough into a ball, transfer it to a large bowl or container, cover tightly, and let rise on the lowest shelf of the refrigerator for 24 hours.

Preheat the oven to 425°F (220°). Line a 9-inch (23-cm) sheet pan with parchment paper.

Remove the dough from the refrigerator and with your hands press it into the prepared pan. Let the dough rest at room temperature for 30 minutes.

Top with the tomato sauce and grilled peppers (or other vegetables of your choosing) and drizzle on a little olive oil. Bake for about 20 minutes.

Variation

✓ SERVES 4 TO 6
GLUTEN-FREE PIZZA CRUST

1 head cauliflower, broken into florets

Salt and pepper

3 tablespoons extra-virgin olive oil

2 egg whites

¼ cup (about 50 g) tomato sauce

Preheat the oven to 400°F (200°C). Line a 9-inch (23-cm) sheet pan with parchment paper.

In a food processor, grind the cauliflower to a fine rice. Mix in a pinch of salt, the oil, and egg whites. Press the cauliflower about ¾ inch deep into the prepared pan.

Bake about 30 minutes. Spread on tomato sauce and toppings of your choice. Bake as above.

Mediterranean Bruschetta

Vivienne loves this so much that she adds herbs. In addition to the oregano? You bet. Never get in the way of an ambitious kid in the kitchen!

✓ **SERVES 6**

2¼ cups (250 g) oil-packed sun-dried tomatoes, drained
½ cup (100 ml) tomato puree
1 tablespoon plus 1 teaspoon muscovado sugar
Pinch of dried oregano
¼ cup (30 g) chopped red onion
2 tablespoons capers, rinsed and drained
1 tablespoon plus 2 teaspoons mild-flavored extra-virgin olive oil
6 slices whole wheat bread, toasted

Slice 4 to 5 sun-dried tomatoes and set aside for garnish.

In a blender or food processor, combine the remaining sun-dried tomatoes, the tomato puree, sugar, oregano, red onion, capers, and olive oil and process into a smooth mixture.

Spread the mixture on the bread. Garnish with the reserved strips of sun-dried tomato.

———————————————

P.S. You can also serve the pureed mixture over barley or farro. Either is a delicious pairing!

Use this sauce on barley or farro!

{ BASKET № 8 }

**Lentils,
Ricotta, Quinoa,
Mushrooms, Spinach,
Cauliflower**

RECIPES

Tagliatelle with Mushrooms and Ricotta-Pumpkin Cream

I made this on TV with the wonderful Antonella Clerici. Everybody loved it, and I hope you'll love it, too.

SERVES 4

11 ounces (300 g) peeled and seeded winter squash, such as pumpkin, kabocha, or kuri (about ½ medium squash), cut into cubes

1 shallot, minced

Generous 1 cup (250 g) Italian-style ricotta cheese or well-drained regular ricotta

1 tablespoon plus 1 teaspoon extra-virgin olive oil

Salt and pepper

1¾ ounces (50 g) sliced dried porcini mushrooms (about 14)

5 ounces (150 g) white button mushrooms, sliced

11 ounces (320 g) dried egg tagliatelle

10 fresh chives, minced

In a large skillet, sauté the squash and shallot in a little water until the squash is soft. Transfer the squash and shallot to a food processor, add the ricotta and drizzle in some oil, and puree. Season with salt and pepper.

Soak the dried mushrooms in water for about 15 minutes. Carefully scoop them out of the water, leaving any grit behind in the bowl. Drain the mushrooms well. In a skillet, heat a little oil over medium heat. Add the dried mushrooms and the fresh mushrooms and season with salt and pepper. Do not add any water to the pan as the mushrooms will give off plenty. Cook until done. Set aside.

In a large pot of lightly salted boiling water, cook the pasta until al dente. Drain and cool under running water. Return to the cooking pot.

Add the ricotta-pumpkin cream, mushrooms, and chives to the pasta and toss to combine. Reheat briefly with an additional drizzle of olive oil and serve.

P.S. This sauce is also great on whole wheat pasta or buckwheat noodles (pizzoccheri).

Seasonal Autumn Quinoa

Quinoa is rich in protein, calcium, and good fat. If you don't have a taste for it, you can use couscous here instead.

SERVES 4

2 cups (320 g) quinoa, rinsed
1 pound (500 g) broccoli, broken into florets
Leaves of 3 sprigs parsley
¾ cup (80 g) oil-packed sun-dried tomatoes, drained
1 cup (150 g) pitted Taggiasca or Niçoise olives
3 carrots, finely diced
Extra-virgin olive oil
Finely grated zest and juice of 1 organic lemon

In a saucepan, bring 4 cups (950 ml) water to a boil. Add the quinoa, cover, and cook until the water is absorbed, about 20 minutes. Halfway through, add the broccoli.

Meanwhile, on a cutting board, mince together the parsley, sun-dried tomatoes, and olives.

When the quinoa is cooked, fluff it with a fork, cover, and let sit for about 5 minutes, then turn out into a large bowl to cool slightly. Add the carrots and the parsley mixture and toss together. Dress with a little olive oil, lemon zest, and lemon juice.

Lentil Salad

I suggest preparing large batches of lentils and freezing them. The freezer is great for storing both legumes and cooked grains.

✓ SERVES 4

1¼ cups (250 g) lentils

¾ cup (80 g) oil-packed sun-dried tomatoes, drained

1 leek, trimmed

Leaves of 1 bunch parsley

Extra-virgin olive oil

Juice of 1 lemon

¼-inch (½-cm) piece fresh ginger, grated

In a large saucepan of lightly salted boiling water, cook the lentils until firm-tender, about 20 minutes. Drain well and transfer to a bowl.

On a cutting board, mince together the sun-dried tomatoes, leek, and parsley—all uncooked—and toss with the lentils.

Before serving, drizzle in some oil, add the lemon juice and fresh ginger, and toss well.

P.S. You can switch up the ingredients here as you like, but always use lemon juice because it helps you absorb the iron in the sun-dried tomatoes and lentils.

Cauliflower Pasta

This incredible first course is made in advance and then reheated in a skillet or warmed in the oven.

SERVES 4

⅓ cup (50 g) raisins
Fresh parsley leaves, to taste
⅔ cup (70 g) walnuts
1 yellow onion
4 oil-packed anchovy fillets, drained
Extra-virgin olive oil
Red pepper flakes
1 head cauliflower, trimmed
Salt
12 ounces (320 g) whole wheat pasta

Place the raisins in a small bowl and add water to cover. Set aside to soak for 15 minutes. Drain the raisins and squeeze them dry.

On a cutting board, mince together the parsley, walnuts, onion, and anchovies.

In a skillet, cook the anchovy mixture with a little oil and red pepper flakes to taste over very low heat until the anchovies have dissolved.

In a large pot of boiling unsalted water, cook the whole head of cauliflower, about 20 minutes. Drain and break into florets.

Transfer about 10 cooked cauliflower florets to a food processor and puree until smooth, then add the puree to the anchovy mixture in the skillet.

In a large pot of lightly salted boiling water, cook the pasta until al dente. Drain and toss with the cauliflower-anchovy mixture and the remaining cauliflower florets.

Variations

You can use Romanesco in place of the cauliflower, or try Brussels sprouts or purple cauliflower.

#tasteandhealth

VITAMIN C is found in more than just citrus. So many foods contain vitamin C. Want a few figures? The daily recommended dose of vitamin C is 60 milligrams (mg). The juice of ½ lemon contains 22 mg; about ¼ cup (100 g) of arugula contains 15 mg; ¾ cup (150 g) of strawberries has 80 mg; a medium tomato contains 50 mg; a quarter pound (100 g) of raw bell peppers has four times as much as an orange. And speaking of oranges, by weight raw cauliflower provides more vitamin C than an orange does. So try some as a crudité dipped in olive oil, salt, pepper, and mustard powder! You'll keep coming back for more!

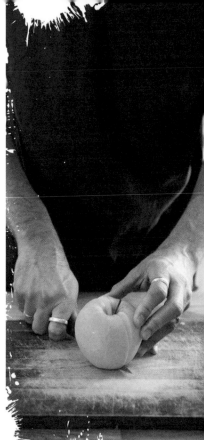

Extra-Light Apple Cake

An apple cake smells like home. To me, there's nothing like it. An apple cake means family, memories, and love.

MAKES ONE 9-INCH (23-CM) CAKE/8 SERVINGS

2 cups (250 g) whole wheat flour

3 tablespoons plus 1 teaspoon (40 g) stevia

1 tablespoon baking powder

Grated zest and juice of 1 organic lemon

½ cup plus 3 tablespoons (200 ml) milk

3 tablespoons plus 1 teaspoon (50 ml) extra-virgin olive oil

⅓ cup (70 g) dried apricots, finely chopped

1 pound (500 g) apples, peeled and diced

Preheat the oven to 350°F (180°C). Line the bottom of a 9-inch (23-cm) cake pan with a round of parchment paper.

In a large bowl, combine the flour, stevia, baking powder, and lemon zest. Stir in the milk, olive oil, and lemon juice. Fold in the dried apricots and apples.

Scrape the batter into the prepared pan and bake until lightly browned, about 45 minutes.

P.S. This recipe was created for a diabetic child so it contains no added sugar. You can add some ground cinnamon to enhance the flavor.

Cream of Cauliflower, Celery Root, and Greek Yogurt Soup

This humble recipe was created on a whim but has become one of my mainstays. It's an excellent opener to a dinner with friends.

SERVES 4

14 ounces (400 g) peeled celery root, cut into big chunks

14 ounces (400 g) cauliflower florets (from about 1 medium head)

Generous ¾ cup (9 oz/250 g) 0% Greek yogurt

Extra-virgin olive oil

Salt and pepper

Saffron, for garnish

In a saucepan, combine the celery root, cauliflower, and water just to cover. Bring to a boil and cook until soft. Drain, transfer to a food processor, and puree into a smooth cream with no lumps.

Add the yogurt and a drizzle of olive oil and puree until smooth. Season with salt and pepper.

Divide among individual serving dishes and garnish with saffron.

#tasteandhealth

Let's talk about **WATER** misconceptions. Depending on where you live, some tap water systems contain lime buildup. The taste may bother some people, but it's nothing more than calcium carbonate, meaning it's a good source of calcium. Ingesting it won't cause you to develop kidney stones or gallstones—those are made of calcium oxalate. You only need to eschew tap water if you're a clothing iron. (Calcium carbonate ruins metal, but that's it!)

Another thing that strikes fear in the hearts of many is the term **TOTAL DISSOLVED SOLIDS (TDS)** that appears on some bottles of mineral water. That phrase doesn't indicate anything bad or negative. It's just a technical term that shows the **MINERAL CONTENT** that remains after a liter of water evaporates at 356°F (180°C).

Water with a high TDS number is richer in minerals than water with a low number. That's all. For specific dietary concerns, consult your doctor to recommend the best water for you.

Green Pasta

It doesn't cost much and we buy a lot of it. I'm talking about spinach, of course. If you don't know what to do with it, I've got you covered: Here's the dish for you. I created this recipe when Veru was pregnant. Since spinach (like all leafy greens) is rich in folate, I took raw tender baby spinach and turned it into a sauce. There's no law against blanching the spinach for a moment before pureeing it!

SERVES 4

Salt

12 ounces (320 g) buckwheat pasta (pizzoccheri)

4 ounces (100 g) baby spinach (3 to 4 cups)

1 cup (120 g) walnuts

3 ounces (80 g) Quartirolo Lombardo or feta cheese

Extra-virgin olive oil

In a large pot of lightly salted boiling water, cook the pasta until al dente.

Meanwhile, in a food processor, combine the spinach, walnuts, cheese, and a little bit of olive oil until smooth and creamy. Add water in small amounts if needed to reach the right consistency.

Drain the pasta and toss with the sauce.

P.S. Buckwheat is gluten-free and high in protein, fiber, and minerals. But if you have whole wheat pasta and want to use that instead, I won't be upset ;-) and the dish will taste just as good!

{ BASKET Nº 9 }

Almonds, Tomatoes, Fresh Apricots, Bell Peppers, Ricotta, Cucumbers

RECIPES

Classic Gazpacho

Gazpacho is a powerhouse full of vitamin C, carotenoids, quercetin, fiber, and anthocyanins. In short, it's a concentrated burst of taste and health.

√ SERVES 4

2 red onions
1 mango
4 tomatoes
2 cucumbers
2 bell peppers (1 red, 1 green)
Tabasco sauce
Juice of ½ lemon
5 tablespoons extra-virgin olive oil
4 cups (1 liter) tomato puree
Salt and pepper
Whole wheat bread, toasted

Mince the onions and place in a bowl. Dice the mango, tomatoes, cucumbers, and bell peppers and add to the bowl. Add Tabasco sauce to taste, the lemon juice, and olive oil. Toss to combine. Add the tomato puree and season with salt and pepper. Refrigerate for 2 hours before serving.

Serve with whole wheat toast.

Alternative

√ SERVES 4

6 small cucumbers
1 white onion, cut into chunks
9 ounces (250 g) baby spinach
  (7 to 8 cups)
2 cups (50 g) basil leaves
¾ cup (20 g) parsley leaves
2 Italian frying peppers, cut into chunks
3 tablespoons (50 g) 0% Greek yogurt
⅔ cup (150 ml) extra-virgin olive oil, plus
  more for drizzling
1 teaspoon muscovado sugar
Salt and pepper
Whole wheat bread, toasted

Green Gazpacho

Peel and chunk the cucumbers and place them in a food processor. Add the onion, spinach, basil, parsley, and frying peppers and process. After a few minutes add the yogurt, the ⅔ cup (150 ml) oil, the sugar, and salt and pepper to taste. Process again until the mixture is bright green.

Refrigerate for 2 hours before serving.

Divide the soup among bowls and drizzle on additional oil. Serve with the toast.

Green

Classic

#tasteandhealth

Scientists have discovered that eating **SOY AND SOY PRODUCTS** such as tofu and (unsweetened) soy milk provides a variety of benefits, from fighting cancer to lowering LDL ("bad") cholesterol: Regular soy consumption as part of a balanced and healthy diet can bring LDL down by 10 to 15 percent. Soy is 42 percent protein, making it one of the best sources of plant protein. Soybeans (mature soybeans as well as green edamame), tofu, and tempeh provide the most benefits, while soy milk is less effective, and soy sauce—a very salty seasoning—offers none.

Apricot and Mango Salad

We should all work to incorporate fruit into our meals. It's not an extra but an important part of a daily diet. So go ahead and add lots of tasty fruit to your salads!

√ **SERVES 4**

6 fresh apricots

3 tablespoons extra-virgin olive oil, plus more for sauteeing

3 tablespoons fresh lemon juice

1 teaspoon honey

5 fresh mint leaves

Pinch of salt

9 ounces (250 g) arugula (10 to 12 cups)

3½ oz (100 g) butterhead lettuce (about ½ head)

1 mango, diced

1 Granny Smith apple, peeled (if not organic) and diced

1⅔ cups (250 g) crumbled feta cheese

Briefly warm the apricots, cut in half without the stones, in a skillet with olive oil until lightly sauteed, then cut them into wedges.

In a mini food processor, blend the lemon juice, oil, honey, mint, and salt to combine.

Tear the arugula and lettuce leaves by hand and make a bed of the two on a large serving platter. Arrange the apricots, mango, and apple on top and sprinkle with the feta cheese. Drizzle on the dressing and serve!

Buckwheat Noodles Trapani-Style

My favorite dishes? Pizza (whole wheat crust, lots of vegetables, tomato sauce), hummus, pasta (whole wheat with tomato sauce topped with feta or aged ricotta), and . . . pizzoccheri, cooked my way!

✓ **SERVES 4**

Salt

12 ounces (320 g) pizzoccheri (Italian buckwheat noodles)

½ cup (50 g) whole wheat breadcrumbs

½ cup (50 g) almonds

5 oil-packed sun-dried tomatoes, drained

5 fresh tomatoes, diced

10 basil leaves

½ to 1 clove garlic, to taste

Extra-virgin olive oil

Black pepper to taste

In a large pot of lightly salted boiling water, cook the pizzoccheri.

Meanwhile, in a nonstick skillet, toast the breadcrumbs. In a food processor, combine the toasted breadcrumbs, almonds, sun-dried tomatoes, fresh tomatoes, basil, garlic, and a few tablespoons of olive oil. Puree until creamy.

When the pizzoccheri are ready, drain them and rinse under running water. Toss with the pesto. Transfer them to a skillet, drizzle with a little olive oil, and reheat. Season with pepper before serving.

Pizzoccheri are one of my favorites. I love them with anything and everything!

Cucumber Water

Cool. Refreshing. That's how I'd describe my favorite flavored water, made with cucumber, lemon, and ginger!

✓ **SERVES 6 TO 8**

One 2-quart (2-liter) bottle
   sparkling water
2 cucumbers, thinly sliced
10 fresh mint leaves
1 organic lime
1 organic lemon
⅓-inch (1-cm) piece fresh ginger

Place the sparkling water in a pitcher. Slice the cucumbers and add them to the water along with the mint leaves. Thinly slice the lime and lemon and add those as well. Peel the ginger, cut it into small dice, and add to the water. Let this beverage infuse in the refrigerator for at least 3 hours before serving. It must be well chilled!

P.S. It looks really "fancy" if you freeze the lemon and lime slices. That way they both cool down the drink and flavor it!

You can create your own favorite flavored water with the ingredients you love!

Variations

You can create your own favorites! One piece of advice: Think seasonally. In summer use peaches, strawberries, and ginger for an excellent flavored water.

In winter you can make an infusion: Bring water to a boil and let the flavoring elements steep for 15 to 20 minutes.

My winter favorite? Ginger, 1 organic lemon, and 1 bay leaf in 2 quarts (2 liters) of water.

Ricotta Spoon Sweet

This is a dessert for coddling friends, family, and, obviously, yourself. Because cooking is an act of love!

✓ SERVES 4

3 egg whites
2½ cups (500 g) Italian-style ricotta cheese or well-drained regular ricotta
25 (150 g) amaretti cookies, crumbled
5 fresh apricots
2 ounces (50 g) dark chocolate (72% cacao)

In a bowl, with an electric mixer, whip the egg whites to stiff peaks. Fold in the ricotta and the crumbled cookies. Work very gently to avoid deflating the egg whites. Transfer to individual serving dishes.

Pit and slice the apricots and arrange them on top, then grate chocolate onto each bowl.

Refrigerate for 5 hours before serving.

P.S. Out of eggs? Simply leave out the egg whites. The dessert will still taste great!

Apricot Cake

Somebody's birthday? An anniversary? This cake—so versatile and so good—is the perfect solution. This isn't a cake that rises very high, but the sweet and sour flavor from the apricots is fantastic.

√ **MAKES ONE 9-INCH (23-CM) CAKE/6 TO 8 SERVINGS**

1½ cups (190 g) all-purpose flour
½ cup (60 g) whole wheat flour
¼ cup (50 g) muscovado sugar
1 tablespoon baking powder
½ cup plus 3 tablespoons (200 ml) milk
¼ cup (60 ml) organic corn oil
10 fresh apricots, pitted and finely diced

Preheat the oven to 350°F (180°C). Line the bottom of a 9-inch (23-cm) cake pan with a round of parchment paper.

In a large bowl, combine the flours, sugar, baking powder, milk, and oil. Fold the apricots into the batter.

Pour the batter into the prepared pan. Bake until lightly browned, 40 to 45 minutes.

P.S. It's best to serve this with 1 cup (250 g) yogurt whipped with 3 tablespoons (60 g) apricot preserves. So delicious! Try replacing the milk with unsweetened soy milk and adding melted chocolate, but it must be 72% cacao dark chocolate.

Detox Juice

I use an extraction juicer to make juice because it is gentler with the fruit than a centrifugal juicer or a blender. It treats the fruits and vegetables tenderly and preserves their nutritional value.

✓ **SERVES 2**

2 cucumbers
1 Granny Smith apple
½ mango
1 pineapple

Extract the juice from all the ingredients and drink chilled! You can also dilute the juice with a little sparkling water.

―――――――――――――――――

P.S. If drinking fruit isn't enough, eat it, too!

Combine any leftover fruit with endive, mâche, and a tablespoon of mustard. It's the perfect salad!

Or eat any leftover fruit with almonds or walnuts or dress with a teaspoon of a mild-flavored extra-virgin olive oil in order to better absorb the carotenoids from the mango.

If you have fruit left over, use it to make a delicious salad!

{ BASKET Nº 10 }

**Black Rice, Farro,
Radicchio,
Milk,
Sun-Dried Tomatoes,
Lentils**

RECIPES

Black Rice with Lentils

This is a fantastic one-dish meal full of fiber; minerals such as iron, manganese, copper, and magnesium; vitamins; protein; and functional molecules, which benefit the cardiovascular system.

✓ **SERVES 4**

1¾ cups (320 g) black rice

Leaves of 1 bunch parsley

¾ cup (80 g) oil-packed sun-dried tomatoes, drained

¾ cup (80 g) walnuts

1 cup (200 g) cooked lentils

Grated zest and juice of 1 organic lemon

5 tablespoons extra-virgin olive oil

In a saucepan, combine the rice with 3 cups (700 ml) water, cover with a tight-fitting lid, and cook over low heat for 20 minutes. Remove the pan from the heat and let the rice continue to steam, covered, until fully cooked, about 15 additional minutes.

Meanwhile, chop together the parsley, sun-dried tomatoes, and walnuts to make a quick sauce.

Add the lentils, lemon zest, lemon juice, and olive oil to the cooked rice. Finally, add the sauce.

P.S. Black rice, brown rice: Pick whatever you like best. They're all packed with fiber!

You can also use basmati rice. Long-grain rice like basmati is less starchy and therefore better for your health!

#tasteandhealth

ANTHOCYANINS (purple, blue, and dark red pigments), ellagitannins, proanthocyanidins, and phenolic acids (such as chlorogenic acid) are some of the most beneficial substances for your health. Blueberries, blackberries, eggplant, plums, red grapes, beets, and radicchio all have them!

These substances are part of the polyphenol family, and polyphenols help prevent chronic degenerative disease. And that's not all—they're antioxidants that have bene-fits for healthy people as well as those with risk factors for degenerative diseases.

One epidemiology study conducted for sixteen years on 34,489 post-menopausal American women demonstrated that a diet rich in flavonoids, and especially anthocyanins, reduces the risk of death due to cardiovascular disease. There are other solid studies that show that anthocyanins regulate various biochemical pathways involved in the development of cardiovascular disease.

Pasta with Radicchio Sauce

Cashews, radicchio, onion, Quartirolo Lombardo cheese—what a fabulous group of ingredients. You won't believe how good they taste together!

✓ SERVES 4

1 head radicchio, cut into strips
1 yellow onion, minced
½ cup (80 g) unsalted cashews
5 tablespoons extra-virgin olive oil, plus more to drizzle
4 ounces (100 g) Quartirolo Lombardo or feta cheese
Salt and pepper
12 ounces (320 g) whole wheat pasta

In a skillet, sauté the radicchio and onion in a couple of tablespoons of water, stirring constantly. When the radicchio mixture is soft, transfer to a food processor and add the cashews, oil, and cheese and puree. Season to taste with salt and pepper, but don't overdo it on the salt. (Restrain yourself!)

In a large pot of lightly salted boiling water, cook the pasta until al dente, then rinse under running water.

Toss the pasta and radicchio sauce together and reheat in a skillet with an additional drizzle of extra-virgin olive oil.

Variation

For a different spin, replace the Quartirolo with smoked tofu and the salt with Niçoise or Taggiasca olives.

Farro and Chickpea Soup

Farro is an ancient variety of wheat. It's rich in fiber, but also in B vitamins, phosphorous, and potassium. This is a staple ingredient you should always have in your pantry!

✓ **SERVES 4**

1 carrot, minced
1 white onion, minced
1 stalk celery, minced
1¾ cups (320 g) farro
Extra-virgin olive oil, as a drizzle, to taste
2 sprigs rosemary
2 bay leaves
1 cup (250 g) canned chickpeas, drained and rinsed
Salt and pepper

In a soup pot, cook the carrot, onion, and celery in water (no oil) until softened, about 10 minutes.

Add the farro, oil, rosemary, and bay leaves and enough water to cover the farro. Bring to a boil and boil for 20 minutes. Add the chickpeas and additional water if needed, depending on the consistency you desire. Season to taste with salt and pepper.

After about 20 minutes, the soup is ready! Remove the bay leaves and rosemary sprigs before serving.

P.S. Not a fan of whole chickpeas? No problem—just puree the mixture before adding the farro.

Variation

Replace the farro with barley and use dried mushrooms in place of the chickpeas.

Radicchio and Apple Salad

This is an unusual salad. It offers a way to work lots of fruit into your meals. A great combination, a wonderful blend of flavors.

✓ SERVES 4

4 medium sweet potatoes
Juice of 1 lemon
1 Granny Smith apple
4 tablespoons raisins
1 head radicchio, slivered
⅔ cup (80 g) pitted Niçoise or Taggiasca olives, sliced
1 cup (150 g) crumbled feta cheese
¼ cup (60 ml) extra-virgin olive oil
½ cup (120 ml) balsamic vinegar

In a large pot of boiling unsalted water, cook the whole sweet potatoes until firm-tender. Drain and set aside to cool. When cool enough to handle, peel and cut into rounds.

Fill a medium bowl with water and add the lemon juice. Peel, core, and dice the apple. Add the cut apple pieces and the raisins to the acidulated water.

To compose the salad, start with a bed of the radicchio. Top with the sweet potatoes. Drain the apple and raisins and add. Then add the olives and feta.

Drizzle with the oil and balsamic vinegar.

P.S. Have a leftover sweet potato? Bake it with a little oil and oregano on top.

To serve, crush lightly with a fork and accompany with goat cheese.

Farro Blancmange

This classic recipe is made of humble ingredients but has flavors fit for a king. It's an ideal dessert or snack and also a nice Sunday breakfast option.

✓ **SERVES 4**

1⅔ cups (300 g) farro
4 cups (1 liter) unsweetened almond milk
¾ cup (100 g) wheat starch
⅔ cup (80 g) organic powdered sugar
Finely grated zest of 1 organic lemon
1 cup (70 g) chopped candied orange peel
2 ounces (60 g) dark chocolate (72% cacao)

In a pot of boiling unsalted water, cook the farro to your desired density. Drain well.

In a large pot, whisk together the almond milk, wheat starch, sugar, and lemon zest. Place over medium heat. When the first bubbles appear, stir in the farro. Once the mixture has reached the desired consistency, remove from the heat, stir in the candied orange peel, and divide among individual serving dishes.

Let cool and then grate the chocolate on top. Store in the refrigerator.

Variation

For a gluten-free version, replace the farro with 1⅓ cups (300 g) semi-polished rice and use cornstarch in place of the wheat starch. That's all it takes! The method is exactly the same.

Radicchio Stuffed with Tofu and Anchovy Mousse

What I like to do in the kitchen is create dishes that are not only healthy, but also pretty and colorful.

SERVES 4

1 head Treviso radicchio
10 ounces (300 g) tofu
1 ounce (30 g) oil-packed anchovy fillets (about 11), drained
Juice of 1 lemon
⅔ cup (80 g) pitted Niçoise or Taggiasca olives
¼ cup (60 ml) extra-virgin olive oil
Chives, for garnish

Break the head of radicchio into leaves and choose 16 of the largest, prettiest leaves.

In a food processor, blend the tofu with the anchovies, lemon juice, olives, and olive oil. With the machine running, drizzle in water in a thin stream until creamy, velvety, and delicious. The tofu will get creamy thanks to the water you're adding along with the other ingredients but it will take a few minutes.

Serve each radicchio leaf with a quenelle of the tofu mixture on top. Garnish with a chive.

Variation

Here's a vegan version: Replace the anchovies with ⅔ cup (70 g) drained oil-packed sun-dried tomatoes and reduce the olives to ½ cup (70 g).

THANK YOU!

There are many surprises in life. Really a lot. This has been an intense year with lots of changes, emotions, and choices. I'd like to thank my family: my mother, Cristina; my father, Umberto; Mirca and Gianni; my sister, Barbara; and especially my girls, Veruska and Vivienne.

Thank you to some special friends: Renato, Alberto, Igor, Taty, Alessandro, Martina, Kevin, Nico, Roberto, Simona, Filippo, Andrea, Romina, Mike, Alessandro, Sofia, Davide, Luca, Albino and Barbara, Federica and Oscar, Teresa, Silvia and Barbara, Patrizia—thank you from the bottom of my heart. Each of you knows why I'm thanking you. Finally, sincerest thanks to the Fondazione Veronesi, my splendid team at Realize Networks (Pasquale, Rosario, Serena, Claudia, Simone, Alessia, Giulia, Ivano, Salvo, Giada, Monica, Silvia, Alex), and my publisher, HarperCollins, who has made it possible to give you what you want, a book in color! Thank you so much—you're the best!

Index by DISH

APPETIZERS AND BREADS

SAUCES AND SPREADS

SOUPS

PASTA AND GRAINS

MAIN COURSES

SALADS

DESSERTS

BEVERAGES

Index by INGREDIENT

Italicized page numbers represent recipe variations.

JAZZ

A Visual Retrospective
Compiled by K. Abé

GIANTS

K. Abe

JAZZ

A Visual Retrospective
Compiled by K. Abé

GIANTS

BILLBOARD PUBLICATIONS, INC./NEW YORK

My deepest appreciation to the many people who provided
assistance in the preparation of this book, especially to Bob
Andrews, Ray Avery, Paul Bacon, Hugh Bell, Eddie Bert,
William Claxton, Frank Driggs, Nancy Elliott, William
Gottlieb, Milt Hinton, Steve LaVere, Jay Maisel, Dan
Morgenstern of the Institute of Jazz Studies at Rutgers
University, T. Ono, Bob Parent, Hajime Sawatari, Arthur
Singer, Chuck Stewart, Arthur Zimmerman, and many
wonderful unidentified photographers. Special thanks to
Shoo Kusano, President of Shinko Music, who gave me this
wonderful opportunity, and to Chic Ogata for his great help
in the compilation.

Copyright © 1986 by
Shinko Music Publishing Company Limited
2-1, Ogawa-machi, Kanda
Chiyoda-ku, Tokyo
Japan

Originally published in Japan by Shinko Music Publishing Company Limited

First published 1988 in the United States and Canada by Billboard
Publications, Inc., 1515 Broadway, New York, NY 10036

Library of Congress Cataloging-in-Publication Data
Jazz giants / compiled by K. Abé.
     p.   cm.
     Includes index.
     ISBN 0-8230-7536-2
     1. Jazz music—Pictorial works.   2. Jazz musicians—Portraits.
I. Abé, K. (Katsuji)
ML3506.J43 1988
779′.978542—dc19   88-14708
                                           CIP
                                           MN

Arranged by Toppan Company Limited, Tokyo, Japan
/Rockport Publishers, Inc., Rockport, Massachusetts, U.S.A.

Printed in Japan by Tosho Printing Company Limited
First U.S. printing, 1988

1 2 3 4 5 6 7 8 9/93 92 91 90 89 88

PREFACE
by K. Abé

T HAS BEEN MORE THAN forty years since my first encounter with jazz. During all this time it has continued to be a great source of inspiration and pleasure.

Photography has enhanced my feeling for the music. I was excited early on by the photographs of musicians that appeared in such magazines as *Metronome* and *Down Beat*. These pictures, which captured the people, places, instruments, and atmosphere of jazz, often affected me as much as the music itself. With my own camera work, I found a new way to explore and connect with this music.

Jazz has continued to evolve, with its younger players embracing styles and blends that the original masters could never have imagined. While immersing myself in these modern sounds, I glance through the old photographs and am reminded of the individuality and the spirit of adventure that have always been present in jazz, whatever its form of the moment.

I have compiled the photographs in this book because of my desire to share them—and the feelings they evoke—with everyone who loves jazz and the great musicians who have been part of its history.

INTRODUCTION
by Nat Hentoff

F ALL THE BOOKS of photographs of jazz musicians, *Jazz Giants* is by far the most permanently immediate. That's not a contradiction in terms, for what this assembly of photographers has captured through the decades, and for all time, are the spontaneity and individuality that are the essence of the music and those who make it.

Pee Wee Russell, who invented sounds never heard before or since on the clarinet, is one of the players here. He claimed not to be articulate off the stand, but he was very perceptive, and once he tried to explain what makes jazz musicians different from all other musicians. Indeed, from all other people.

Said Pee Wee: "A certain group of guys—I don't care where they come from—have a heart feeling and a rhythm in their systems that you couldn't budge, a rhythm you couldn't take away from them even if they were in a symphony organization."

The "heart feeling" he talks about is what others have called "soul." You have to know an awful lot about your instrument to play jazz, but technique, however astonishing, is meaningless in this music unless you tell a story, your own

story—a story that has so much feeling in it that the listeners suddenly recall their own losses and anticipations.

Charlie Parker, also indelibly present in this book, said it most succinctly: "Music is your own experience, your thoughts, your wisdom. If you don't live it, it won't come out of your horn."

And if you don't let what you've known and felt come out of your horn, then you'll never stand out on the jazz scene.

There's another requirement. To have been a powerful enough storyteller to be included in this photo microcosm of living jazz history, all that emotion and technique had to fuse into a personal *presence* that made the player immediately identifiable as *only* himself or herself. There is not a person in this book—instrumentalist or singer—who could be mistaken for anyone else after the first few notes are heard. Actually, after the first one or two notes, there is no doubt who is commanding your attention.

Duke Ellington, who is, of course, grandly and variously represented in this book, was telling me one day: "The other night I heard a cat on the radio, and he was talking about 'modern' jazz. So he played a record to illustrate his point, and there were devices in that music I heard cats using in the

1920s. These large words like 'modern' don't mean anything. Everybody who's had anything to say in this music—all the way back—has been an individualist."

What lasts is the legacy of these individualists. Not the big and porous categories. The players in *Jazz Giants* shaped the music in such penetrating ways that they influenced many other players in their own generation, and far beyond.

There isn't a page in this book that doesn't evoke the thrusting distinctiveness of each of these shapers of the universal language that is jazz. As Lorraine Hansberry used to say, a universal language can only be made up of very particular voices.

Often, there are photographs here of musical giants when they were just beginning to become aware of their potential force: Miles Davis, for instance, at a table at Birdland in 1949, when he had just begun the passage from innocence to experience that changed the way he looked at himself and his music.

Because jazz musicians are less likely than most people to wear masks, their faces make for marvelous portraits of the person within. Jimmy Rushing, so wise in much-traveled years, smiles with the look of someone who has seen it all

but isn't in the least jaded because he figures there still might be a surprise around the corner.

And Cecil Taylor, who paid harder dues for a longer time than most other musicians before he was finally recognized, smiles here with the immense satisfaction of knowing he is now of worldwide renown, and he hasn't compromised one note of his music to get there.

Going through these pages I can hear and see the past merging into the present and foretelling the future. There is the youthful Ornette Coleman, with just as much determination and plain stubbornness in his eyes as finally brought him, too, into the consciousness of jazz listeners from New York to North Africa to Tokyo.

And here is John Coltrane, seemingly serene among the trees, but unable to thoroughly control that energy—the ceaselessly searching energy that you can see in his eyes.

As for the onliest Ellington, just as in life, so in these photographs is he revealed as protean. Each shot offers a different dimension of a complex identity that had to be so complex in order to create so huge and wide-ranging a body of music.

The contrasts between Count Basie and Thelonious Monk further illuminate these pages: Basie, who had found swinging order in the universe of his band and so had peace, pulsating peace; Monk, who kept hearing new challenges from inside and restlessly insisted on continually surprising himself. Sometimes, the surprises were so marvelously exhilarating that he had to get up from the piano to dance.

Lady Day wanders through the book, sometimes in control, sometimes on the edge, always putting her life into her music. And the music showed that some of that life, contrary to legend, was even merry. I remember an evening with her in a friend's apartment during which Billie did hilariously accurate takeoffs of booking agents and record company executives. She was better than most stand-up comics. She did indeed have the blues, too, though she sang few of them. They're also here.

There are so many more—jazz musicians who, as record producer Milt Gabler once said, "got such big souls." So big, in some cases, that they could change, in a minute, from the essence of gentleness to a hurricane. Ben Webster and Charles Mingus, for instance. Look at them here.

The photographers represented in this book, long recognized internationally as singular artists themselves, are like the musicians they have shot. All have technical prowess. But in photographing these jazz improvisers, much more than technique is required. Soul, the jazz spirit of risk-taking, and an understanding of the inside of the music are all essential. And that's what all these photographers brought to the jazz experience. They, too, are part of it.

Louis Armstrong in a scene from the Columbia product. "Jam Session"/1944

8

Dizzy Gillespie, a leader of the bebop movement, 1944

Louis Armstrong, Seattle, Washington, c 1954

Miles Davis at Birdland, New York, January 6, 1949

Promotional shot of Louis Armstrong autographed to drummer John Riley Scott, 1931

12

W. C. Handy, c 1948

13

SWISS KRISSLY

SATCHMO-SLOGAN
(Leave It All Behind Ya)

Louis Armstrong's greeting card to friends

W.C. Handy and Louis and Lucille Armstrong

Paul Whiteman

Paul Whiteman in Berlin

Bunny Berigan

St. Mary's Cemetery, in Fox Lake,
Wisconsin, Berigan's birthplace

Bix Beiderbecke

*Oakdale Cemetery in Davenport,
Iowa, Beiderbecke's birthplace*

Bunny Berigan, New York, 1939

Fats Waller, 1938

Quincy Jones, 1959

Dizzy Gillespie, 1960

Johnny Griffin/May 1961

Doug Watkins/Feb. 1962

Duke Ellington and Freddy Guy, 1925

Buck Clayton and Jimmy Maxwell, New York, 1982

Meade Lux Lewis, Los Angeles, 1962

Right, Willie "The Lion" Smith, Harlem, 1947

26

William Claxton

Ornette Coleman

Kenny Dorham, May 1954

Jay Maisel

Ruby Braff, New York

Right, Buck Clayton, February 18, 1959

Charlie Parker at a photographer's studio

Rex Stewart, musicians' union leader, Kansas City, June 1960

George Wettling, November 3, 1952

Buck Clayton, New York, 1981

Woody Herman, New York, November 1961

36

Thad Jones, 1965

J. J. Johnson, April 1967

Kai Winding

Lee Konitz and Warne Marsh, New York, 1961

John Coltrane

Quincy Jones in Athens, Greece, on a State Department tour with Dizzy Gillespie's band, 1956

Unidentified musicians

Jay Maisel

Donald Byrd practicing in a subway train, New York, June 1960

Unidentified musician, New York

46

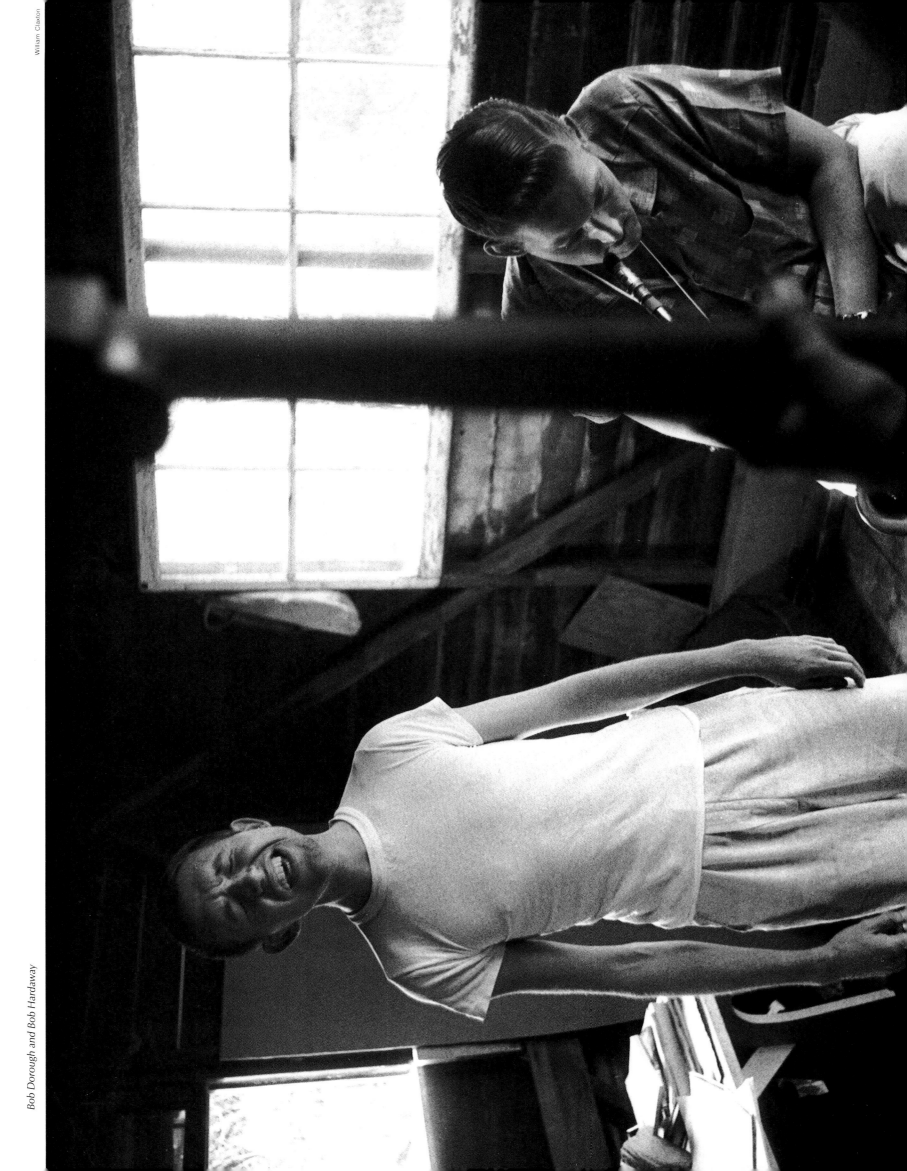

Bob Dorough and Bob Hardaway

47

The jazz postman, Washington, D.C., April 1960

Bourbon Street, New Orleans, 1968

K. Abé

A New Orleans Jazz Museum exhibit, 1968

K. Abé

George Lewis in Japan, May 23, 1964

K. Abé

Benny Morton, autographed to
Eddie Bert at the Famous Door,
New York, Summer 1938

Duke Ellington, Billy Strayhorn,
and Willie "The Lion" Smith at
Columbia University, New York, May 1964

Duke Ellington

Count Basie

Teddy Wilson and Benny Goodman at Carnegie Hall, June 28, 1976

Thelonious Monk at Sankei Hall, Japan, May 11, 1966

K. Abe

Julian "Cannonball" Adderley at Sankei Hall, Japan, August 13, 1966

George Shearing at a recording session, October 1961

Herb Geller, Russ Freeman, and Shelly Manne at a recording session

Duke Ellington at Fine Recording Studio, New York, December 1962

Wes Montgomery at a recording session, October 1960

Betty Carter

Billie Holiday

Johnny Hodges at RCA Victor Studio, New York, September 1967

The Hi-Lo's recording for Starlight at Four Star Studio, Hollywood, 1956

Sarah Vaughan recording for Black Coffee

William Gottlieb

Frank Sinatra recording for Columbia, 1960s

Thelonious Monk and Gerry Mulligan, August 12, 1957

Ben Webster and Gerry Mulligan

Leroy Vinnegar, Carl Perkins, and Tony Bazley recording for Contemporary, Fall 1957

Stu Williamson and Zoot Sims, 1954

Shelly Manne, Shorty Rogers, and Jimmy Giuffre recording for Contemporary, 1954

Wardell Gray and Conte Candoli recording for Frank Morgan at GNP (Gene Norman Presents), 1955

William Claxton

74

Dinah Washington recording for EmArcy, June 15, 1954

Billie Holiday with Mal Waldron, Vinnie Burke, and an unidentified guitar player, October 28, 1958

Clifford Brown with Zoot Sims and Shelly Manne recording for Pacific Jazz, 1954

Ray Avery

Recording session for the Jess Stacy and the Famous Sidemen LP Tribute to Benny Goodman (Atlantic), with Murray McEachern, trombone; Vido Musso, tenor sax;
Ziggy Elman, trumpet; Heinie Beau, alto sax and arrangements; Chuck Gentry, baritone sax; Allen Reuss, guitar; Nick Fatool, drums; and Artie Shapiro, bass, 1954

Jay Maisel

William Claxton

William Claxton

Conte Candoli and Lou Levy

Carson Smith and Bob Brookmeyer

Ray Charles at a recording session

Ray Charles with Gerald Wilson

Right, Ray Charles with one of the Raylettes, 1962 **86**

Lester Young, Buck Clayton, and Dickie Wells recording for Keynote, 1944

Count Basie recording for Mercury, January 1952

Fats Waller, piano, recording with Cedric Wallace, bass; Al Casey, guitar; and Gene Sedric, clarinet, in Chicago, January 1940

John Kirby, bass, recording with O'Neil Spencer, drums; Charlie Shavers, trumpet; Buster Bailey, clarinet; Russell Procope, alto sax; and Billy Kyle, piano

Above, Coleman Hawkins, tenor sax, recording for Signature with Ellis Larkins, piano; Shelly Manne, drums; Andy Fitzgerald, clarinet;
Al Casey, guitar; Bill Coleman, trumpet; and Oscar Pettiford, bass, December 8, 1943   Below, Charlie Shavers, trumpet;
Allen Eager, tenor sax; Shelly Manne, drums; Pete Brown, alto sax; Mary Osborne, guitar; Al McKibbon, bass; and Leonard Feather, October 3, 1946

Miles Davis, Lee Konitz, and Gerry Mulligan at a recording session for the Birth of the Cool *LP, January 21, 1949*

Junior Collins, French horn; Bill Barber, tuba; Kai Winding, trombone; Max Roach, drums; Gerry Mulligan, baritone sax; Miles Davis, trumpet; Lee Konitz, alto sax; Al Haig, piano; and Joe Shulman, bass

At Lennie Tristano's studio, Warne Marsh, tenor sax; Peter Ind, bass; Lennie Tristano, piano; and Al Leavitt, drums, August 15, 1953

Recording session with George Morrow, bass; Hank Mobley, tenor sax; Max Roach; and Kenny Dorham, trumpet, 1956

Earl "Fatha" Hines at Rudy Van Gelder's studio, 1964

Paul Quinichette and Mel Powell recording for Vanguard at the Masonic Lodge Auditorium, Brooklyn, New York, August 17, 1954

Elvin Jones recording at Rudy Van Gelder's studio, 1964

Max Roach and Buddy Rich at a recording session for Mercury, 1959

Duke Ellington at a recording session for Columbia

101

Erroll Garner on a television show

Shelly Manne on "Stars of Jazz," KABC-TV, Los Angeles, 1956

The Harry James Big Band on "Stars of Jazz," with Denis Budimir on guitar, Ray Sims and Bob Edmondson on trombones, 1956

Harry James relaxing with pianist Jack Perciful, 1956

Mel Tormé on "Stars of Jazz," 1956

Billie Holiday on "Stars of Jazz," 1956

Ray Avery

Mel Tormé on the CBS "Color TV Show," October 1951

Eddie Ber

ddie Bert

The Red Norvo Trio on the "Color TV Show": Tal Farlow, guitar; Clyde Lombardi, bass; and Red Norvo, vibraphone, October 1951

Jim Hall, Ralph Pena, and Jimmy Giuffre on "Stars of Jazz," 1956

Jack Teagarden on "Stars of Jazz," 1956

Ray Avery

Chet Baker and Bobby Timmons on "Stars of Jazz," 1956

Jay Maisel

Gerry Mulligan

52nd Street, New York, late 1940s

Buddy Childers and Stan Kenton backstage at the Baltimore Theatre, 1948

William Gottlieb

117

Chris Connor

Lambert, Hendricks & Ross: Dave Lambert, Annie Ross, and Jon Hendricks

Carmen McRae and Norman Simmons

Bill Evans, Shelly Manne, and Eddie Gomez

Ellis Larkins and Al Hall, New York, 1972

Kenny Burrell at A&R Studio recording for Blue Note, New York, 1968

K. Abe

Art Farmer

Chet Baker

Bud Powell, August 24, 1957

Right, Julian "Cannonball" Adderley in San Francisco

Dave Brubeck, September 1962

Stan Getz and his son Nicky, Connecticut, 1972

Duke Ellington at Freedomland, Bronx, New York, August 1964

Cootie Williams at Freedomland, August 1964

Sonny Stitt at the Monterey Jazz Festival

Chet Baker on "Stars of Jazz," 1956

Ben Webster and Gerry Mulligan

Charles Mingus, bass; Roy Haynes, drums; Thelonious Monk, piano; and Charlie Parker, alto sax, at the Open Door, New York, September 13, 1953

134

Charlie Parker at the Open Door, New York, September 13, 1953

Charlie Parker and Miles Davis at the Three Deuces on 52nd Street, New York, 1948

Coleman Hawkins and Miles Davis at the Three Deuces, 1948

Dizzy Gillespie Big Band with Miles Davis on second trumpet, John Lewis on piano and Ray Brown on bass, at the Club Downbeat, 44 West 52nd Street, New York, 1948

William Gottlieb

William Gottlieb

William Gottlieb

*Top, Ella Fitzgerald with Gillespie
at the Club Downbeat, 1948*

*Right, Ray Brown and Milt Jackson
at the Club Downbeat, 1948*

Charlie Parker and Red Rodney watch Dizzy Gillespie at the Club Downbeat, 1948

Charlie Parker at the Three Deuces, New York, 1947

Fats Navarro, Miles Davis, and Kai Winding at Birdland, New York, January 6, 1949

Juilliard student Miles Davis with Howard McGhee at Nola Studio, New York, 1948

Thelonious Monk, Howard McGhee, Roy Eldridge, and Teddy Hill at Minton's Playhouse, New York, 1948

Thelonious Monk at Minton's on the same day

Thelonious Monk

*Thelonious Monk
and Charlie Rouse*

Hugh Bell

William Claxton

*Eric Dolphy and
Thelonious Monk*

Hugh Bell

Charles Mingus at Café Bohemia, New York, July 30, 1955

Bill Evans

Ray Avery

Red Mitchell and Hampton Hawes, Los Angeles, 1954

Overleaf, Art Tatum, Rochester, New York, 1948

Page 153, Red Norvo, c 1947

Dizzy Gillespie and Ornette Coleman at the Jazz Gallery, December 5, 1960

The Billy Taylor Trio: Taylor, piano; Charlie Smith, drums; Earl May, bass; at the Downbeat, New York, September 10, 1952

Sarah Vaughan with the Count Basie Orchestra at Birdland, New York, December 16, 1954

Conte Candoli and Sal Salvador at Birdland, New York, April 26, 1953

Stan Kenton with road manager and baritone sax player Bob Gioga, Baltimore, Maryland, 1948

The Phil Moore Four, 1947

Cafe Bohemia in Greenwich Village, New York

Snookie's on West 45th Street, New York

Hugh Bell   William Gottlieb

Tony Scott on alto saxophone

Allen Eager and Curly Russell at the Royal Roost, New York, 1948

163

Lester Young

Lester Young, December 28, 1956

Nancy Elliott

Lester Young on Art Ford's
Jazz Show, WNTA-TV, 1958

Left, Lester Young on 52nd Street, 1948

Frank Driggs Collection

The Lester Young Sextet at Kelly's Stable, New York, 1941, with Hal West, drums; Shad Collins, trumpet; Lester Young, tenor sax; Nick Fenton, bass; Clyde Hart, piano; and John Collins, guitar

Eddie Bert at the Band Box,
April 26, 1953

Band leader Marty Napoleon

Charles Shavers, Kenny Clarke, Zoot Sims, Oscar Pettiford, Kai Winding, and an unidentified pianist at Club Downbeat, New York, September 10, 1952

Coleman Hawkins in Kelly's Stable dressing room, New York, 1939

*Charles Mingus and Bud Powell at the
Open Door cabaret, New York, September 1953*

Bob Parent

*Top, the Charlie Parker group at the Blue Note, Chicago, June 1949, with
Tommy Potter, an unidentified singer, Kenny Dorham, and an unidentified drummer*

*Left, Big Sid Catlett and John Field
at Storyville, Boston, November 6, 1950*

Tony Scott, clarinet; Kenny O'Brien, bass; Eddie Wasserman, tenor sax; Irv Kluger, drums; Jackie Paris, guitar; and Eddie Bert, trombone, at the Circle in the Square in Greenwich Village, New York, March 10, 1952

Hugh Bell

Brew Moore

Hugh Bell

Zutty Singleton

Sonny Greer and Tyree Glenn

Benny Goodman

Gene Krupa and Benny Goodman

Benny Goodman with Vido Musso and Big Sid Catlett, c 1946

Gene Krupa at Basin Street, New York, August 9, 1956

The Eddie Condon group at Eddie Condon's, New York, August 12, 1953, with Condon, guitar; Cutty Cutshall, trombone;
Wild Bill Davison, trumpet; Edmond Hall, clarinet; Dick Cary, piano; and Walter Page, bass

Bob Parent   Hugh Bell

Eddie Condon

William Claxton

Above, Muggsy Spanier in San Francisco, 1962

Below, Bob Crosby's Bobcats at the Hickory House, New York, with Ray Bauduc, Yank Lawson, Warren Smith, Matty Matlock, Eddie Miller, Bob Haggart, Bob Zurke, and Nappy Lamare

Left, Muggsy Spanier at Eddie Condon's, New York, 1946

Institute of Jazz Studies, Rutgers Univ.

Pee Wee Russell, Brad Gowans, Bobby Hackett, Joe Sullivan, and Marty Marsala at Jimmy Ryan's on 52nd Street, New York, c1939

Bobby Hackett and Louis Armstrong at Child's Paramount Restaurant, New York, September 16, 1952

Pee Wee Russell

183

Bob Wilber and Sidney Bechet at Eddie Condon's, New York, 1947

Sidney Bechet at Child's Paramount Restaurant, New York, August 23, 1953

George Wettling, Edmond Hall, and Wild Bill Davison

Willie "The Lion" Smith

Jimmy McPartland

Tony Parenti

Howard Rumsey and Barney Kessel at Laguna Beach, California, June 20, 1955

The Lighthouse All Stars in concert at Laguna Beach, June 20, 1955, with Frank Rosolino, trombone; Bud Shank, alto sax; Bob Cooper,
tenor sax; Howard Rumsey, bass; and guest guitarist Barney Kessel (not shown: pianist Claude Williamson and drummer Stan Levey)

The Lighthouse All Stars at the Lighthouse, Hermosa Beach, California, 1952, with Shelly Manne, drums; Milt Bernhart, trombone; Shorty Rogers, trumpet; Frank Patchen, piano; Jimmy Giuffre, tenor sax; and Howard Rumsey, bass

The Lighthouse All Stars in Tucson, Arizona, 1956: Howard Rumsey, Bob Cooper, Bud Shank, and Frank Rosolino

Chet Baker

The original Gerry Mulligan Quartet, Los Angeles, August 1952: Mulligan, baritone sax; Bob Whitlock, bass; Chico Hamilton, drums; and Chet Baker, trumpet

Willie "The Lion" Smith at Newport, July 6, 1958

Anita O'Day at the Newport Jazz Festival, July 7, 1958

The Newport Jazz Festival, July 1958

Tony Scott Quartet: Scott, clarinet; Jimmy Knepper, trombone; Henry Grimes, bass; and Ed Levinson, drums

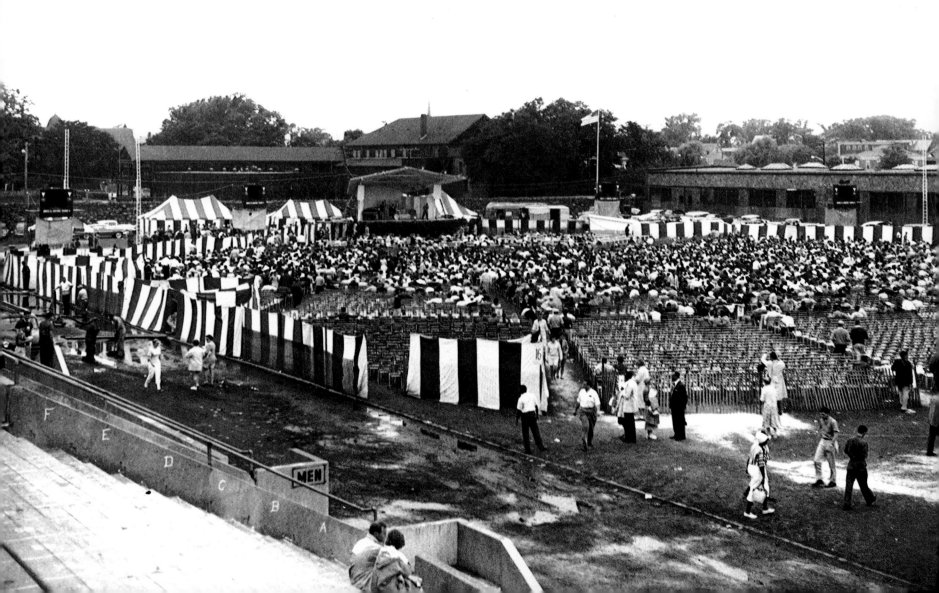

Gerry Mulligan

Dinah Washington

Addison and Art Farmer, July 10, 1955

Dizzy Gillespie and Milt Hinton at the Newport Jazz Festival, July 6, 1957

Joe Williams with the Count Basie Orchestra

Wes Montgomery at the Newport Jazz Festival, July 4, 1965

Jay Maisel

*Lester Young and Tony Scott at
the Newport Jazz Festival, July 5, 1958*

A music fan with a jazz sketchbook

Max Roach accompanying a jazz ballet, July 1960

William C|

Sonny Rollins at the Newport Jazz Festival, July 7, 1958 (not shown: Henry Grimes, bass; Roy Haynes, drums)

The Jazztet at Randall's Island, New York, 1960: Benny Golson,
tenor sax; Art Farmer, trumpet; and Tom McIntosh, trombone

Thelonious Monk at Randall's Island, New York, 1959

Charles Stewart

Gigi Gryce at Randall's Island, New York, 1959, with Hank Jones, piano; Donald Byrd, trumpet; and Wendell Marshall, bass

Red Garland at Randall's Island, New York, 1957

Bobby Timmons

Johnny Hodges in Tennessee

Duke Ellington in Tennessee

Billie Holiday backstage at Carnegie Hall

*Maxine Sullivan with the Dizzy Gillespie Orchestra
at the Strand Theater, New York, December 1948*

Helen Humes

Left, Anita O'Day at Basin Street, New York, August 9, 1956

Anita O'Day at the New York Jazz Festival, August 24, 1957

Hajime Sawatari   William Gottlieb

Top, Chris Connor at the Latin Quarter,
Tokyo, January 3, 1962

Left, Les Brown and Doris Day
at the Paramount Theater, New York, 1946

William Gottlieb

Nat King Cole Trio in Washington, D.C., c 1940

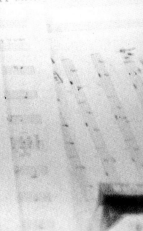

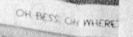

Bob Parent

Clifford Brown, December 30, 1955

Art Blakey at Koseinenkin Hall,
Tokyo, December 1963

Hajime Sawatari

Horace Silver at Sankei Hall,
Tokyo, December 31, 1961

Hajime Sawatari

222

Joe Williams

Jimmy Rushing

William Gottlieb

Django Reinhardt backstage at the Paramount Theater, New York, 1948

Right, Dave Tough backstage at Eddie Condon's, New York, c 1946

Charlie Ventura and Bill Harris, New York, 1947

Sonny Rollins

Illinois Jacquet, 1947

Stan Kenton and Johnny Richards, 1955

Art Pepper in a photo session for an Intro album cover, 1955

Ray Avery

Bud Shank, flute

Count Basie

K. Abé

Eric Dolphy

234

235

Gil Evans

Archie Shepp

John Coltrane

Ron Carter

K. Abé

Jim Hall

238

Ruby Braff

Lee Konitz

K. Abe

John Lewis

K. Abe

Cecil Taylor

Helen Merrill

K. Ab

Max Roach

Milt Jackson

Bird
1952

The Modern Jazz Quartet

K. Abe

Count Basie

K. Abe

251

Willie Smith and Charlie Shavers on a JATP (Jazz at the Philharmonic) tour, Tokyo, 1953

Ben Webster on a JATP tour, Tokyo, 1953

Left, Phil Woods in New York, 1973

Dee Dee Bridgewater and Thad Jones in Tokyo, March 1974

K. Abe

K. Abé

Duke Ellington

Toshiko Akiyoshi at Berklee College of Music, Boston, 1956

Toshiko Akiyoshi and George Wein at the Newport Jazz Festival, July 5, 1956

Shelly Manne and His Men—Contemporary Records

WFL DRUM CO. 1728 N. Damen Ave.. Chicago 47. Ill.

ART BLAKEY • Blue Note Recording Artist

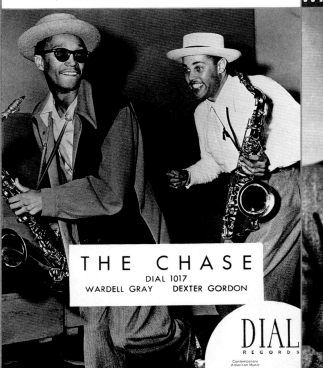

THE CHASE
DIAL 1017
WARDELL GRAY   DEXTER GORDON

Lionel Hampton—Associated Booking Corp.

PROMO
SHOTS

JAMES MOODY • Blue Note Recording Artist

Duke Ellington

Jimmie Lunceford—William Morris Agency

Artie Shaw

SIDNEY BECHET

BLUE NOTE RECORDS

Cab Calloway

Maynard Ferguson—Associated Booking Corp.

WYNTON KELLY • BLUE NOTE RECORDING ARTIST

Stan Kenton

Dizzy Gillespie—Shaw Artists Corp.

Modern Jazz Quartet—Monte Kay

Wayne Shorter—Vee Jay Records

Jackie Cain and Roy Kral—Associated Booking Corp.

Mel Tormé—General Artists Corp.

Blue Mitchell—Riverside Records

Ginnie Powell and Boyd Raeburn—General Artists Corp.

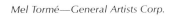

Lee Wiley

Eddie "Lockjaw" Davis—Shaw Artists Corp.

Ahmad Jamal—Associated Booking Corp.

Chris Connor—Shaw Artists Corp.

ol Sloane, Larry Elgart Orchestra—Willard Alexander, Inc.

Rose Murphy—Associated Booking Corp.

Marilyn Moore, Charlie Barnett Orchestra—MCA

Dinah Washington

Mary Ann McCall, Woody Herman Orchestra
—General Artists Corp.

Helen Merrill—Shaw Artists Corp.

Jo Ann Greer, Les Brown and His Band of Renown

Betty Carter—Shaw Artists Corp.

Sarah Vaughan—Shaw Artists Corp.

*The Palace Theatre Orchestra,
Beale Street, Memphis, Tennessee, c 1922*

*The Paul Whiteman Orchestra, 1928, including
Bix Beiderbecke, Frankie Trumbauer, Harry Goldie,
Lenny Hayton, and Charlie Margulis*

The Paul Whiteman Orchestra, c 1923

Tyree Glenn and
Chu Berry in Alabama, c 1939

Milton J. Hinton

Mildred Bailey and Glen Gray, 1938

T. Ono Collection

Lee Wiley recording at Liberty Studio,
December 1939, with Artie Shapiro, bass;
George Wettling, drums; Max Kaminsky,
trumpet; Joe Bushkin, piano; Wiley, vocal;
Bud Freeman, tenor sax (not shown:
Pee Wee Russell and Eddie Condon)

Institute of Jazz Studies, Rutgers Univ.

*Charlie Christian and Teddy Bunn
on guitars with Slam Stewart on bass
at a Gibson guitar demonstration,
New York Band Instrument Co.,
New York, 1939*

Tommy Dorsey with Frank Sinatra
and The Pied Pipers, New York, 1942

*Howard McGhee, Flip Phillips, and
Charlie Parker on a JATP tour, 1947*

The Stan Kenton Orchestra at Sweets Ballroom,
Oakland, California, September 18, 1950:
Al Porcino, trumpet; Eddie Bert,
Bob Fitzpatrick, Harry Betts, and Burt
Varsallona, trombones; Bob Cooper,
Art Pepper, and Bud Shank, saxes

Charles Mingus, Red Norvo, and
Tal Farlow (the Red Norvo Trio)
with Bob Cooper of the Stan Kenton
Orchestra in Salt Lake City,
September 21, 1950

JATP on tour in Japan, 1953

Jeri Southern, Johnnie Ray,
Rosemary Clooney, and Stan Kenton, 1952

Sam Price, Walter Page, Jo Jones, Pat Jenkins, Jimmy Rushing, Henderson Chambers, Ben Richardson, and Buddy Tate, December 1, 1954

The Dizzy Gillespie Big Band
in Athens, Greece, on a State Department tour,
1956, with Gillespie on the left and
Quincy Jones third from right

A gathering of musicians in Harlem, c 1959

Charles LaVere with the Chordettes
on the George Burns Show, Sahara Hotel,
Las Vegas, August 8, 1960

Eddie Condon's All-Star group on NBC-TV, New York, October 1961. Front row, from left: Pee Wee Russell, Bud Freeman, Joe Sullivan (glasses), Meade Lux Lewis, Lil Armstrong, Mae Barnes, Blossom Seeley, Milt Hinton, Bob Haggart. Second row: Baby Dodds, unidentified banjo player, unidentified percussionist, Gene Krupa, Johnny Guarnieri, Eddie Condon, Yank Lawson, Henry "Red" Allen, Jimmy McPartland, Buster Bailey. Back row: second from right, Jack Teagarden

Sarah Vaughan, Pearl Bailey, and
Ella Fitzgerald on a television show, California, 1979

Milton J. Hinton

Dick Hyman and Ruby Braff,
New York, 1985

Nancy Elliott

George Simon's 50-year anniversary in the
music business, New York, June 1985.
Front row, from left: Jimmy McPartland,
Lester Lanin, Gerry Mulligan, Les Paul.
Second row: Marian McPartland,
Cab Calloway, Bill Simon, George Simon,
Sammy Kay, Benny Goodman, and
Ed Polcer (co-owner of Eddie Condon's)

Nancy Elliott

The Wild Bill Davison Quartet

The Photographers

K. Abé is known around the world for his singularly beautiful photographs of jazz musicians and for his expert knowledge of the jazz field. Born in Tokyo, Abé was first exposed to American popular music in the mid-forties. While he was a student at Waseda University, in the late forties and early fifties, he performed jazz at U.S. Army and Navy camps. After graduation, he worked as a radio deejay and an album cover designer, and taught himself photography. His pictures have been published in several books on jazz and have appeared in a number of newspapers and magazines.

Abé's photographs appear on pages 2, 50, 51, 56-57, 58, 59, 62, 119, 121, 123, 125, 126, 128, 129, 232, 233, 235, 238-248, and 250-259.

Ray Avery was born in Canada, but at the age of six moved with his family to Big Bear Lake, California. He attended the University of California at Los Angeles. Avery became interested in photography in 1945 when he went overseas as an air force pilot. He began to specialize in jazz photography in Los Angeles in 1953. His photographs have appeared on more than 100 album covers. However, he says that photography has always been his hobby, and his rare records business is his principal occupation.

Avery's pictures appear on pages 49, 60, 61, 65, 70-73, 79, 80, 81, 103-107, 110, 111, 112, 126, 130-131, 151, 190, 191, 193, and 231.

Hugh Bell was born in New York City and was a jazz fan from the time he was a teenager, when he also became interested in photography. He took courses at New York University in journalism and film production. In his early career Bell worked as a film crew assistant doing documentaries and television commercials. He also shot portraits of actors in his home studio and eventually began to photograph jazz musicians.

Bell's photographs appear on pages 147, 162, 164, 172-175, 179, 186, 187, and 211-214.

Eddie Bert was born in Yonkers, New York. His long-term career as a jazz trombonist included work with Red Norvo, Woody Herman, Stan Kenton, Charles Mingus, Benny Goodman, Thad Jones and Mel Lewis, and appearances as leader of his own group. He supplemented his musical activities with forays into photography.

Bert's photographs appear on pages 52, 108, 109, 159, 161, 168, 230, and 269.

William Claxton, who is a native Californian, has two degrees in psychology and an M.A. in the psychology of art, but no formal training in photography. He sold his first picture story while still in college and went on to achieve recognition as a top photographer of jazz. He has received 36 awards for pop, jazz, and classical album covers. His photographs are in the collections of the Chicago Institute of Art, the Museum of Modern Art in New York, and the University of Chicago. He has collaborated with Vincent Price on two books and with Terry Southern on another, *The Journal of the Loved One.* Claxton's latest book, *Jazz,* was published in 1987.

His photographs appear on pages 26, 28, 32, 33, 40, 44-48, 68, 74, 75, 84, 85, 87, 102, 132-133, 146, 150, 181, 188-189, 204, 215, 216, 223, 228, and 232.

Nancy Elliott says, "I started as a painter, and I have always been fascinated by the human face. My work as a photographer continues this exploration." She began her photographic work in 1958, doing portraits of such jazz legends as Billie Holiday, Lester Young, Benny Goodman, Ella Fitzgerald, Sarah Vaughan, Count Basie, Buck Clayton, Joe Williams, Artie Shaw, Eubie Blake, Jo Jones, Mel Lewis, Roy Eldridge, Benny Carter, and Thelonious Monk. Her photographs have been published in the *Time-Life* "Giants of Jazz" series, the *New York Times,* the *New York Daily News,* the *New York Post, New York* magazine, *Down Beat, Jazz Journal,* and many other jazz periodicals. She started her "Portraits of the Poor" series in 1980 with a 35mm camera given to her by musician Buck Clayton. Since then she has been photographing her subjects on the streets of New York.

Elliott's photographs appear on pages 25, 35, 167, and 273.

William Gottlieb, who was a writer and editor for *Down Beat,* shot hundreds of photographs of well-known jazz musicians in the 1940s. Many of them have appeared in books, TV documentaries, art shows, and museum collections. He learned to take pictures in the late thirties when the *Washington Post* refused to pay for a staff photographer to illustrate his jazz column. Gottlieb continued to photograph jazz subjects until 1948, when he became a producer of educational film strips. Gottlieb's most recent book is *The Golden Age of Jazz.*

Gottlieb's photographs appear on pages 9, 27, 67, 82-83, 114-115, 116-117, 136-141, 143, 144, 145, 152, 153, 160, 161, 163, 166, 176, 180, 184, 218, 219, 226, 227, 228, and 229.

Milt Hinton, who has been shooting photographs of jazz subjects for many years, is one of the most influential and respected of all jazz bassists. Hinton has performed with Cab Calloway, Count Basie, Louis Armstrong, Teddy Wilson, Benny Goodman, and a host of others.

Hinton's photographs appear on pages 10, 267, 271, and 273.

Jay Maisel, who was born in Brooklyn, New York, studied graphic design at Abraham Lincoln High School and painting with Joseph Hirsh. He graduated from Cooper Union in 1952 and earned a B.F.A. at Yale a year later. Since 1954, he has become well-known as a freelance photographer for magazines, advertising agencies, and major U.S. and international corporations. He has received many awards, including Photographer of the Year in 1986 (A.S.M.P.), the Infinity Award for Applied Photography in 1987 (International Center of Photography), and a Gold Award for Photography for two years in a row (Art Directors Club of New York). In 1986 Maisel had a major one-man show, "Light on America," at the International Center of Photography.

Maisel's photographs appear on pages 30, 43, 63, 84, 101, 113, 118, 124, 183, 194, 195, 202, 204, 223, and 225.

Bob Parent, an amateur photographer since 1937, developed an interest in jazz in 1941. He subsequently became involved in the Boston jazz scene and the activities of the Jazz Society. Among his early photographs were shots taken of Sidney Bechet and Pops Foster at the Savoy Cafe. Parent is still active in the jazz world and recently had a group exhibition of jazz photography with William Gottlieb and Charles Stewart in New York City.

Parent's photographs appear on pages 29, 31, 34, 69, 76-77, 78, 94, 97, 124, 134, 135, 148, 149, 154-158, 165, 169, 170, 171, 177, 178, 182, 185, 200, 201, 205, 216, 217, 221, 224, 270, and 274-275.

Popsie Randolph was Benny Goodman's band boy and later his band manager. As a photographer he took promotional shots of popular musicians and singers, as well as many significant photographs of jazz artists.

Randolph's photographs appear on pages 11, 66, 89, 92, 93, and 142.

Hajime Sawatari was born in Tokyo and studied photography at Nihon University. After graduation in 1963 he worked at the Japan Design Center for three years and then began freelancing. His fashion and commercial photographs have appeared in magazines and other media. Most of his jazz photography was taken while he was at school, and many of his shots were published in the Japanese edition of *Down Beat* at the time. Sawatari published two books in 1973—*Nadia* and *Alice*—both of which are still in print.

Sawatari's photographs appear on pages 218, 220, and 222.

Arthur Singer attended Cooper Union Art School in New York and began work as a commercial artist. In the early fifties he began to focus on subjects drawn from nature. His first break was an assignment to illustrate several articles for *Sports Illustrated*. In 1982 he was commissioned by the U.S. Postal Service to create a sheet of 50 stamps showing the official bird of each state. Singer is unquestionably at the front rank of American painters of birds. His love of nature is supplemented by a fondness for the music of Duke Ellington.

Singer's photographs appear on pages 52, 61, 64, and 127.

Charles Stewart studied music for eight years as a youngster but says he couldn't even master "Chopsticks." Realizing he'd never become a great musician, he set his sights on photography. Stewart studied fine art at Ohio University, and later moved to New York to work with Herman Leonard. He began meeting and photographing people like Lennie Tristano, Warne Marsh, Charlie Parker, and Tadd Dameron. Since the 1950s, many of Charles Stewart's photos have been used on album covers and have appeared in newspapers and magazines. Stewart recently published his first book, *Chuck Stewart's Jazz Files*.

Stewart's photographs appear on pages 20-23, 36, 37, 39, 41, 53, 54, 55, 95, 96, 98, 99, 100, 120, 203, 206, 208, 209, 210, 234, 236, 237, and 272.

Additional Photo Credits
Bob Andrews Collection, pages 192, 195; Ray Avery Collection, 266; Eddie Bert Collection, 269; CBS, 14; Columbia Productions, 8; Columbia Records, 220; Down Beat, 90; Frank Driggs Collection, 11, 88, 89, 92, 93, 142, 167; Irvin Glaser, 91; Mike Gould, 18, 169, 268; John Graudenz, 15; Hooks Bros., 13, 266; Institute of Jazz Studies, Rutgers University, 14-17, 19, 24, 38, 42, 86, 90, 91, 181, 220, 267, 268, 269, 270, 271; Steve LaVere Archives, 12, 18, 169, 266, 268, 272; MCA, 16; MGM Records, 38; John W. Miner, 16; Music Life Magazine, 260, 261; T. Ono Collection, 215, 267; Pell-Thomas, 195; Wide World Photos, 15; Arthur Zimmerman Collection, 32, 66, 141, 170, 196, 197, 198-199, 207, 268

Julie MacDonald, who died recently, was a well-known sculptress, writer, critic, and jazz enthusiast. Among her art subjects was her close friend Charlie Parker. Her portrait of Parker appears on page 249.

Index